NO FAITH OF MY OWN

With a New Introduction by C. Don Keyes

GRACEFUL REASON

The Contribution of Reason to Theology
With a Foreword by John Heuss

J. V. Langmead Casserley

UNIVERSITY
PRESS OF
AMERICA

LANHAM • NEW YORK • LONDON

Copyright © 1984 by

University Press of America,™ Inc.

4720 Boston Way
Lanham, MD 20706

3 Henrietta Street
London WC2E 8LU England

NO FAITH OF MY OWN was first published in 1950
by Longmans, Green and Co., Ltd., London, England

GRACEFUL REASON © 1954
by The Seabury Press, Incorporated

ISBN (Perfect): 0-8191-3793-6

INTRODUCTION

The writings of Julian Victor Langmead Casserley
(1909-1978), philosopher, theologian, and sociologist,
contain a prophecy of hope which is urgently needed as
we approach the twenty-first century. Casserley's hope
was not the kind of shallow optimism that comes
through captivity to the trends of the times, but instead it
was rooted to the perennial tradition of Western
philosophy, the historic Christian revelation, and
political socialism. The traditional Anglican perspective
from which he interprets Christianity is based on
Richard Hooker's "light of reason" and thereby the
mainstream of the Western spiritual heritage; he is not
partisan and one-sided, but inclusive and ecumenical. His
Anglicanism is simultaneously Anglo Catholic,
Evangelical, and Liberal, in the most positive senses of
those three terms. Casserley's concepts possess the kind
of wholeness that resists fragmentation into such
seemingly irreconsilable opposites as: reason and
emotion, theory and practice, orthodox and liberal, etc.

We are living in a time in which there seems to be a
shortage of hope. In August of 1982, when I was at Mrs.
Casserley's house in Maine, looking at Dr. Casserley's
unpublished manuscripts I found one called "Theology
of Man". At that time I was in despair, but I found a
statement about the meaning of human transcendence
that provoked me to hope:

> To transcend is to be there and known in a
> more or less casual sort of way and yet to
> preserve an inner impenetrability which not
> only is not pierced but could not be
> pierced.

I

One reason for today's shortage of hope is the widespread forgetfulness of our transcendence as human beings. *Transcendere* means to climb over, surpass, or go beyond. Human transcendence involves climbing over, rather than being enslaved by, the spirit of the times, especially when the popular culture has enshrined cynicism, boredom, and apathy. Casserley's hope for surpassing these spiritual vices was not naive, for he took the grimness of human existence well into account in formulating his hope, as this statement from "Theology of Man" suggests:

> In Tewkesbury Abbey in Gloucestershire in England there stands the 15th century tomb of Archbishop Wakeman. The monument consists of two tiers. At the top, we see the dead Archbishop carved in stone lying in state in the splendor and dignity of his Arch-episcopal robes. On the lower tier, beneath him, a rat and a worm are gnawing at a handful of bones which are all that remain of the once powerful and dreaded prelate. This is the theme that Pascal in the 17th century was to call 'the grandeur and misery of man.' Even Teilhard de Chardin, almost drunk as he sometimes seems with the thought of man's advancing technological mastery of this world, writes also of each man's diminishment as he approaches death with the sensitive mastery and acuteness of perception which reveal him as by no means unaware of the paradox and tragedy of the mortality of the hero. Yet, of the two, the misery of man is perhaps the more typical 20th century theme. Book after books seems

II

to debunk man in almost masochistic fashion, by dwelling on the dethronement of man as knowledge progresses.

Casserley also knew how forcefully today's cynicism can destroy hope by debunking all that has value, as he explains in the same manuscript:

> There are, of course, many human beings today, as always who hide from life so successfully, who are so stupifyingly diverted, rather than stimulated by their experience, that they know no peak moments at all. For them, both irreligion and religion are alike impossible. For many modern writers our's is a time in human history in which such a bleak apathy and mediocrity has wrapped itself around the consciousness of man more successfully, perhaps, than ever before. For them modern or contemporary man is 'come of age', blasé, unresponsive to the beauties, subtleties and surprises of life, blighted and blasted with a icy, aged maturity. How should man, who has lost all consciousness of his own transcendence, understand the transcendence of God? Knowing neither what it is to transcend, nor to be transcended, he can neither affirm nor deny God. He is incapable of both theism and atheism alike. For the word of God, meaning absolute and ultimate personality, no longer conveys anything to him. Not knowing what the word of "God" means he finds himself forgetting what the word man means.

III

Human transcendence and divine transcendence are not opposites that exclude each other, according to Casserley. Nor did he believe, as some do today, that theism and humanism are incompatible. Forgetfulness of the one is forgetfulness of the other. Similarly recovery of the consciousness of either kind of transcendence facilitates recovery of the other. Hope for Casserley comes through transcendence, as the four following observations about his position show.

First, hope is transcendence through having a meaningful future. That is true for individual persons as well as for groups, both large and small. Casserley taught that technology does not have to destroy us. It may do so, but there is no inevitability that it will, for it is conceivable that modern technology could be put to good use. He believed that evolution may continue to improve the human species, and he argued that the Christian revelation is not essentially tied to any specific political system, economic system, or class consciousness. Casserley's position on theology transcends all such distinctions as those and can be reduced to none of them. He also wrote that Christians must be prepared for radical change. His description of what that change will be like is striking in the manuscript "Theology of Man". He is looking ahead to the twenty-first century, and this manuscript comes, I believe, from the late sixties. I shall quote a paragraph or so.

> The theology of the 21st century will be of enormous importance. It is safe to say that by 2050 the world in which we have grown up and with which we are familiar, our type of civilization, culture and society, will have been entirely swept away. No doubt some old landmarks will survive but many will have

IV

disappeared altogether. Yet, of course there will be a real continuity. That new technological and social world will be inhabited by our grandchildren or greatgrandchildren, and they will be aware of us as part of their history. No doubt many of them will tend to laugh at us, or even to dismiss us as representatives of an odd or immoral phase of their development which will by then have been condemned out of hand almost universally. Nevertheless the wisest historians of the time will no doubt find in us something to admire as well as much to censure. But perhaps the most familiar landmark that will still be surviving in undiminished vigor will be the Christian Church. It has sometimes been observed that in a world of total change nothing whatever has come to stay but the gospel. But the Church and the gospel will survive, if they do survive, not because they have refused to change but because they will have been humble enough to accept inevitable change and wise enough to confine themselves to the modes of change that conduce to survival. In this mutable world, immutability is in a subtle process of change.

I do not think anyone can say that Casserley's theology is unmindful of the present and the future.

Many people look upon the kind of historical change that Casserley hints at with fear, despair, and anxiety. Casserley, however, did not look at it that way. He thought of the crisis that will be brought about by that

kind of change as opportunity and challenge and he
wrote this in "Theology of Man":

> When the Christian tradition is truest to
> itself, Christian existence is conceived in
> eschatological fashion. It is life lived on the
> edge of the world, life in which all is
> perpetually energizing and stimulating crisis.
> It is an absorbing drama without
> intermission. Perhaps another way of
> expressing what I mean by the edge of the
> world would be on the eve of the next great
> evolutionary transformation.

Teilhard de Chardin was the thinker that suggested to
Casserley as well as to others a way in which to
synthesize evolution and eschatology. And so, in these
and yet other ways, Casserley's hope asserts that history
has a goal, one that justifies our sacrifices, one that
challenges us to high adventure rather than despair.

Second, hope is transcendence through being rooted in
a spiritual heritage, that is to say, having meaningful
continuity with the past. Casserley could be affirmative
about the future, could treat the present as adventure,
because his resources were not limited to the present,
because he did not bow to trends of the times. He
transcended fads. He understood the trends of the times
and the fads of the present age extremely well. He could
see through them, but was not captured by them. And, as
I think back over the times in which I studied with Dr.
Casserley, the people who did not like his thought were
chiefly captives of the trends of the times. Casserley's
sources, however, were universal. In matters of religious
belief, Casserley had no faith of his own. His faith was

simply that of the universal Christian revelation, not limited to any particular historical epoch. In matters of philosophy, Casserley's resources were at least two thousand seven hundred years of Western thought. Casserley had the kind of mind that the ancient Roman Stoic philosopher, Seneca, described. "A great and noble thing," Seneca said in his 102nd Letter to Lucilus, "is the human mind. . . . Its fatherland is all the arch that encompasses the height and sweep of the firmament, this whole dome within which lies sea and land, within which the ether separates human and divine and also joins them to one another . . . No era is closed to great intellects, no epoch impassable to thought." Casserley's spiritual resources have that sort of universality, and this rooting in the Western spiritual heritage is what some have called Casserley's cultural conservatism. Casserley makes it quite clear that a person can be culturally traditional without accepting political and economic conservatism. In fact, Casserley held that his own socialist political stand was completely compatible with his cultural conservatism. It is not the sort of conservatism which is hidebound to past folk-lore. His traditionalist attitude is not Victorian but is based instead in that vast expanse of the epochs which Seneca talks about. Casserley believed in preserving that cultural heritage and claimed that it is what ought to be stable in a changing world. He wrote about the Judeo-Christian heritage, "that it is to society as the spirit is to the body, as the intellect is to the instincts, as the memory of the past and the preservation of the future are to the mind absorbed in the existing joys of the moment." Sometimes Casserley refers to this Judeo-Christian spiritual heritage as the noösphere, using Teilhard de Chardin's term, meaning science, religion, the arts, and so forth. In his book, *No Faith of My Own*, Casserley claims that the

Church has a responsibility to the cultural heritage: "in our modern, increasingly non-Christian world the traditionally reverenced ideals of historical, scientific and rational integrity, and the essential truths and values of humanism, are as gravely challenged as Christianity itself, and . . . as the present situation develops, the task of defending them will tend more and more to be undertaken by Christian thinkers and the Christian Church."[1]

Casserley sees the debunking of man as the undermining both of Christianity and of humanism and believed that Christianity, with its interest in the transcendence of God, may have to defend humanism. It is humanism based on God's transcendence, not one-dimensional reductionism. Hope comes, in part, from transcending into the past in the right way. This does not mean being limited to past conceptions, for transcendence also involves growth, but it does mean keeping and defending what is truly humanizing in the tradition.

Third, hope is transcendence through following the light of reason. I use Richard Hooker's term, "light of reason", because of Casserley's interest in that sixteenth century thinker as the archetypal Anglican theology. The belief that reason is important in our relationship to God is, as I see it, what distinguishes a Catholic theologian from other kinds of theologians. Casserley, as I said, followed Hooker rather than the English Puritans' interpretation of Calvin. Casserley rejects the kind of interpretation of Calvin that says that we can use reason on worldly things but it has nothing really to do with our knowledge of God. Casserley also rejected the view that

[1] J. V. L. Casserley, *No Faith of My Own* (London: Longmans, Green, and Co., 1950), p. 159.

the fall of man is total and that human nature is completely depraved. The fall of man has affected every aspect of human existence, but it has not utterly destroyed all that is of value in human beings. What would happen if we believe that in the fall of Adam man became depraved in all respects? We might start acting accordingly.

> Indeed, would the tragedy of man be so tragic if his Fall were total? Surely, the tragedy of human existence as we know it lies precisely in the way in which it brings conflict and deformation into the very length and breadth and depth of our human being. A total Fall, a complete corruption, might at least have spared us that, for it is not our experience that the conflict is known only in the mind of the converted man who still belongs to a fallen world, who is still tempted and still sins. We find, on the contrary, crowding in upon us every day, evidence of the immense destructive scale and scope of the conflict in every man, whatever he may be. In other words, a picture of man deeply and gravely wounded by the Fall, desperately ill as a consequence of the Fall, and yet still in some sense man, fits the actual situation of being a fallen human being and our existential experience of that predicament, very much better than any doctrine of total fall.[2]

As Casserley sees the situation, therefore the fall has

[2] J. V. L. Casserley, *Graceful Reason* (London: Longmans, Green, and Co., 1955), p. 49.

permeated all aspects of life and made them ambiguous, but it has not utterly put out the light of reason.

Further explanation is needed to clarify what Casserley means by reason. I suspect that most people in America today, when they hear the word reason or rational, think only of calculative uses of the intellect, namely its technological application. In this way they assume that if someone is rational, then he or she is no longer emotional. Many think of reason as somehow throwing emotion out the window. This is not so in the case of Casserley, for his use of the word reason means more than calculative thinking. It means a state of mind that can include emotion, the desirable emotions, and, therefore, as he uses the term rational he does not mean what we ordinarily mean by it. I suspect that the contemporary popular religious attitude in America is probably more anti-rational in all branches of Christianity than it is traditional. Casserley believes that the debunking of reason amounts to a devaluing of human existence. He agreed with the tradition which claims that grace perfects nature and does not destroy it, and therefore what is best in paganism is not annihilated by revelation but rather preserved and elevated by it. The spirit of the times today is prejudiced against anything except the calculative use of reason.

In contrast to this disparaging of reason, Casserley and the Western tradition affirm its value in our relation to God. A few examples will help illustrate this. According to Plato, reason is the means by which our minds are able to grasp eternal realities such as beauty and justice. Aristotle's rational contemplation is the most divine activity in which human beings can engage. St. Thomas Aquinas' beatific vision of God is an intellectual act. Hooker's light of reason leads us to knowledge of what is sensible. Tillich claimed that the philosopher's concern for being and non-being is correlated with the religious person's faith and doubt. And Teilhard de Chardin held that the claims of science and religion do not contradict one another. At the same time, reason is not merely a theoretical activity, for it also has practical consequences. At least three of these seem to be implied by Casserley's position.

A. Casserley believed in what he and others have called the "perennial philosophy". Among other things this means recognizing that no one system has all the truth. Believing in the perennial philosophy means that we are able to retrieve the truths that various positions have. It means that the big issues are always present and can be found in each age. Believing in the perennial philosophy means that despite the very great disagreements of philosophers with each other, there is nevertheless an underlying unity. We do not have to take a merely partisan stand, but we can be open to truth wherever it's found. This is what is Catholic, universal, about Casserley's hope. I quote him from "Theology of Man":

> The important thing in Catholic Christianity
> is not the extent of our basic agreement but
> the way in which we agree about the
> importance of our disagreements.

Casserley is a both-and thinker. When I went to study with him at Seabury-Western I had come there from the University of Oklahoma where I had studied philosophy with Gustav Mueller, a Hegelian thinker. I went to ask Casserley his impression of Hegel's method and he said that he believed that there was a great deal of value in it. Casserley was perfectly understanding of how I could be Anglo Catholic and, in matters of philosophy, Hegelian.

Other people told me that I had to be a Thomist if that was my churchmanship position, but Casserley saw my position as perfectly reasonable and consistent. So I wondered if there might not be just some Hegelian element in his thought, too, and I believe there is in his book Graceful Reason. The intent of his statement is not to describe Hegelianism but to describe Anglicanism with its interest in trying to grasp both sides of a position.

> In some respects it does seem to me that the whole mind and bent of Anglicanism is rather synthetic or Hegelian. Many so-called dialectical theologians seem to delight in multiplying "either-or" situations, by impaling the reader on the horns of one dilemma after another. But the Anglican mind always dislikes arbitrary "either A or B" situations and tends to say, "surely, we can have both A^1 and B^1". I say both A^1 and B^1 and not both A and B because a true synthesis does more than merely lump together its two terms in a bare paradox. Instead, it transforms and enriches the meaning of each term in the very process of reconciling it to the other. A true synthesis is neither a compromise nor a self-contradiction, but a profounder apprehension.[3]

Neither Casserley nor I accepted man of the conclusions of Hegel's philosophy, in particular, his tendency to glorify the state in his later writings. Certainly, one can repudiate that side of Hegel and still find value in his method, which tries to preserve both

[3] *Graceful Reason*, p. 22.

sides of conflicting truth claims through going up to a higher position that allows both of them to exist. Similarly Casserley's theological message is capable of seeing the truth of both sides of an issue and surmounting the conflict; it is not either-or, but both-and.

B. Casserley believed that there was truth in minority positions. He is not the kind of systematic thinker who requires other people to fit his system He is the kind of systematic thinker that sees that minorities have their truths. And I quote here from No Faith of My Own:

> When Ibsen's Dr. Stockman remarked: 'Majorities are always wrong; minorities are always right', he was no doubt exaggerating. It is possible for minorities to sink well below as well as rise above the community standard. In a well-ordered society, professional thieves are as much a minority as saints. Nevertheless if majorities usually contrive to avoid what is grossest in life it is also true that what is highest escapes them with equal persistence. Minorities are sometimes right but majorities never, and a wise majority will cherish its minorities as a man in the dark will value his torch.[4]

C. The most obvious practical result of Casserley's mainstream rationalism is moderation. This is not the same as compromise. Moderation is not having low standards. Moderation is what makes high standards

[4] *No Faith of My Own*, p. 139.

XIII

possible. In practical matters it is the intelligent use of resources. And, according to Casserley in "Theology of Man", neither God nor man should be defined chiefly in terms of power. There must be a moderation of that concept. I quote something that is an insert to the manuscript. He apparently thought of it after he had written the main part of the work.

> I not only object to a conception of God that thinks of him merely or even primarily in terms of sovereignty and power but I object also to any conception of man that thinks of him merely or even primarily in terms in terms of sovereignty and power and I object to both doctrines for the same reason — that they mis-apprehend the true value and excellence of human personality. The person, whether divine or human, finds authentic self-expression in the range and integrity of its loving and in the wide variety of its values.

Casserley is not saying that God lacks power, but that it is even more important to think of God as loving. I presume that this is a facet of Casserley's moderation in practical affairs. As I have said, in political matters, Casserley's position is basically socialist; and, of course, if we take the long-range view of Western political theory, socialism probably is the moderate Western position as opposed to an anti-religious type Marxism and as opposed to an anti-religious type capitalism. Thus, I suspect in matters of politics as well as other practical things that Casserley would represent his own position to himself and to us as being moderate.

Fourth, hope is transcendence of triviality through the awareness of aesthetic value. Casserley had an aesthetic

XIV

consciousness not only of liturgy and the fine arts but of theological and biblical concepts as well. His interest in the aesthetic dimension of the Christian faith is something that he talks about especially in his earlier period, but he never loses sight of it even when his thinking goes through some changes. Casserley's aesthetic consciousness of faith is an important ingredient in his theology of hope. He wrote in an early work that lack of faith comes partly from the inability to appreciate the aesthetic meaniing of religious symbols and partly from the inability to look at theological concepts artistically. I believe that this kind of sensitivity to beauty and aesthetic matters in Casserley is really a grass roots Anglicn concept. I don't know how many Anglican theologians you find defending it, but I do think that if we were to examine the theological consciousness of the majority of church people we would find a particular sensitivity to the aesthetic dimension of the Christian revelation.

Casserley's position resists debunking the sublime and beautiful, so popular in the 1960's and 1970's. Even his theological method appreciates the heights and the depths of the symbols of Christian faith, appreciates their aesthetic nuances. This same aesthetic grasp of the symbols is also what gives life to Casserley's way of interpreting theology and keeps it from becoming dry. Furthermore it prevents his traditionalism from becoming authoritarian as in systems that present religion as a set of alien laws imposed upon individuals from the outside. For Casserley, on the contrary, the tradition is to be appreciated in its beauty and sublimity and entered into and participated in freely as one does a loved art work. This spirit also marks the difference between Casserley's "cultural conservatism" and reactionary thought.

I conclude that something like Casserley's grasp of the aesthetic dimension of faith is a necessary part of our Western tradition, for it is the feeling appropriate to peak experiences, namely those events of human transcendence that infuse hope and awaken an awareness of God's transcendence. Casserley's openness to the future, his rooting in the tradition, and his insistence on following the light of reason get their validity partly through his aesthetic awareness of the human predicament and God's redemptive action in Christ.

C. Don Keyes
Professor and Chairman
Department of Philosophy
Duquesne University

NO FAITH OF MY OWN

Since
this is closer to being a 'popular' book
than the kind of thing I usually write
I venture to dedicate it
with great gratitude for her unfailing goodness
to me and mine
to

MARY

who says she cannot understand
my other books
and is much too sensible
to try.

CONTENTS

CHAPTER ONE

REMEMBRANCE OF THINGS PAST

This is not a book about me. Devotees of autobiography and intimate self-revelation are advised to turn to the writings of more flamboyant personalities. They will find nothing to their taste here.

My outward life has been uneventful, and would perhaps be described as 'blameless' by those mildly malicious writers who have made this word a satirical equivalent for 'insipid'. I am one of that minority of the men of my generation who have lived through two wars without fighting in either. I was a child at school in 1918 and I had become a busy parish priest well before 1939. I studied philosophy, psychology and theology at a modern university, although from the first with a bias towards sociological problems and inquiries which has grown more and more pronounced with the passage of time. I was ordained and later married. I am the fond father of three children. After some fifteen years continuous practical experience of parochial life I have become the rector of a tiny country parish in Devonshire and a teacher of sociology at the nearby University College. It must be clear from this unexciting summary that such a career as mine hardly provides the raw materials of a readable autobiography. Of course, my life has been interesting to me, and it is my Christian belief that, like all human lives, it is a matter of absorbing interest to God, but it contains little to arrest the attention of other people, and so, not being blessed ·with the ready

wit and verbal ingenuity to make literary bricks without
straw, I can assure the reader that I have no intention of
inflicting on him one more of those dreary volumes of
not very memorable memoirs which are so fashionable
nowadays.

Still there has perhaps been one episode in my life
which might be held, at all events by the more indulgent
spectator, to possess a certain measure of interest. If anything can justify my temerity in writing this book, it is
this one episode, which I acknowledge to be incompar-
ably the most important in my life.

I have at least this in common with those for whom
this book is written: I grew up in complete isolation
from the Christian Faith, as a member of a family which
had entirely abandoned both the practice and profession
of religion. Others may write of dull Victorian Sundays
chiefly composed of orgies of church-going which bored
their infant souls to distraction, of dull Sunday-school
lessons, of grace at meals and family prayers, but as the
world gets older—and not noticeably better—those who
can look back upon a childhood of this kind must be a
steadily decreasing minority. Indeed, I imagine my own
early years provide a more typical example of childhood
and youth in this twentieth century—no church, no
sunday-school, no prayers at my mother's knee, just the
pleasant existence of a spoiled child in moderately pros-
perous circumstances, growing up in a spiritual vacuum,
as jealously guarded against the love of God as against
the sins of men. That is where I began, and this is where
I am now, writing a book that seeks to commend
Christianity. It is a long journey from there to here. The
fact that, by the Grace of God, I have made it, may perhaps lend some spark of interest even to a career so externally uneventful as mine.

If my childhood, so remote from religious influences, was from one point of view a typical twentieth-century childhood, it possessed another feature which was and is highly unusual. The influences which surrounded me in my earlier years were not merely indifferent to Christianity but actively hostile. In these days conscious and deliberate irreligion is even more rare than enthusiastic membership of the Christian Church. We talk much of the decay of belief, but the decay of unbelief is an equally significant feature of modern life. Few people conform nowadays, except perhaps very occasionally, to the established practices and beliefs of any Christian denomination; yet all but a tiny minority of Englishmen would, if asked, unhesitatingly describe themselves as Christians, and such organized anti-religious movements as still persist in this country are feeble to the point of nonentity. This absence of any strong and vocal opposition to the practice and profession of the Christian Faith is, from the Christian point of view, a great misfortune. Bold and outspoken opposition to religion has at least the merit of focusing public attention on religious and spiritual issues. I was brought up under the influence of a comparatively small and unimportant anti-religious body known as 'The Rationalist Press Association'. I can give personal testimony to the splendid services which such movements, unintentionally of course, render to the cause of Christianity by their persistent stress on the necessity of making some definite personal decision about religion.

Indeed, what little I learned about Christianity during these early years was entirely derived from the publications of this particular society. I can just remember a quaint little book called *Savage Survivals*, from which a portion was read to me by my father every night on going to bed. I must have been six or seven years of age at the time. No doubt my parents had an uncomfortable feeling that something concerned with religion should be transacted at a child's bedside, and so, since they did not believe in God or prayer, we studied the *Savage Survivals* instead. The book's theme, so far as I can recollect, was the way in which modern civilized life is spoiled by the survival of savage and superstitious practices and customs from a pre-scientific age, and the wonderful time which will be had by all when they finally disappear.

Later, in my early teens, I was presented with a volume called *The Churches and Modern Thought* by a gentleman named Philip Vivian. I still keep it by me and I have, indeed, a sentimental affection for it. Re-read today, its most amusing feature is its touching admiration of the Japanese, whose virtues are extolled to the point of extravagance, and who are put before us by the author, 'as a concrete and magnificent example of a nation whose character is formed entirely by non-theological instruction'. What interested me at the time, however, was not the author's enthusiasm for the infant militarism of distant Japan but his description of Christianity. It was, as I have since become aware, inaccurate and misleading in the extreme, for the method adopted by these anti-religious propagandists is almost invariably that of knocking down a man of straw, of putting before the reader an absurd and grotesque caricature of the beliefs which it is proposed to criticize, so that it only remains for the critic to point out how absurd and grotesque they are. But Mr. Vivian's account of Christianity, however misleading, was at all events near enough to the truth to be interesting and, since he described his book in a sub-title as 'an appeal for candour', it occurred to me that the most candid thing for a youthful inquirer to do was to find out what was to be said on the other side. I knew what Mr. Vivian thought about Christianity, but the code of rigid intellectual honesty in which I had been trained from childhood—and for my rationalist father's conscientious insistence on the importance of this prime virtue I shall always be grateful- -seemed to demand that I should now endeavour to find out what intelligent Christians thought about Christianity. I had been taught that in all circumstances it is a man's duty to sift for himself until he finds a truth which utterly convinces him, and that, above all, he should never treat the intellectual authority of any other man as absolute.

There was never any danger of my over-estimating the importance of the views of Mr. Vivian. Even at fourteen I found him unsatisfactory. There was too much venom and prejudice in his tone, even when he tried most of all to sound sweetly and conscientiously reasonable. No doubt he had personal and psychological reasons for hating Christianity, but I had none, and his obvious bias weakened for me the force of his arguments. To tell the truth, Mr. Vivian was in this matter typical of the R.P.A. writers. I could understand that those who believed in a particular religion should love it passionately, but I found it difficult to comprehend or sympathize with the violent hatred of Christianity which seemed so often to accompany irreligion. I did not notice it at the time, but perhaps the fact that, at all events within the little world of my experience, unbelief meant spitefully denying something whereas belief meant enthusiastically affirming something, provoked in me an adolescent tendency to find religion and religious people more attractive than their critics.

So it was that the question of the truth or falsity of Christianity became a living issue for me, and my rationalist training imposed on me the duty of never letting it drop until I had found an answer to it which could satisfy my reason and dominate and direct my life. This stress on the importance and necessity of intellectual persistence, on the inherent sinfulness of mere apathy and indifference to the solemn questions which life puts before us, is the finest element in the rationalist tradition. It was the best thing that my parents and the friends of my youth had to give me and I gratefully admit that they gave it without stint and placed me in their immeasurable debt. When I came to know Christianity better I discovered that I need not cease being a rationalist in order to become a Christian. Those who call themselves rationalists in the narrow and partisan sense of the word are not necessarily outstandingly rational persons. It is possible to worship the Goddess Reason from afar, to offer lip service to her image without partaking of her spirit. The rationalist who becomes a Christian may well find himself not merely as rationalist in theory as ever, but also much more reasonable in practice.

I now began to seek further information about Christianity from the writings of intelligent Christians. It was not long before I discovered that the rationalists were engaged in attacking a position which, from the intellectual point of view, was much more formidable than they in their somewhat jaunty, over-confident writings had seemed to suppose. I learned with increasing surprise how astoundingly ignorant of the intellectual content of Christianity, of the ultimate purposes which the Christian life pursues and the characteristic emotional attitudes which accompany it, the majority of anti-

Christian writers are. That superficial persons who are merely indifferent to religious problems should be uninterested in specific forms of belief and unbelief alike was quite understandable, but that people should openly reject the Christian religion, and even regard their views on the subject as of sufficient importance to merit publication, without having taken the trouble to obtain any very clear or detailed knowledge of precisely what they were rejecting, seemed to my young mind, indoctrinated with the rationalist ideal of intellectual integrity, to be both shocking and reprehensible. Yet such was very plainly the case, and subsequent experience has only confirmed this first impression. If intelligent Christians knew what Christianity was, and presumably they did, it was evident that writers like Mr. Vivian had nothing more than a vague and ill-informed nodding acquaintance with the subject. I well remember reading some essays of the late Baron von Hügel during this period of intellectual development. I did not at the time altogether understand them, nor should I now entirely agree with them, but even then I was able to see that the comprehensively intellectual religion of the Baron was one to which Mr. Vivian's strictures and criticisms were almost totally irrelevant. Thus I was led to the conclusion that in order to satisfy that hunger for truth which is the noblest element in the rationalist tradition, I must embark upon a more prolonged and open-minded study of Christianity.

I do not wish to suggest that this study, which occupied the second half of my teens and was necessarily immature and defective in the extreme, was of itself responsible for making me a Christian. The personal decision to take one's stand in life on the side of Jesus Christ is always and necessarily much more than a merely intellectual one. It is the decision of the whole man. It is that to which he consents with his entire being. The man who arrives at such a decision experiences a sense of compulsion in making it. It is one which has become for him inevitable. 'Here stand I, I can do no other.' Many other factors are operative beside purely intellectual ones. There is, for example, the disillusioning experience of personal moral failure which throws him back on the Grace of God, and the intimate, and still to me wholly mysterious, process of personal development in the course of which Jesus Christ, who would appear from the superficial point of view to be a remote personage who died many centuries ago, becomes for the subject of the experience a living, dominating personality, with an unexpected power to attract and compel him even against his will. But since every man has some sort of intelligence, such a decision of the whole man must always include an intellectual element, and an inquiry into the content of Christian belief, and into the reasons which render it possible for highly intelligent men to believe in it sincerely, may at all events co-operate with the process of spiritual growth by clearing its paths of obstacles which might otherwise not easily be overcome.

This early study of Christianity as Christians know it led me to make two other observations. For me they were important and intellectually decisive, but I still believe that they have also an objective validity, that they are important not only for me but for everyone.

Broadly contrasting rationalism with Christianity, unbelief with belief, I perceived, and still perceive, in the former a parsimonious tendency to deny the complexity and variety of reality, to commend some of our characteristically human interests and activities while condemning others. The unbeliever is persistently saying, in effect, 'A is true but B is false,' or even, 'Because A is true, B must be false,' whereas the more comprehensive religious mind inclines to the double affirmation, 'Both A and B are true'. Thus it is often maintained that because the physical scientists have achieved conspicuous successes it necessarily follows that the religious attitude towards life is invalid and must be rejected. On the other hand no intelligent Christian, so far as I know, has ever argued that because his faith is true physical science is all moonshine. The Christian philosopher frankly accepts the complexity of the creation, and is neither surprised nor discouraged by the difficulty which he sometimes experiences in his efforts to relate one random truth to another, to harmonize the diverse interests and activities of his fellow-men. He knows that more penetrating thought and profound information than his will some day succeed where he has failed, that patience is among the greatest of the intellectual virtues, if only because it preserves us from the narrow arrogance of the one-track mind which will reject one partially assimilated truth in the name of another.

From the first I found this greater breadth and comprehensiveness of the religious mind one of its most attractive features. I had been brought up among people who were so interested in earth that they denied the reality of heaven. I was, of course, aware that some eastern religions are conversely guilty of such a concentration on heaven that they tend towards a denial of earth, but Christianity, at all events, was emphatic about the existence of both. Indeed, it went beyond a mere affirmation of their twin reality in its practical grasp of the fact that some men are temperamentally more interested in heaven whereas others are more inclined towards serving

B

God by doing something here and now about the problems of earth, and that both attitudes are legitimate and complementary. It takes all sorts to make a Church. There is a primarily contemplative Christianity and there is a primarily active Christianity, and both are regarded as valid in the rich and complex ethical tradition of the Church because both are concerned with reality. Accustomed as I was to the tiny island of affirmation situated in a vast ocean of denial inhabited by the rationalist, this broader and more tolerant attitude towards life introduced me to a larger, more complex and therefore more interesting world. We rationalists believed in natural science, economic progress and social reform, democratic politics and (possibly) art. Now, without foregoing one of these interests, the vast realm of classical metaphysics and theology became for me one in which a self-respecting intellectual could wander at will and without shame.

The rationalists had tried to impose upon me a kind of philosophical censorship. All questions which sought to discover the truth about ultimate reality—which inquired as to the origin, purpose, destiny and innermost nature of things—were dogmatically declared unanswerable and it was therefore forbidden to ask them. But once our human curiosity is aroused, it is not so easily silenced, and the young philosopher who finds himself thus sternly enjoined to put aside all metaphysics and theology, and confine himself to mere matters of fact, may well ask how it is that his intelligence, which is certainly capable of propounding metaphysical and theological questions, must necessarily be incompetent to discover or appreciate the answers. Besides, the assertion that a whole realm of reality is inherently unknowable is plainly self-contradictory. The

fact that at the present moment I am unacquainted with
something does not justify me in saying more than that
for the time being I know nothing about it. Before I am
in a position to declare that this unknown thing is not
merely unknown but unknowable, I must know a great
deal about it. A reality could only be unknowable because it possessed certain characteristics, completely distinguishing it from all knowable realities, which must
forever elude my powers of observation and conception.
I should not be justified in roundly declaring that it was
unknowable unless I knew for certain that it possessed
these characteristics. It would therefore appear that I
cannot know a thing to be unknowable without implying that in fact I know a great deal about it. This is the
reductio ad absurdum of all sceptical attempts to dictate
arbitrary limits to the adventurous human intelligence,
to paralyse those thoughts that wander through eternity. Thought is by nature free and it will not consent to
the abject and slave-like existence to which the positivists would condemn it.

And so I entered a sphere in which no question which
the human mind could conceive was forbidden, in which
the intellect could spread its wings and fly, in which not
even the loftiest and most abstract themes of philosophy
were taboo. The pedantic insistence that all knowledge
must be concerned with earthly matters of fact, that all
thought must confine itself to the calculation of temporal advantages, lost all power to restrain me. I imagine
my feelings were not unlike those of an old-time emi-
grant from one of the smaller Balkan states on settling
down in America. I experienced a thrilling and growing
intellectual freedom as I moved step by step towards the
Christian Faith. The horizon before me was indefinitely
expanded. I found that the problems which confront the

human mind are more various and greater than I had been led to suppose, and as I looked towards the present limit of my mental vision I realized that there was still an infinity and eternity of them to come.

My second observation was forced upon my notice not so much by reading and reflection as by the character of the times in which people of my generation had to grow up and discover a philosophy of life. Those who were young in the nightmarish period between the two wars were not able to do their thinking peacefully, in a kind of intellectual paradise, inhabited only by purely logical ideas entering into chaste and serene relationships with each other. Our thoughts had be related to events of an increasingly dramatic and ominous kind. The twenties, on the whole, were not so stormy as the thirties, but even then it was possible for the listening ear to catch without difficulty the sound of 'ancestral voices prophesying war'. An age was dying. We were those upon whom the end of our world was come. By slow stages what we long continued to call the 'post-war period' unmasked itself as yet another 'pre-war period'. The bright hopes raised by the victory of 1918 rapidly faded. The victorious allies quarrelled about almost everything. The economic collapse of western civilization was followed by the rise to supreme political power in Germany of a philosophy which explicitly denied all that western civilization regarded as most certainly true. It was a new Gethsemane. 'Father if it be Thy will, let this cup pass from us.' But why should it be His will? We must drink our own brew, and, in so doing, drink to our own judgment. And there were not lacking those who were ready to take at all events the first sip with considerable relish. In such a tormented atmosphere, thought was inevitably conditioned by events. The age which began with the Renaissance and the Reformation, the age which sought money and power before everything else, which created the vogue of natural science and cynically employed its discoveries in the service of its reigning purposes, was coming to an end. It had become primarily an age of efficiency. Men were learning how to kill each other with increasing efficiency. They were learning how not to reproduce their kind with increasing efficiency. Civilization was mass-producing copies of its own death-warrant in vast quantities. It was busy writing words of doom all over its walls which it seemed tragically unable to interpret.

It seemed to me that the scepticism and intelligent worldliness in which I had been reared was the reigning religion of this dying epoch. For the last two hundred years at least the white peoples of the world have not as a whole taken their religion really seriously. Some have openly rejected it, but more have outwardly conformed to it on condition that it made no effort to guide and direct their lives. Churchmen and non-churchmen alike in practice treated the business of the world, its steadfast pursuit of wealth and power, as more important than the quest for God and His Kingdom. To the world as they understood it and to its demands as they were accustomed to formulate them they devoted the major portion of their time and energy. In the day-to-day conduct of business and politics the behaviour of the man who went to church was indistinguishable from that of the man who did not. Ours is a world which has for centuries devoted itself, its intellectual resources and physical and moral energies, to the service of purposes from which God is excluded. The fact that throughout this period a considerable number of people have continued to sing hymns on Sundays can neither modify, conceal

nor excuse its fundamental godlessness. When a man
of the twentieth century puts worship and prayer out of
his private life he is merely giving open expression to
the spirit of an age which thrust them out of its public
life centuries before he was born. But now this age is
coming to an end. We are the horrified spectators, and
sometimes the stricken victims, of its ultimate consequences. In short, the philosophical outlook in which I
had been brought up seemed to me to be the characteristic outlook of the modern world. (It is significant that
the classical literature of rationalism, which I had been
taught to admire, belongs for the most part to the
eighteenth century.) History, in setting before us the
grim spectacle of the self-destruction of our world was,
for me at all events, refuting its dominant philosophy
with weapons more deadly than the most incisive argument.

By such a process of mental development I was led to
a point at which conversion to the Christian Faith became for me a possibility. At all events the purely intellectual barriers were down. I no longer regarded Christianity as absurd, for I now knew too much about it to
adopt the attitude of smug and complacent mental
superiority characteristic of most rationalists. On the
other hand I had lost all faith in the austere but negative
outlook which I had learned at my father's side, and
which had always in practice and sometimes in theory
dominated the life of my world and times.

Conversion itself was still to come. The longer process
of persuasion must precede the short, sharp hour of
decision. In my case it was delayed a little longer by a
brief flirtation with Marxism, which even then was becoming a fashionable phase of the process of sowing
one's intellectual wild oats. But every man's conversion

is his own affair—like, very like, his falling in love—and
we need not concern ourselves with it here. But this at
least ought to be said: These who think of conversion in
terms of the soul being drawn towards the attractions
and comforts of a real faith—the so-called 'consolations
of religion'—quite misunderstand the nature of both
Christianity and the human soul. When the soul finds
itself near enough to the faith to look it, so to speak, in
the face it is repelled quite as strongly as attracted. Like
a child who has disobeyed his mother to his own hurt,
the soul seeks the faith longing for the comfort and fear-
ful of the admonition. in the depths of himself the man
maturing towards conversion knows that the faith will
insist on doing uncomfortable things with him once it
gets him into its power. No man relishes the prospect of
having the accepted pattern of his life redesigned for
him. There is that in Christianity which persistently
humiliates and ruthlessly criticizes the believer, and it
will be not denied. When God calls, man sometimes
comes, but he comes, if he comes, reluctantly and ner-
vously at first. There is an excitement and joy in the
faith which overcomes the reluctance and the fear, but
not immediately.

The major portion of this book is devoted to a brief
summary of what in fact Christians believe and how
they try to live. It is useless to discuss whether Christianity is true or not until we know what it is, and nowadays such a knowledge is a very rare thing. The reader
should bear in mind that the author is a member of the
Church of England, and naturally his presentation of the
universal faith is influenced by his Anglican background
and point of view. The divisions between Christians are
deep-seated and it would be foolishly optimistic to sup-

pose that they can or will be easily or swiftly overcome.
But they can be exaggerated, and I believe that in fact
most of what I have written here would be endorsed by
Free Church or Roman Catholic readers as much as by
my fellow Anglicans. No doubt I have included some
things which my Protestant friends would prefer to
omit, and excluded others which Roman Catholics
would insist on emphasizing. Nevertheless, I have
thought it best to outline the Christian Faith as I have
received it through the life and witness of the ancient
Church of this land, in the hope and confidence that it
consists for the most part of that universal Christianity
which has bridged the gap between the diverse spirits
and outlooks of many nations and generations.

I neither have nor desire to have any faith of my own.
A real religion is not something which a man can make
for himself, by piecing together his own experiences and
opinions with what he can learn from those of other
people. It is something which makes him rather than
something which he makes. It is of the essence of religion to demand human solidarity and fellowship. Of all
the activities of the human spirit it is the one in which
most of all mere subjectivity and undisciplined 'private
opinion' are out of place. If I had a private religion of
my own I hope I should have also the good sense to keep
it private, for such things cannot be spoken of successfully. But Christianity is a religion which can and must
be communicated. It is because it was communicated to
me that I dare to hope that I may be able to communicate it to others in my turn. It is precisely because I have
no faith of my own that I dare to pray that my faith
may become, even through me, the faith of other men.
The main purpose of this book is objective exposition
not subjective self-expression.

And so, once more and with renewed emphasis, this is not a book about me. I have ventured to produce my credentials, such as they are. I have spoken the prologue. But now I make my bow and hasten to depart before the play begins. But the reader will perhaps forgive me if I yield occasionally to the temptation to peep out at him from the wings!

CHAPTER TWO

THE GOSPEL

If you ask a non-Christian philosopher what he believes to be the truth about ultimate reality, he will, if he is the kind of philosopher who is prepared to make any answer at all to a question of this kind, propound some sort of theory. The Christian, in response to the same question, will tell a story. The non-Christian replies in terms of a neat scientific, mathematical or logical scheme; he will speak of atoms, molecules, quanta, biological cells, the absolute, or what not, but always for him reality will be reduced to abstract, impersonal, dead concepts which are endowed with precisely those properties which they require in order to fit the argument, and no others. They are types, not individuals. For such philosophers the ultimate truth which lies behind all life is death. Behind the dramatic clash of personalities and purposes which we call life and history, they perceive only the impersonal, serene and orderly workings of a nicely proportioned, scientific and mathematical or philosophical and logical scheme.

Reality as Drama

The Christian interpretation of life, on the other hand, is dramatic from top to bottom. However deeply he delves into the heart of reality, the Christian still continues to find evidence of personality, purpose and life, of free choice between equal possibilities, of aspiration,

sacrifice and love. We may call his the dramatic interpretation of life. For him life as we know it now is begotten of the wider, fuller life 'which was in the beginning, is now and ever shall be'. Behind the personality
of man he discerns the personality of God in whose
image man is made; behind the drama of time, the drama
of eternity; behind the wars of earth, the 'war in
heaven'. And so the Christian, asked to give an account
of his convictions about the nature of ultimate reality,
begins by telling a story. Any theories which he may
subsequently formulate will be the fruit not of abstract
speculation but of his reflection on the story, which is
the solid foundation of his life and thought alike.

We may describe such a story as a myth, provided we
are careful to avoid the error of supposing that a myth is
necessarily a fiction. A myth is a dramatization of truth.
We may dramatize a truth imaginatively for ourselves,
or we may find it dramatized for us already in some
historical episode. Other things being equal, historical
myth is more vivid and arresting than legendary myth,
but in the case of primordial and prehistoric events
which lie beyond the range of our historical vision—
like the creation of the world and the beginning of conscious and deliberate wrongdoing—we have no choice
but to rely on myths of an imaginative character.

Some writers have supposed that the mythical way of
expressing truth is characteristic of the child-like primitive mind, whereas the more mature and civilized
modern mind prefers to express beliefs in terms of abstract conceptual theories. This is quite misleading.
Primitive man had his theories and modern man, particularly if he is a political propagandist, makes his
myths. The fact is that myth and theory are parallel and
alternative means of expression. Most truths and beliefs

can be stated either mythically or theoretically, according to the purpose and convenience of the speaker. Thus
in Christianity we have both the biblical myth of the
fall and the theological doctrine of man's fallen condition, and many popular books written to explain the
results of modern scientific discovery to the non-scientific reader abound in imaginative mythical illustration.

Nevertheless, there is an important difference between
these two modes of expression. Theory always carries
with it the suggestion that the reality is impersonal process.
Myth, on the other hand, always assumes or implies that
the reality is personal drama. For this reason the language
of theory is more appropriate when we are giving an
account of the processes of nature, and the language of
myth more serviceable when we are dealing with human
existence and history. The twin errors of being too
mythical about nature and too abstract and conceptual
about man are so familiar and generally recognized that
each has been given a name of its own. Depicting nature
in personal terms is called the 'pathetic fallacy'; schematizing life and history in impersonal terms the 'apathetic
fallacy'. Most people will perceive these two fallacies
for what they are easily enough, but one problem remains. Which kind of language is most appropriate
when we are dealing neither with nature nor with
human life and history, *but with the Ultimate Reality which
lies beyond and behind both?* What I have called the
dramatic view of reality insists that the drama is prior
to the process, that it is quite credible to think of the
chief character in the metaphysical drama initiating the
natural process, to serve as the stage or setting of the
historical drama, and equally incredible to suppose that
the immediate and obviously real drama of our own
existence is a misinterpretation of a rather more than

usually complicated kind of impersonal process. Hence it prefers to express its beliefs about ultimate reality and human destiny through the medium of myth in the first place, and to pass on to theory only at a later stage in the discussion. In this chapter I shall try to tell the story which is the basis of all Christian belief and practice frankly as a story, with a minimum of comment and moralization. But I would emphasize that this Christian myth is above all others one which is composed chiefly of sober and ascertainable history, and which uses imaginative and legendary material to only a minimal and relatively insignificant extent.

In the Beginning

The beginning of this universe to which we belong was not the beginning of everything. There was no absolute beginning. We speak of the beginning of this and that, but not of an absolute beginning of everything. Indeed, the latter would be a self-contradictory notion, for it would imply that before the beginning of everything there was nothing, and out of nothing nothing comes. Before anything began there was and must have been that which has neither beginning nor ending, which is from all eternity to all eternity. Our name for Him is God. In the beginning, therefore, not of everything, but of this universe in which we are, God, because He did not wish to monopolize the privilege of life, called into being spiritual personalities distinct from yet dependent on Himself, out of whose loyalty and love He might fashion a kingdom of living beings freely and joyously co-operating with Him and with each other. Because He sought a kingdom in which these offspring of His would freely do His will,

rather than a mere machine for the automatic registra-
tion of His commands, He was compelled to endow
them with a mysterious capacity to disobey Him if they
chose, although He subtly wedded such acts of disobedience to unsatisfying and disillusioning consequences. These beings, because they were begotten of
His own eternal purpose, may be called His children,
for He loved them with an everlasting love.

Among this vast multitude of the offspring of God
we human beings are included. Our peculiar characteristic, so far as we know, is that we are embodied
spirits, as distinct from the pure spirits or angels who began before we did. Some of these pure spirits misused
God's great gift of freedom, so that before our universe
began there were spiritual forces working against that
very purpose of God for the sake of which they had been
created. No doubt these 'fallen angels' were in part responsible for the tragic fact that as soon as man reached
a stage in his intellectual and spiritual development at
which it was possible for him to distinguish between
good and evil he began to display that proneness to the
latter which has been his most pronounced characteristic
from the dawn of history until now. Thus through all
their generations men have been and are born into a
world in which sin has been going on for a long time.
In other words, both our heredity and our environment
militate against the purpose of God and spoil our lives
by estranging us from Him and from the destiny which
He ordained for us.

True, enough good remains in human life to indicate
to us how glorious a thing life was meant to be and is
still, at all events in theory, capable of becoming. All
down the ages men have dreamed of a better world and
sought a better country, of a heaven hereafter or a

utopia on earth. Such dreams are dim and fitful recollections of our real destiny, a more sublime heaven then has dawned upon the inspired imagination of any saint, a more splendid and satisfying utopia than has entranced the mind of any sage. But man has risen higher in aspiration than in deed. He has proved tragically unable to make his actions match his dreams. He cannot climb so high as he can see.

And so, as the centuries of estrangement between God and man mounted up one upon another, men tended to forget what He was like from Whom they came, to dismiss, as an idle dream, all thought of their imposing destiny, and to lose even the capacity to imagine what human life would be like if it were unspoiled by sin. They forgot where they came from, where they were going and why they were here.

But men are not merely the instruments of God's purpose; they are also the children of His purpose. He is not only their Master but also their Father. They were created not for exploitation but for love. A defective instrument can be discarded in favour of a better, but the nature of parenthood is such that an ungrateful, faithless child must be loved until the heart is broken, with a love which may perhaps survive even the breaking.

Because God is Father He will not accept the fall of man as final. His, as the hymn writer says, is 'the love that will not let us go'.

But we must consider the human situation which confronted God before we can begin to understand and appreciate the subtle mastery with which He dealt with it.

As a result of sin all men are the victims of a threefold ignorance and a threefold weakness. Sin may be variously, but in each case correctly, described as disobedience to the commandments of God, as rebellion against the natural laws and necessities which govern our earthly existence, and as a preference for self-centred to God-centred modes of thought and ways of life.

Man's Threefold Ignorance

The sinner is estranged from God because he is so preoccupied with the problems and perplexities of his own existence that he cannot clearly perceive that infinitely greater Reality, so much more important and interesting than himself, in which 'he lives and moves and has his being'. Because he was made for God, and is therefore incapable of attaining any real peace of mind or spiritual satisfaction without God, religious questions still interest him; he is fascinated by the problem of the great unknown out of which he came. But he finds it easier to ask questions than to answer them. Human answers to human questions, even the best of them, are haunted by a sense of uncertainty, by an inherent lack of authority. Man cannot by searching find out God. All human theories about the nature and attitude of the great realities which transcend our observation, of whatever kind—theistic or atheistic, pantheistic or polytheistic—are more or less doubtful. *God cannot be known by man unless God shews Himself to man.*

Man's sin is not only against the laws of God, but also against the law and purpose of his own being. Sin has become a human characteristic so universal that man has lost his capacity even to imagine what life would be like without it. The humanity which a man sees when he looks inwards at himself and outwards at his neighbours is a spoiled humanity, little more than a grotesque caricature of the real thing. The sciences which seek to

study and describe the career and personality of man as
we know him now are similarly unable to give us any
idea of what unspoiled humanity would be like. Psychology—which studies the mentality of man, physi-
ology—which scrutinizes his physique, history—which
investigates his past, sociology—which analyses his
social structures, are alike sciences which study man as
sinner, inevitably so, for life presents them with no alternative datum. What is real, unspoiled manhood like?
Our ethical writers and imaginative utopians have
laboured to provide us with an answer to this urgent
human question, but their answers are haunted by the
same inherent uncertainty that pervades our religious
speculations. *Unless God revives and reveals the original
pattern of humanity, man cannot know for certain even what
he himself truly is.*

Man's ultimate destiny is as darkly mysterious to him
as his origin and present nature. If he knows not for
certain whence he comes and for what purpose he is
here, his final destination is equally in doubt. After
death, what? This question has fascinated and perplexed
every human century, and the same familiar uncertainty
robs every human answer, of whatever kind, of the confidence and cogency it seeks. Another life in another
world, rebirth in this one, nothing at all, all these answers have been advanced, with local and ephemeral
variations, and all of them are more or less debatable.
We do not know for certain what awaits us. *Man cannot
know his destiny unless God shows him a concrete example of
its fulfilment.*

Man's Threefold Weakness

But ignorance is not the only fruit of sin. Self-centred-
c

ness is a colossal stupidity, for although a man may pretend for practical purposes that he is the centre of his own world, he is certainly not the centre of the real one, and hence, in building up a self-centred existence, he is constructing a world of fictions. Not the least tragic of the results of this futile process is the inability which it brings with it even to utilize such knowledge as we have. Even when man knows God it does not follow that he will be able to seek and serve Him. Even when he becomes satisfied that a certain form of action is right, it does not follow that he will be able to perform it. Even when he conceives and embraces the true idea of his destiny, it does not follow that he will be able to achieve it. Man needs more than knowledge. He requires also a revolutionary transformation of his affections, so that he can begin to desire and love the truth which is shewn to him; he needs a will-power greater than his own so that he can begin to obey the laws which are revealed to him; he needs an inspired perseverance, a harmonious concentration of all his vital and spiritual powers, if he is to pursue without deviation the destiny which is set before him.

To sum up, in Christian terminology, man needs grace as well as truth, and 'grace and truth came by Jesus Christ'.

Enter the Hero

In order to illuminate our threefold ignorance and remedy our threefold weakness God, who made us and loves us, 'for us men and for our salvation', in the midst of history—'in the fulness of time', as St. Paul says—became man. The Word who in the beginning was with God and indeed was God, was made flesh and we beheld His glory. Thus St. John sums up the essence of the Christian story—a thrilling adventure of which God is the hero, crossing infinite spiritual distances and over-coming seemingly insuperable metaphysical obstacles in order to re-establish contact with man, a spiritual romance in which God is the lover clamouring passionately at the gateways of the human heart. As a result of this divine action, an episode as unexpected and unlooked for by the children of this world as the arrival of Columbus by the aborigines of the Americas, contact was re-established between man and God, between time and eternity, between earth and heaven.

When the Christians say that God became man, they use the words literally and not at all figuratively. God really became man without ceasing to be God. He did not merely disguise Himself as a man, as the Greeks, for example, have often portrayed their merry and attractive but fatally fictitious gods and goddesses as doing. His was a real babyhood and youth, a real growth in mind and stature, a desperately human hunger, an exquisitely human pain, an agonizingly human death. In His thirty years of incarnate existence, God was touched and harrowed by all that is most menacing in the lot of man—physical pain, economic insecurity, subtle temptation, a tragic death foreseen and awaited, the frustration of noble purposes, intellectual misunderstanding, the wearisome, disillusioning absence of sympathy, slander, unpopularity, injustice, persecution, rejected love. All that most easily overcomes the spirit of man He faced without defeat, all that is most prone to embitter and distort the human character He absorbed without bitterness or spiritual loss, smiled kindly through the endless frustrations which so often cynicize and disillusion

romantic and idealistic men, loved unwearyingly
through the rejection of love with a love which not even
hatred could remould in its own image, confronted
temptation with an invincible perfection of character
and purpose against which the hitherto victorious
powers of evil were powerless, and finally placed in the
hands of death a life so intense and concentrated on its
destiny that death's age-old mastery over life was revealed as a broken thing.

Truth comes by Jesus Christ

He is the image of the invisible God. Whoever sees Him
sees the Father. He answers, not merely in words but in
concrete and heroic human living, not in the abstract
and speculative terms of philosophy but by bitter and
bloody participation in the storm and stress of history,
all man's religious questionings. Where, perhaps Who,
do we come from? The God whom man cannot find by
searching shows Himself in the life and death and resurrection of Christ.

But Christ is human as well as divine. He is not only
the image of the invisible God, but also the image of the
forgotten man. He reveals the truth about manhood as
well as the truth about Godhead. He is the true man. 'All
we like sheep have gone astray.' We have fallen beneath
the level of our own manhood. In Him we see an unspoiled, truly natural manhood. In Him we see what we
cannot see in ourselves and in each other, God's purpose
in conceiving, designing and creating manhood fulfilled.
In Him, with Pilate, we 'behold *the* man'. But if the
earthly perfection of Christ's human nature reveals to us
fully for the first and only time in history our own
latent capacities, His risen glory, the transfiguration of

the perfect manhood by an unparalleled act of God, is
also a reminder and a foretaste of our brilliant destiny.
Christ is the first fruit, we are the main crop. In Him,
then, we see not only what we must become here and
now if our way of life is to correspond to our real
nature, and to the purpose of Him who created us, but
also what we are to become hereafter.

Grace comes by Jesus Christ

He dispenses not knowledge only but also power. In
Him we find redemption as well as revelation. He makes
possible much more than a merely external knowledge
about God. Rather the characteristic fruit of His work
is a living fellowship between God and man, a mysterious union of the Creator and the creature, in which the
Creator's creative purpose is fulfilled and the creature's
life is infinitely transfigured and enriched. Faith in
Christ unlooses new moral and spiritual forces in the
life of the Christian. At its best, as we see it in the saints,
the Christian life is distinguished not so much by its
more intimate knowledge of God as by its sacrificial
love and reckless desire for Him; not so much by its
profound and therefore more humiliating self-knowledge as by its capacity for radical and creative repent-
ance—an internal personal revolution so comprehensive
in its results that its comparative rarity outside Christianity has given birth to the widespread illusion that our
characters and temperaments are fixed and unalterable
from birth to death; not so much by its romantic prevision of an enticing destiny as by its possession of a very
efficient spiritual technique—mystical, sacramental and
moral—of attaining it. In short, Christ gives us not only
new and otherwise unobtainable knowledge but also

the power to make some practical use of it. This power
is what Christians call Grace.

The Hero's Less Heroic Family

Grace passes from God to man through contact. It is
in the Christian Church that men enjoy the most intimate and sustained contact with God which is possible
in this life. For the Church is in a profound sense a part
of Christ. Every baptized Christian is a *member of Christ*,
using the word *member* in its literal sense of *limb*. The
Church is so much part of Christ that the story of the
Church is an episode in the whole story of Christ, so
that in a sense the life of Christ is still unfinished because
Church history has not yet come to an end. The Church
has nothing in common with a merely commemorative
fellowship, like the Dickens Society, which looks back
admiringly at its dead hero and devotes itself to honour-
ing his memory and studying his works.

For the Christian, Christ is not a dead hero but a living
Lord. The function of the Church is not to preserve His
memory but to enjoy and proclaim His presence. He
who was dead is alive and with us always, to the world's
end and beyond.

The story of the Church is therefore, from one point
of view at all events, the story of the activity of the
Risen Christ.

He is still the same Christ. For example, to this day He
continues to show His old preference for this world's
disreputables. He, the saviour of sinners, still prefers to
keep company with the publicans and sinners. The great
Physician is still of opinion that He can spend His time
more usefully with those who are sick than with those
who are whole. And the Pharisees have not changed

very much either. They are still scandalized by the Lord's liking for low company. They are still tricked into a denial of His claims by their not unnatural contempt for His friends. To this day many unbelievers continue to declare loudly to the world their own moral superiority to the believers. No doubt they are right. Christians spend a great deal of their time in their corporate worship frankly confessing that they are unworthy of the name of Christ, and anyone closely acquainted with them will know that they are by no means exaggerating. Even such virtues as they do attain they ascribe not to their own excellence but to the power of God. The unbelievers, on the other hand, can at least call their virtues their own, and they frequently do.

But the Christian will obstinately insist that he is the richer of the two. 'You are an excellent fellow', he says to the good pagan, 'and your many splendid virtues are richly rewarded by your comfortable sense of possessing them, by your pleasure in their exercise and your natural pride in their achievement. My faith compels me to contrast myself with Christ and the sense of being a sinner must therefore haunt me for all eternity. But although I am doomed never to find satisfaction in my self-knowledge, this is more than compensated by the joy of fellowship with God through Christ. When you turn to that inner core of your life which transcends your intercourse with natural things and human society, that innermost incommunicable part of you which must either be shared with what is more than man or never shared at all, then you, unfortunate sir, are alone. I know that I am never alone. You have your virtues, but I have my Lord. The comparison contents me.'

So much for our attempt to compress into a few pages

the fundamentals of the Christian experience and out-look. All reality is vividly personal and dramatic. It is not superficially personal and profoundly impersonal as many scientists and philosophers suppose. Behind the drama of time lies the drama of eternity. And these are not two dramas but one, for the characters of the eternal drama are intensely preoccupied with the predicament of those in the temporal drama. God so loves the world that He comes into it, and the fruit of His unheralded entry is a new way of life which men can share with Him. The first effect of this new way of life upon those who endeavour to live it—or, more accurately, to live in it—is not so much to make them better than their fellows as to make them more acutely conscious of their grievous moral defects and of man's desperate need for some power greater than his own to enter his life, to work for him an interior personal transformation of which his own unaided capacities would be utterly in-capable. This transforming process is sometimes swift and sometimes slow. Sometimes it begins dramatically in the broad daylight of youthful or adult self-conscious-ness, and sometimes in infancy, before the dawn of memory and conscious reflection, the process is incon-spicuously started in the immature soul through the agency of the Christian environment into which the child is born. In any case God's policy with man is a long-term policy and the finished product is not visible from here.

That, in brief, is what the Christian calls the Gospel. The rest of this book will be devoted to the amplification of this theme, to a sketch of the philosophy of life which it has begotten in the minds of those who accept it, and some consideration of the objections and misconceptions which its proclamation has sometimes aroused in the audience. But before we turn to our main exposition, we must first indicate the relation between the Gospel, God's answer to our human questions, God's response to our human predicament, and the various attempts, some of them very splendid, which men have made, impelled by needs inherent in their nature, to answer their questions for themselves and to diagnose their own malady independently of the Gospel, perhaps because they lived before the days of its proclamation, perhaps because, although they have heard it, they have been unable to make it their own.

The Alternatives to the Gospel

What then is the relation between the Christian Gospel on the one hand, and non–Christian philosophy and religion on the other? The simplest and therefore most attractive theory is that which would reduce this relationship to the stark contrast between absolute truth and absolute falsehood. The Gospel answers man's questions correctly, whereas all other philosophies and religions answer them incorrectly. The Gospel makes the only practical and appropriate response to our human predicament, whereas all other philosophies, although they purport no doubt sincerely to make adequate provision for man's spiritual needs, in effect fail to make any response at all. But this simple and direct antithesis is one which the intellectual honesty and common sense of Christians renders unacceptable. The great philosophical, ethical and religious systems of mankind do at least bear witness to a diffused awareness of God and a profound impulse towards God, inherent in human nature, which even sin has proved powerless to eradicate. This blind groping for God, this hunger and thirst after a righteousness, sometimes conceived as abstract and impersonal, an ethical code, and sometimes in visions perceived to be active and intensely personal, the Living God, is a universal phenomenon running through all history. It bears witness to the important truth that the Spirit of God has never separated Himself from the spirit of man, that human nature, because it was destined and created for the purpose of God, cannot content itself with a godless existence.

In the great philosophies we see man's submerged and confused awareness of God, and of the reality of the invisible world, rising to the light of day and becoming articulate in the conscious reflections of wise and gifted men. In the great religions we witness man's effort to make contact with the unseen, to pass from an intelligent awareness of God's existence to some kind of direct experience of his living personality, or at least, where this idea of ultimate divine personality has been rejected, to the immersion and loss of our own finite personalities in what is regarded as the boundless and all-pervading impersonality of the Absolute. The saints and mystics who originated and developed the great religions were not content, as the sages who begot the great philosophies so often were, with mere awareness of God's existence. They wanted to know what He was like and what we must do, what kind of life we must live, in order to enter into fellowship with Him. Out of their experiences in meditation, vision or trance, or in vividly dramatic moments of prophetic inspiration, they endeavoured to piece together a spiritual picture of Him and to formulate His demands on men.

Always the essence of this demand was that men should strive after likeness to God, so that their doctrines of God determined the type of conduct which they recommended to their fellows. If they thought of God as personal, they sought to become more intensely and harmoniously personal in themselves, emphasizing the importance of self-control and fixity of purpose, and recommending a deliberate cultivation of will-power, so that the self-conscious personality of man should emerge triumphantly out of the tangle of impersonal and directionless emotion and impulse beneath which it is too easily buried. If they thought of God as impersonal, they distrusted human personality and advocated the systematic extinction of purpose and desire. If they thought of God as good, they demanded in His name the utmost ethical endeavour from men. If they thought of him as non-moral, their recommendations as to human conduct displayed a like indifference to ethical standards.

Even to-day our idea of the good still remains fundamentally dependent on our idea of God. Thus, for example, one of the characteristics of thought in an age greatly influenced by the successes of physical science has been a widespread tendency to substitute the idea of an impersonal nature, uniformly obedient to mechanical laws, for the idea of a personal God. This has introduced a subtle inclination to depreciate the claims of individual personality in contemporary schemes for the reform and reconstruction of our social life. More and more we incline to think in terms of a large-scale planned society, devoted to satisfying, by the mass production of standardized products, the elementary physical needs that all men have in common, rather than in terms of one which aims at the production and nurture of unique personalities and the satisfaction of their unique requirements. We are moving towards a world in which personal eccentricity, even of the noblest kind, will be in-

creasingly at a discount, a world which, having labori-
ously constructed an elaborate and correspondingly
fragile social and economic system, will more readily
think in terms of fitting human beings into it than of
undertaking the delicate and dangerous task of readapt-
ing it to meet the rich complexity and variety of personal needs. It is equally significant that an epoch which
has tended to put nature in the place of God has also
seen a reassertion of the will to power and a revival of
systematic cruelty on an undreamed of scale. This is because nature can as easily be thought of in terms of
biology as in terms of physics, and in this case men will
tend to interpret it not as a serene impersonal efficiency,
impelling those who contemplate it towards an equally
serene and impersonal planned and collective social
order, but as a bloody struggle for existence producing
in its admirers a sadistic reverence for ruthlessness and
brutality and an insatiable delight in war. Thus Nazi
Germany was one of the typical products of a narrowly
scientific age—by which term we refer, not to the fact
that in our modern period the quest for a knowledge of
nature has prospered more than ever before in history,
but to the widely prevailing tendency to regard nature
as science reveals her as the ultimate reality, that is, to
put nature in the place of God. The soulless efficiency
and mechanical discipline, the all-embracing collectivism of Nazi Germany and Soviet Russia reflected and
still reflects the cult of nature as it is at all events supposed
to be revealed by the physical sciences. Their ruthless
self-assertion and brutality seem necessary, and therefore
appear to 'make sense', in the context of what is again
popularly regarded as the conception of nature to which
we are led by the biological sciences, a struggle for existence in which success waits upon the strong. This is a

digression, but at least it illustrates the permanence of the tendency to base our doctrine of the good on our doctrine of God.

Thus in philosophy man expresses and articulates his confused consciousness of the fact that he is not alone in the universe, that he lives and moves and has his being in a wider and more inclusive life than his own. In religion man shows his dissatisfaction with a mere knowledge of God's existence, his desire to love and serve what he knows and to make human life an imitation of the divine. But the various philosophies and religions of mankind all fall more or less short of their aim. Some approach it more closely than others, but the Gospel alone supplies that which philosophy and religion seek.

Only God can tell us the real truth about God. Only the Creator of man can tell us the real truth about our present nature and our ultimate destiny. But the Gospel when it comes does not hesitate to use the noblest achievements of the men of philosophy and the men of religion. Thus, in the providence of God as Christians would say, the highest development in the sphere of religion, that of the Hebrews from the patriarchs through Moses to the prophets and thence to the zealous reverence for the law of God of first-century Judaism, prepared the way for the first proclamation of the Gospel. Later the superb outburst of philosophical genius which was the glory of ancient Greece provided indispensable aid to the early Christian Church when, on the basis of the Gospel, it began to work out a comprehensive Christian philosophy of life. No Christian can deny that the Spirit of God was in the Old Testament writers, for their words are now incorporated in his own Bible. Similarly, Christians would find it difficult to deny that the Spirit of God was in early Greek philosophy, for the wisdom of men like Plato and Aristotle has influenced and interpenetrated Christian thought from its very beginnings.

CHAPTER THREE

THE FAITH

The purpose of this chapter is to provide the reader with a brief and simple account 'of those things which are most surely believed' among Christians. For the moment we are concerned only with exposition. The immediate question which concerns us is not, 'Is Christianity true?' but, 'What is it?' I believe that the religious education of the last few generations has so been neglected that a large number of both those who call themselves Christians and those who do not, and perhaps an even larger number of sincerely perplexed people, would be quite unable to give an adequate answer to this second question if it were put to them.

I have selected as the basis of this exposition what is among the most ancient and unquestionably the most widely accepted of all summaries of the Christian Faith —'The Apostles' Creed'.

The assertions contained in the Apostles' Creed fall into three classes: (*a*) Metaphysical assertions about the nature of ultimate reality. These statements are theological in the strict sense of the word, that is, they are concerned with the character and purpose of God; (*b*) Anthropological assertions about the nature, predicament and destiny of the human race; (*c*) Historical assertions about events alleged to have taken place in Galilee and Judea nearly two thousand years ago. The metaphysics and anthropology of the Creed are based on the history. What a Christian believes about God and man is derived

47

from the truth about Godhead and manhood given to us once and for all in the life, death and resurrection of the 'GOD-MAN', Jesus Christ. The central, historical portion of the Apostles' Creed is therefore the very heart of it. Without any rearrangement, however, we will discuss its affirmations in their familiar order.

I believe in God the Father Almighty, Maker of Heaven and Earth

This brief statement makes in a few words no less than five major assertions:

(1) That God exists.
(2) That He is our Father.
(3) That He is Almighty.
(4) That there is an invisible and spiritual world just as truly as there is a visible, material world.
(5) That God created both these worlds.

That an ultimate power of some kind exists has been obvious to men at all times. We are all aware, sometimes painfully aware, that we are not the most powerful beings in the universe, that there is a power greater than our own and greater than that of any finite thing known to us, and that we must live as best we can in its presence. There are, of course, other names which have been given to this ultimate power beside the familiar word 'God'. The Absolute, Nature, the Life-Force, the Dialectic, are all names given to what the Christian calls God and each of them implies a different type of belief about Him. Those who use the word 'God' believe that this ultimate power, whose existence all men recognize, is personal. The essence of personality is the capacity to choose without external constraint between equal possiblities. Wherever there are persons there are things

done which need not have been done and possibilities
neglected which could equally well have been realized.
Those who believe in God hold that a selective activity
of this kind is implied by the very existence of the universe of which we are a tiny part. It cannot be said that
the creation was something which simply had to take
place. There is nothing absurd or self-contradictory in
the idea of no creation. As we know, there is a world,
but there might equally well have been none. Nor, even
if there was to be a world, can we perceive any reason
for supposing that it must necessarily have been the kind
of world we know ours to be. It might equally well have
differed from this world in an almost infinite variety of
ways. Thus we seem driven to the conclusion that the
ultimate reality is personal, that its activity is selective,
deliberately realizing some possibilities and neglecting
others—just as I do myself when I decide to go to the
cinema rather than spend the evening at home with a
new book. This conclusion would appear to be not
merely one for which the evidence is exceedingly strong
but rather one of quite overwhelming rational necessity.
The onus of proof, that is, would appear to rest on
those who reject it rather than on those who assert it.
The ultimate reality is therefore personal and hence we
speak of Him, not It, of God, not of some impersonal
Absolute.

The Christian holds God responsible not merely for
the origin of the universe but also for its maintenance in
being from the beginning until now. The idea of a God
who created the universe and thereafter took no further interest in it is called 'Deism', a heresy popular in
the eighteenth century. It is a doctrine which satisfies one
particular intellectual need of man while frustrating all
his religious needs. Those who believe in it are in a

D

position to account for the origin of the universe by
saying that God created it. But a God invented by men
simply in order to get them out of one particular
philosophical perplexity is not one who can be adored,
worshipped and obeyed. According to the Christian
belief, God is the Governor as well as the Creator of the
world, which could no more continue without Him
than it could begin without Him. The word 'Providence' is used to describe this government of the world
by God. The Christian belief that God is in absolute
control of all that happens 'in His creation gives rise to
the most familiar and probably the most profound of
all religious difficulties, for it would seem to imply that
God must be held responsible for evil occurrences as well
as for good.

Another implication of the doctrine of Providence is
that God perfectly understands every created thing.
Nothing is excluded from the all-embracing' comprehensiveness of His knowledge. Perfect knowledge of
created things must necessarily belong to the Creator
alone. Even in this life we understand most intimately
what we ourselves have made. Other men's constructions
we observe from without, but we comprehend the true
purpose and formation of our own achievements from
within. It is God's entire comprehension, at once of the
actual state and latent capacities of the universe, that
makes Him its Master. Even among men, knowledge is
power. Absolute knowledge is absolute power.

But the Christian sees in God not only absolute power
but also absolute love. At this point we begin to rely for
our knowledge of God not on our own reasoning, nor
on the confused sense, universal among men, of the
existence of a power far greater than our own which
can and must ultimately determine our destiny, but on

the historic figure of Jesus Christ. The God who shows Himself to us in Jesus is perfect Fatherhood, absolute Power absolutely blended with absolute Love.

We are more accustomed to the separation and opposition of power and love than to their unity and conjunction. We know how disappointing and inefficient human sympathy and sincere goodwill can become, how easily love degenerates into mere sentimentality; and we have learned also, at great cost, how ruthless and unloving human power can be. We shall see that Christianity repeatedly emphasizes bold contrasts of this kind between what happens on earth and what is eternally true in heaven; for sin is a distortion of reality, and not the least tragic consequence of living in a sinful world is that it makes the truth seem, at all events superficially, incredible. Certainly there cannot be a more striking or dramatic contrast than that between the brutality of modern power—as we see it, for example, in Soviet Russia—side by side with the miserable failure of modern goodwill—of which the frustrations of U.N.O. provide a melancholy example—and the strong love of God, invincibly strong and invincibly loving, revealed to us in Christ.

In God's creation there is an invisible and spiritual part just as truly as there is visible and material part. The spiritual and material are not two separate worlds but two interpenetrating and interacting realities which together compose the one world in which we live. We ourselves are examples of this complex but complete unity of body and spirit. My soul and my body are not contemporary but distinct realities. They are so subtly mingled and united that it is impossible to tell precisely where the one ends and the other begins. In our experience the response of the body to the purposes which the spirit embraces is so swift and immediate, a transaction taking place so deep down in the roots of our being, that it entirely eludes our consciousness. As I talk, for example, my awareness of an intention to employ the words appropriate to my meaning is followed so instantly by my awareness of using them that I am not conscious of any interval between the two, and my theoretically distinct experiences of intending to do something and actually doing it fuse into one.

Just as the spiritual and bodily part of the man make one person, so the spiritual and material parts of the creation together compose one world. All of it is created and governed by God; all of it is essentially good; all of it is injured by sin; all of it redeemed by Christ. Clearly, the Christian Faith repudiates utterly the very prevalent notion that the material part of the world is so inferior to the spiritual as to be unworthy of association with it, a view which has often been exaggerated into such dismal and dangerous heresies as that of the Manicheans, who believe that matter is inherently evil and that our possession of bodies is the cause of our sin, or that of those Gnostics who taught that God created only the spirit and that matter emanates from an evil power opposed to His will, or that of some of our more hysterically pagan modern poets, who seem to suppose that they can only affirm the goodness of the life of the body by denigrating the life of the spirit and agitating slanderously against all morality. Against such false antitheses the Christian insists on the validity of physical needs and the wholesomeness of the emotional and aesthetic joys which accompany their satisfaction. The physical life of man, like his spiritual life, is spoiled by sin, and therefore, so that our redemption in Christ may be complete, we see in Him a physical life as well as a spiritual life restored to perfect health and complete accord with the will of its Creator. The Word is made flesh and the sacred flesh of Christ plays its necessary part in His work of revelation and redemption. Indeed, the mystery of the empty tomb and the visions of the Glorified Body of the Risen Christ which followed it, a Body so like and yet so unlike ours, has impressed upon the Christian mind the conviction that in some way, the methods and implications of which we are clearly not in a position to analyse and elucidate, our physical life will share in the blessings of the peace which Christ will re-establish between ourselves and God, and will have its place in our attainment of our final destiny, so that the life with Christ in God which awaits us will be a life to be lived by the whole man and not merely by the spiritual part of him alone.

And in Jesus Christ His only Son Our Lord, who was con-ceived by the Holy Ghost, born of the Virgin Mary

In a comparatively unimportant region of the Roman Empire, among a peasant people who treasured in their minds a centuries-old expectation that God would send them the Messiah, a heaven-sent Prince or King who would deliver His people from aggression and establish a golden age of justice and freedom, there was born nearly two thousand years ago the most important figure in the history of mankind. Rightly He has been regarded by the historians of the Christian era as the turning point in our human story. All that happened before His birth is dated B.C., 'before Christ'. All that has happened since is dated A.D., meaning not, it is important to notice, 'after Christ', but 'in the year of Our Lord', in that part of history that belongs to Him, that is dominated by His

Spirit, that either rises and progresses because of its knowledge and love of Him or falls and decays in futile rebellion against its Lord. His mother called Him Jesus, leader or saviour of men, but men subsequently hailed Him as Messiah or Christ, dimly discerning that this saviour was from heaven. Thus the double name, Jesus Christ, accurately sums up the complex truth about His personality, which was and is at once divine and human.

He might conceivably have been born at any time or in any place. The precise moment and locality of His birth was determined by the will of God. (We have already seen that God's way of selecting freely, and therefore inscrutably, between equal possibilities, just as we do, is convincing evidence of His will and Personality.) Other children are born as the fruit of the intercourse, sometimes loving and deliberate and sometimes not, which has taken place between their parents. They emerge out of the world process, each one a fresh instance of what the creation is capable of producing, a new and unique variation on an old and familiar theme. This child, however, came not out of the world but into it. He was the Creator's gift to the creation and not the creation's gift to the Creator. At His birth God intruded into the world-process what could not conceivably have emerged out of it—Himself, the Creator sustaining the role of a part of the creation, as an author might appear in his own play. Of necessity so unique an event had to take place in a unique manner. Jesus was born not of a man and a woman but of a woman become the instrument of God.

The miracles of the gospel are best understood as the unique consequences of a unique cause. An absolutely extraordinary career, such as that of the God-Man, must inevitably be accompanied by circumstances of an equally extraordinary character. The miracles of the gospel do not prove the doctrine of the Incarnation. They merely corroborate it. To believe in the gospel miracles without believing in the Incarnation would be absurd, but not more absurd than a belief in the Incarnation which rejected the miracles. The unique cause must have its unique effects. It is impossible to suppose either without the other. The two together make a convincing picture.

It should be emphasized that the Virgin Birth is in no sense to be interpreted as casting a slur on marriage. There is no suggestion that the normal way of being born is somehow a bad or disreputable thing. On the contrary, Christians regard it, with all natural things, as something given by God and therefore inherently good. But the normal way of being born is not necessarily a suitable way for the God-Man to be born, for, as we have seen, normal human birth implies a 'coming-out-of' whereas the birth of Christ was a 'coming-into'.

The idea of the 'God-Man' is not one which the human mind has at any time found it easy to grasp. The intellect tends to dislike the unfamiliar and to be horrified and scandalized by the unique. From the moment of its first proclamation to the world there has been an almost continuous stream of attempts to explain away the Incarnation. There have been those who insisted that Our Lord was divine but not truly and completely human; and those, on the other hand, according to whom He was primarily human and only divine in a more or less figurative sense. One interesting early heresy, known as Nestorianism, although it originated at the end of the fourth century A.D., has quite a modern psychological flavour and seems to interpret the mystery of Our

Lord's being in terms of dual personality, two separate
although harmonious personalities inhabiting and using
the same body. Another early heresy, Arianism, thinks
of Jesus as neither divine nor human, but as a being
intermediate between the two, resembling both in
striking but different ways. Thus the ancient world exhausted all the possibilities—divine but not human,
human but not divine, neither divine nor human, an
external conjunction of divinity and humanity. No
heresy can be original. No heresy can claim to be
somehow more modern and 'up-to-date' than orthodoxy.

Of these four forms of heresy, the second is probably
the most widespread in the twentieth century. The
humanity of Our Lord is insisted upon and His divinity
is either explicitly denied or explained away as little
more than a figure of speech. According to some writers
there is a spark of divinity in us all, but a much brighter
spark in Jesus than in anyone else. Others interpret Him
as a great prophet and teacher and nothing more.
Others again think of Him in terms of human genius
and regard Him as a being endowed with a supreme
talent for moral and spiritual activity analogous to the
equally consummate although very different gifts manifested by such men as Shakespeare in poetry, Beethoven
in music, Newton in physical science and Napoleon in
war. All such writers agree in picturing Jesus as a gentle
and humane preacher of earthly righteousness, declaring
to men the fatherhood·of God and the brotherhood of
men

The primary difficulty about such theories is their
remoteness from all the written records of the earthly
career of Jesus which are still in our possession. In each
of the four New Testament gospels and in the epistles

of St. Paul, which were probably written at an earlier date than any of them, Jesus is presented to us as the Messiah, in whom all the prophetic hopes and visions of the Hebrew people recorded in the Old Testament are fulfilled and more than fulfilled. The picture of Jesus as a kindly ethical teacher is an entirely fanciful and fictitious one which runs counter to all the historical evidence we possess. The sole recommendation of such a picture, and for many modern men and women it has seemed to be a sufficient recommendation, is that it rids us of what has been called 'the scandal of particularity'.

The human intellect abhors the unique. It never feels comfortable until it has succeeded in placing any new thing which is presented for its inspection in a class alongside a number of other more familiar things, and so it is rendered happy and comfortable by the thought that Jesus is no more than one ethical and religious teacher among many—although, no doubt, the best of them, or one human genius among many—possibly the greatest, or a being possessed indeed of a divinity, but a divinity which is similar in character to that with which ordinary human beings are endowed—even if, in his case, it is greater in degree. But is there any real reason for supposing that what is unique and sharply distinct from everything else never occurs? Certainly, the human intellect would have an easier time of it if this were so, but it would be foolhardy in the extreme to suppose that one of the functions of reality is to minister to the laziness and conventionality of man's intelligence. Once we admit the bare possibility of the unique, and we can find no rational grounds for refusing to do so, the argument for these modern reconstructions of Our Lord's career falls to the ground, and their extreme divergence from all the surviving historical records will compel us, as a matter of sheer intellectual honesty, to reject them.

There is another objection to this modern picture of Jesus as a gentle and movingly sincere preacher of moral purity. Men like that do not get themselves crucified. The cynical men of the world, who are the rulers of its present darkness, tend on the whole to be very tolerant of ethics. They are well aware that in a fallen world such as this the teaching of ethics, telling men what they ought to do and how much happier they would all be if only they did it, is a futile proceeding which is unlikely to make any noticeable difference to the course of history. The Christian gospel is quite a different thing. It deals not with ethical obligations but with present and pressing realities. It proclaims not duties but facts. The gospel, it has been truly said, is good news not good advice. It fights against sin not so much by moral exhortation as by shewing that sin is absurd.

The facts revealed and declared in the gospel about the attitude and purpose of God, and the nature and destiny of man, were such as to make nonsense of the political and social systems, the personal and corporate assumptions, which dominated, and to a great extent still dominate, the life of mankind. In a social system built on slavery, for example, the sensitive, kindly person who goes about declaring that slavery is wrong can in practice be tolerated with safety. Human self-interest, and the ingenuity of the human intelligence when self-interest employs it in its service, aided and abetted by human conventionality, by the average man's inability to believe that what all his neighbours, even the nice ones, are doing can conceivably be wrong, may be trusted to fulfil their normal function of freezing and paralysing the conscience.

The challenge of Christ and Christianity to Jewry and Rome was of a more radical character. The danger to the established order of the ancient world was fully revealed when one of its citizens, preaching a new interpretation of reality and without any particular interest in attacking slavery on moral grounds casually remarked, in drawing out a few of the implications of his philosophy, that the slave, after all, is the Lord's free man, while the free man is the Lord's slave. Those who were led to accept this picture of ultimate reality would perceive from this new intellectual standpoint not that slavery is wrong—which in a fallen world might even add to its attractions—but that slavery is nonsense, contradicting not merely humane ethical laws but the fundamental facts of life. In an empire whose laws proclaimed that slavery exists, St. Paul the Christian declared not that it ought not to exist but that in fact it cannot exist, that the law is not so much an outrage as a fiction, not bad morals but bad theology; and as men in increasing numbers accepted St. Paul's teachings about the nature of God and man they revolted increasingly against what seemed to them the legally imposed farce of pretending that what is not is. To crusade against the law is just one more way of bearing witness to its majesty and power. To appeal from law to reality is to expose it as a hollow sham. A social order, like the Roman Empire, brought face to face with a theology which makes nonsense of its most cherished and basic institutions is fighting for its life, and fighting perhaps in vain. But kindly ethical teachers are not worth crucifying. It was not for an ethic that the Saviour and His first apostles died but because they brought with them a new picture of reality, human and divine, which seized the social order by the throat.

Human and divine. In order to reveal to us the hidden truth about Godhead and the forgotten truth about manhood, Christ had to be, in the most literal sense of both words, at once divine and human, and to this belief in the double nature of the one personality of Christ the Church has obstinately clung through many centuries of incredulity. Disbelief in the Incarnation, as we have seen, is no modern phenomenon. All the heresies are as old as orthodoxy. Evidence of their existence is to be found in the New Testament and no doubt they will continue to have their protagonists even to the Day of Judgment. But is it possible to have two natures and yet remain one person? The Athanasian Creed replies, in effect, that such double-naturehood is not only a possibility but even a familiar every-day reality. 'For as the reasonable soul and flesh is one man: so God and man is one Christ.' In more modern language, the conjunction of divinity and manhood in Christ is analogous to the blending of animality and manhood in us. All the biological processes characteristic of what we call animal life are equally characteristic of the physical life of the human being. It is even possible to pretend, with at all events a certain degree of plausibility, that a man is nothing more than an unusually complicated animal, a heresy very similar to that of supposing that Jesus Christ is nothing more than an unusually good man. Yet we should almost all of us agree that the former of these two heresies, however plausible, is false and misleading. In the sense that we possess complete animal natures we may indeed truly be called animals, but we have also our specifically human characteristics, quite unlike anything to be recognized in the animal kingdom —self-consciousness, reason, conscience, the sense of sin, the power to make deliberate choices and to respond sympathetically to the beautiful and the sublime, a capacity for disinterested love. These are the more important and significant aspects of our being. The relationship between our specifically human and our more universally animal characteristics, the necessity of fusing them into one harmonious personality, causes many of the most perplexing of our personal problems. We can very easily imagine that analogous problems confronted the God-Man but, having no personal experience of them, we are no more in a position to say precisely what they were than a dog is able to picture for himself the interior personal life of his master. The inner life of the God-Man must necessarily remain for us a hidden mystery. No man is in a position to write a psychology of Jesus Christ. But the Christian will not be guilty of the unpardonable intellectual arrogance which denies what it cannot understand. He affirms the reality of the dark mystery and finds that, while remaining dark in itself, it illuminates brilliantly everything else in his life.

Suffered under Pontius Pilate, was crucified, dead and buried

The Creed passes swiftly from the birth of Jesus to His death, summing up all that intervened between the two events with the terse remark that 'He suffered'. He was born, He suffered, He was crucified. Neither the suffering nor the crucifixion were accidental. They were the inevitable consequence of the clash and inter-play of His perfect with our spoiled manhood.

A somewhat free and imaginative interpretation of the scriptures may see in the Cross of Christ man's solution of a problem first propounded at His birth. How was Jesus, the Son of Man who is also Son of God, to be fitted into our self-centred scheme of things? Man had so arranged his world and his life in it that it contained no place obviously fitted for the reception of the Son of God. It was ominous and appropriate that there was 'no room at the inn' at the time of His birth. There was never to be any room for Jesus on earth until men made room for Him on the cross. 'He came unto His own and His own received Him not.' In a world in which the foxes have holes and birds of the air have nests, He had nowhere to lay His head. We cannot fit Christ into our present scheme of things, neither into our scheme of thinking nor into our scheme of living. Always He is a revolutionary and disturbing influence. He comes into our house either as what seems to us a disagreeable and critical visitor or as a welcome deliverer who will lead us out of it into a better. In which of these two guises He appears depends upon the degree to which we are satisfied or dissatisfied with what we are and have. The man who is tolerably satisfied with the existing scheme of things, with his present way of life, will resent the entry of this intruder with his unpleasing habit of con- trasting the way things are done on earth with the way they are done in heaven, the conduct and attitude of God with the conduct and attitude of men. The more self-critical, however, may conceivably welcome one who lends their criticisms not only a new intensity but also a more substantial intellectual foundation, for whereas the human critic of humanity contrasts what is with what might be, thus laying himself open to the charge of arraigning fact in the name of fiction, this divine critic of humanity contrasts fact with fact, earth with heaven, the more superficial with the more pro- found realities, man's life with his calling, his few and comparatively feeble historical achievements with his

God-like nature and sublime destiny. In the days of Our Lord's flesh the majority of men, and they the most powerful, were numbered amongst those who are prone to resent the Divine Intruder. Probably the same is true at any time, but however that may be, it was certainly true at the material time of which we are speaking; although there was no room for Christ at the inn, there was room enough and to spare for Him on the cross.

When the Christian surveys the 'wondrous cross', his emotion is emphatically not one of pity and sympathy for Jesus. Such an attitude towards the cross is only possible so long as we are ignorant that the man who is being crucified is the Son of God. There were, as He journeyed to Calvary, the women who wept for Him, but they were greeted with a characteristic rebuke. 'Weep not for me but for yourselves and for your children.' In a world in which men crucify the Son of God, what will they do to each other? Our own twentieth-century experience teaches us the tragic answer to that urgent question. The consequence of sin is blood, now as much as then.

The horror of the cross is to be found in its vivid and dramatic presentation once and for all of what it is to which our self-centred mode of existence leads us, to the brutal murder of Incarnate Love. The kind of sin which plots and accomplishes the death of Christ is not the crude and generally recognized kind, neither fornication nor drunkenness nor petty theft, but the unimaginative, calculating protection of their own interests by the worldly wise, the characteristic sins of widely respected and no doubt, in a sense, respectable men. The Temple clergy, for example, were partly anxious about their class interests, partly concerned for the future of their nation and partly zealous for what they regarded as the integrity of their faith. No doubt most of them fused these three anxieties into one. Pontius Pilate was concerned partly for public order and partly to avoid disturbances which might imperil his tenure of office. Such men belonged to that large class of human beings who contribute perhaps more names than any other to our history books, the class of petty politicians, petty enough to be the true democratic representatives of the common man—which the great national leader never is —slightly corrupt, rather sincere, extremely muddle-headed, unimaginatively selfish and absurdly self-opinionated. Every court and parliament and political party teems with such creatures and, if there were enough Christs, they would doubtless crucify one of them every day. But there is only one Christ, and that is why Caiaphas and Pilate look so much blacker than their brothers. The appearance is deceptive and a little unfair to them.

But if the horror of the cross is to be found in its revelation of the consequence of human sin, the splendour of the cross lies in its equally vivid and dramatic revelation of the power of Divine Love. For the Christian, the cross is the most decisive of all victories. There the love of God which will not let man go confronts the stark hostility of the sin of man which will not let God come. Sin summons up all its latent powers and achieves its crowning masterpiece. It does its damnedest and prevails nothing. From the human point of view the crucifixion is an utter failure. The only triumph which human sin could conceivably enjoy against the Love of God would be to extinguish it in weariness and anger. When sin has done its worst it has only succeeded in demonstrating once and for all how powerless it is to

abate the love of God, to deflect the Creator even by a
hairbreadth from His purpose.

What would have happened if sin had proved victorious on Calvary? There can only be one answer:
It would have precipitated the end of the world. Such a
triumph would necessarily result in a great act of Divine
wrath, obliterating the whole creation. But this is mere
empty speculation. The truth is that human sin could not
conceivably have been victorious. It was doomed from
the start. 'God is greater than our heart', and so it is that
the crucifixion of the Son of God is the victory that
overcomes the world.

But the Christian sees in the cross more even than
that. He sees not only the inherent weakness of human
sin, frustrating itself even in its strongest hour, and the
invincibility of the love of God. He sees also the perfect
humanity of Christ rising to supreme heights of self-
expression in this voluntary and mortal act of obedience.
Inevitably Our Lord's humanity shrank back in horror
from the prospect of an agonizing death. But His natural
shrinking is an utterly obedient shrinking. 'Father, if it
be Thy will, let this cup pass from Me, nevertheless, not
My will but Thine be done.' Selfless, ungrudging
obedience such as this is the very perfection of manhood. The creature exists only to carry out the Creator's
will. What we call the automatic creatures obey Him
automatically. A stone glorifies God by being a stone.
The impulsive, animal creatures obey Him impulsively,
the cow by chewing the cud, the wild horse by courting
his mate in the spring. But free-willing, self-conscious
and reflective creatures must obey Him, if they obey
Him at all, in accordance with the laws of their own
being, freely, deliberately and rationally, knowing what
they do and why they do it.

E

The relationship between our spoiled humanity and the perfect humanity of Christ is a theme of crucial importance for Christians. Our Lord's humanity is a humanity in complete and unbroken harmony with His divinity. Jesus is one with God. Can we hope to become one with God also? That is precisely what Christ came to do for us, to work an atonement, or at-one-ment, between us and God. We become at one with God by becoming first of all one with Him who is one with God already, by joining our humanity to His, by harmonizing our humanity with His. 'No man cometh unto the Father', He says, 'but by Me.' How is this done? There are two classic phrases which Christians have used for centuries to express the ways in which we may hope to foster and express our solidarity with our Lord— *Incorporation into the Body of Christ* and *Imitation of Christ*.

The meaning of the second of these terms is clear enough. We must seek and find a more and more Christ-like way of living our daily lives. The former phrase is perhaps a little less familiar and, to any but the instructed Christian, more elusive in its meaning. To be incorporated into Christ means to be joined to Him, secretly, as it were in the very depths of one's being, through membership of His Church and through participating in that intimate spiritual life of prayer and sacrament which the Church strives to live with its Lord. But the simpler phrase cannot stand by itself. The imitation of Christ means much more than merely selecting a dead hero as our model and striving to be as like him as possible. Were we to attempt it, we should certainly find it a quite futile and unrewarding process.

Some writers have been so obsessed with the idea of merely imitating Christ in this remote and external way, rather as a young sailor might swear to imitate Nelson in a fit of very natural hero-worship, that they have been led by it into a denial of His divinity. If we are to have any hope of imitating Him, they say, He must resemble us in every respect. If He is divine, then His divinity gives Him a moral advantage over us which makes it impossible for us to have any hope of imitating Him. The argument is plausible but fallacious. The one thing which cannot be imitated is genius. We do not say that because Shakespeare was as human as we are we can therefore hope to write plays like his; but if we supposed that Shakespeare was divine as well as human, and able to live again in the lives of those who loved him, then we might all of us perhaps begin to entertain the highest literary aspirations. It is precisely because Christ is not a dead hero who lived two thousand years ago, but a risen, living Lord who is with us always, that we dare to speak of the imitation of Christ, which means not that a man is able, by a sheer *tour-de-force* of personal and private will-power, to make himself like Christ, but rather that Christ can and will reproduce Himself in the life and character of His Christians. The imitation of Christ presumes the spiritual incorporation of the imitator into the body of Christ, and cannot be understood apart from it. The outward and visible Christ-likeness of the saint is the fruit of the inward, invisible presence and operation of Christ in the heart of his life.

For the Christian, then, one consequence of the cross is the life of the Christian Church or community, for it is by sharing wholeheartedly in that life that the Christian becomes one with Christ. But Christ is one with God, as the supremely costly act of obedience on Calvary so vividly demonstrated. The mystery of churchmanship is an essential part, therefore, of the mystery of the cross, that reunion of God and man first made possible by the union of the divine and the human in the one Christ.

He descended into Hell, the third day He rose again from the dead, He ascended into Heaven, and sitteth on the right hand of God the Father Almighty, from thence He shall come to judge the quick and the dead.

Resurrection. Descent. Ascent. The Christ after the flesh, who made Himself visible to men at a particular place and time conquers death and, in so doing, transforms Himself into the Universal Christ who entirely transcends the limitations of space and time, the Saviour of all mankind. The gospel story of the resurrection and the ascension is thus the story of an essentially transitional process. It shews us 'Christ after the flesh', as St. Paul calls the Lord and Master whom he had probably never seen, becoming the omnipresent Lord encountered by subsequent generations of Christians in their communions and prayers.

No Resurrection, no Gospel. The gospel was in the beginning and still is the proclamation of the resurrection. The ultimate reality, the mysterious power which presides over the life of the universe, is not against Jesus but on His side. The courage and integrity of Jesus in the jaws of death is not a pathetic gesture of defiance flung in the face of a cruel fate. Rather it is the manifestation of a tenderness and righteousness at the heart of the universe which the life of a fallen world had first concealed and then forgotten. This hero is not a dead hero but a living Lord. The point of the Gospel is not that Christ is better than we are in a merely ethical sense, that He is good while we are evil—a comparison which might do little more than hurt our pride—but that the resurrection of Christ bears witness to the existence of a sovereign reality which we have contradicted, so that ⸱⸱ live apart from Him is to violate the laws of life, a futile process which can only end in their vindicating themselves against us, and avenging themselves upon us, by exposing to us and the universe the inner vanity of our pretentious achievements. To proclaim the resurrection is to proclaim Christ as Judge and man as under judgment, to proclaim the reality, the eternal validity of His life and the divorce from reality of our own, to declare that His death is life and that our life is death. The proclamation of the resurrection moves the hearer to conceive and put the appropriate question, 'What must I do to be saved from this life which turns out to be a form of death?' In all ages the reply is inevitably the same. 'Repent, transform your character, adjust your desires and purposes to this new revelation of the true nature and destiny of man; and be baptized, join yourself to Christ —or, better, let Christ join Himself to you—and henceforward live and move and have your being, with your fellow-Christians, in the wider life of Christ. Follow the shepherd with the rest of the flock, operate as a limb of the Body under the direction of its Head.' Such was and is the gospel, the same yesterday, to-day and forever.

No Gospel, no Resurrection. Those who will not or cannot accept the gospel, either because they dislike the uncomfortable readjustments which it demands of their comfortable lives, or because it hurts their pride and makes nonsense of their cherished claim to self-sufficiency, must necessarily reject the resurrection. In the last resort there are only two alternatives to believing the resurrection story. If the apostles were not telling the truth when they declared that Christ had risen, then either they were the sincere victims of hallucination or they were the perpetrators of an ambitious and self-interested fraud. The original enemies of the gospel chose the latter alternative. They declared that the apostles had deliberately stolen the Master's corpse in order to give colour to a fiction calculated to enhance their power and prestige. The subsequent career of the apostles rendered this story incredible. Men capable of such deceit will not sacrifice themselves through many years and at last crown their unrewarding careers with martyrdom in order to maintain what they know to be a lie. The most vigorous of the early opponents of the gospel, St. Paul, watched St. Stephen die and could not for long continue to resist the conviction—destructive though it was of his chosen way of life, of his cherished traditions and rising ambitions—that this insignificant Christian was dying for what he knew to be true. The conversion of St. Paul is for us who, like him, have not known Christ after the flesh, one of the most significant episodes recorded in the New Testament. This man of magnificent intellect, whose self-interest would certainly have prompted him to discover and cling to any available reasons for denying the resurrection, was driven to the conclusion that in fact there were none, and his fundamental sincerity compelled him at last to acknowledge the truth and embrace with joy its unpleasant implications.

Brief as was its vogue, this first reaction of the anti-Christian party to the gospel is very significant. It provides us with a conclusive objection to the hallucination theory universal, in some form or other, amongst the anti-Christians of later generations. Those who declared that Christ was risen and those who circulated the slander that the apostles had stolen His body were at least agreed about one vital fact—the emptiness of the tomb on the first Easter morning. Had the tomb not been empty, it is inconceivable that the Jerusalem authorities would have neglected the most obvious way of exposing the whole resurrection story. The allegation that the body had been stolen could never have been more than a very inferior second best. It could have only occurred to men who were compelled by circumstances to deny the resurrection and at the same time to account for the empty tomb. Had the apostles been merely the victims of hallucination, the tomb would not have been empty and the pentecostal episode would have been easily and speedily brought to an end. The self-sacrifice of the apostles makes nonsense of the theory that they were commonplace tricksters, and the survival of the gospel beyond those first days at Jerusalem makes equal nonsense of what has become the more prevalent view that they were simple enthusiasts, beguiled by their enthusiasm and grief into beholding what was not.

But although the hallucination theory cannot quote a single piece of historical evidence on its side, and although it flatly contradicts all the available evidence, it will doubtless continue to find believers. Still those who will not accept the gospel dare not admit the resurrection. Always they will be driven to the invention of spurious arguments with which to defend a position which is, in fact, both spiritually and intellectually untenable.

And so Christ after the flesh passes through death to resurrection to become the Universal Christ of Christian spiritual experience. He descends to the place of departed spirits—or 'Hell', as the Creed says, using that word in its more primitive sense—thus shewing that He is also Lord of those who had predeceased Him on earth. The joyous reunion with God through fellowship with

the God-Man is as much a possibility for the citizens of
the world B.C. as for the citizens for the world A.D. He
ascends, passing from time to eternity, Lord of the future
as well as the past. He remains on earth in the lives of
those who love Him. He will be with them always to the
end of time, that moment of final reckoning when the
differences between real and unreal ways of life, between
God-centred existences—in which what is consciously
taken to be the centre, the most important element of
life, is in fact the real centre—and self-centred existences
—which absurdly locate the centre on the circumference
—will be starkly exposed to the mind of the simplest
spectator.

That is what judgment means—a striking of contrasts,
a vivid revelation of the difference between the real and
supposed worth of our activities and objectives. 'The
first shall be last and the last shall be first.' The triviality
of what had supposed itself majestic shall be set beside
the majesty of much which had been dismissed as trivial.
Last judgment is not, of course, the only judgment.
Judgment is a permanent activity of God in history. The
calamitous consequences of the ambitious design, the
repeated frustration of our more imposing purposes, the
paradox of modern man, talking incessantly of an
earthly paradise and living tragically in what more often
resembles an earthly hell, judgment is implicit in it all,
relentlessly indicating, not with words but with facts,
the defectiveness of the design, the unreality of the purpose, the misconception of utopia, man's interminable
failure to comprehend his true nature and envisage his
proper destiny. God's judgment on what men do is the
consequence of what they do. The laws of life are such
that only through complete obedience to God can man
find abiding satisfaction. All else is in the long run un-

satisfying and disappointing. It is in the frenzied hour of disillusion with his secular ideals and self-centred, earth-bound purposes that man is most dangerous to man. But this is not the place in which to embark upon an inquiry into the spiritual causes of war. Here we need only remark that because provisional judgment is going on all the time, there must necessarily be final judgment at the end of time, for judgment, in which the ultimate consequence pronounces the verdict sometimes for, but more often against, the cause is an essential characteristic of life in time.

I Believe in the Holy Ghost

The Christian life is not a solo but a duet. Christianity is not a religion of law but a religion of grace. It does not think of God as a remote and majestic law-giver Who, having issued His commands, leaves us alone while we struggle to obey them, abandoning us to sink or swim by our own efforts, and then reappears at the end of the process as a stern judge, rewarding the successes and punishing the failures. On the contrary, the Christian knows God to be one who gives His own personal assistance to those who sincerely attempt to carry out His wishes and submit to His will, to do outwardly what He would have them do and to be inwardly what He would have them be. To do God's will we need God's help. The Christian life cannot be lived without Christ. This divine assistance which comes from God to man through Christ is called Grace. But it is essential to understand that this assistance is not a thing but a process. It is God living in the life of man and man living in the life of God. It is an intensely active and creative partnership between God and man, in the course of which the activities of the two so mingle with and interpenetrate each other that it is impossible to tell precisely where the one ends and the other begins. Indeed, the question: 'Which of my virtues and achievements must be ascribed to God and which of them to my own efforts?' is one of which the Christian never even conceives. It would be like asking, 'Which plays the more important part in the conception of a child, the father or the mother?' Orthodox Christianity has always steered a middle course between such an emphasis on God's grace as would imply that human effort is useless or superfluous and such a concentration on the importance of earnest and unremitting moral and spiritual endeavour as would seem to set God's grace in the background. Without grace human effort cannot prosper and without human effort, humbly co-operating with God, grace is not given. None the less, in any partnership between God and man, God is inevitably and infinitely the senior. And so it is that when the Christian considers the best, the redeeming features of his life, he cannot but interpret them as the fruit of the activity of the Spirit of God let loose within him, rather than as the product of his own labours. Experience reduces him to the humble conviction, simply expressed in the words of the familiar hymn, that:—

> . . . Every virtue we possess,
> And every conquest won,
> And every thought of holiness,
> Is His alone.

The only alternative to the Christian way of crediting God with our human virtues and victories is the highly unpleasant one, which cannot be avoided by mere morality or even by a religion of law, of crediting ourselves with them. When human goodness is not frankly and unreservedly attributed to the grace of God, it inevitably ministers to human pride, and that is why so many 'good' people possess such remarkably unattractive personalities. Human achievement tends to become self-conscious and pretentious. Only when it is sincerely regarded as primarily divine achievement can it be successfully blended with that humility and self-forgetfulness which is the most graceful and compelling characteristic of the lives of the great saints.

This personal power of God, alive in the life of every Christian, ceaselessly fulfilling its sanctifying and humbling task, making the Christian a better man than he had ever supposed himself to be, and at the same time convincing him that he is very much worse than he ought to be, rendering him great in the eyes of other men and small in his own, is called the Holy Spirit. As we have already emphasized, the dynamic of grace is not a thing, not a lump of stuff, or a quantum of energy, it is an inherently personal process, indeed a Person, the third Person of the Blessed Trinity, as the Christian has learned to call the Eternal Three Who is eternally One.

The Trinity

The Christian belief in the Trinity and the Unity of the Godhead, the Three who is One and the One who is Three, is perhaps the most characteristic and unique of all Christian beliefs. It must be emphasized that this doctrine is not a mathematical or metaphysical conundrum invented by people with a perverse taste for thinking in riddles. The doctrine was one to which Christians were driven by the steady pressure of their personal experience of God on their thinking. The facts

which compel us to accept the doctrine are clearly put
before us in the New Testament, and they are recapitu-
lated in the spiritual life of every Christian.

The Christian fully shares the fundamental insight and
conviction of the Old Testament. 'The Lord our God
is one God.' He who supposes that there can be more
than one God has not even begun to realize what the
word God means. God is the beginning and cause and
explanation of all things; on Him all things depend and
in Him they live and move and have their being. The
nature and purpose of all things have been ordained by
Him. His unity is the source of the very unity and coher-
ence of the universe. The philosopher can no more think
clearly in terms of more than one God than he can think
clearly in terms of no God. One God, one ultimately
Sovereign Power, one final principle and interpretation
of all things he must have, whether he calls Him God or
not. Two or more gods would be useless to him; for
where a plurality of gods is supposed to exist, the truth
is that in the literal sense of the word none of them is
god at all. That which is ultimate, supreme and absolute
can tolerate no rival.

Similarly the religious man cannot even begin to
understand the depth and meaning of worship until he
knows that there is only one God. Such a man cannot
worship two gods. He cannot offer to two distinct
divinities his self, his soul and body, all that he is, all that
he has, all that he hopes to become. So long as he believes
in several gods his acknowledgment of each of them is
haunted and qualified and made unreal by his sense of
the existence of the others, and of his parallel obligations
towards them. To worship many gods is to worship no
god; to worship many gods is in effect not to worship
at all. Philosophy and religion, man's reason and rever-

ence alike, drive him to the inevitable conclusion that God is one and cannot conceivably be more.

But the first Christians, the Jewish lieutenants and companions of Jesus, Who taught them to call God their Father, utterly convinced as they were of the unity of God, yet found themselves, and particularly after the resurrection, in effect worshipping Jesus, paying Him divine honours which belong to God alone. They knew that in Jesus they had seen the Father and they knew that He was and is one with the Father, for He had told them so, and yet they knew at the same time that He was not the Father. To suppose that Jesus was the Father would be to make nonsense of His whole life of prayer and communion with the Father, and of His way of distinguishing Himself from the Father, even while affirming his underlying spiritual solidarity with the Father. But they were not conscious of anything in their attitude towards Jesus incompatible with man's all-inclusive obligations towards God. They did not feel that they were taking God's glory and giving it to another. Their conscience never accused them of idolatry. The earliest Christians coupled together the sacred names of God the Father and Jesus Christ without any sense of impropriety. 'Grace to you and peace from God our Father and the Lord Jesus Christ,' writes St. Paul to his Corinthian converts. Clearly he had no feeling that these words in any way take in vain the name of God. If someone were to write, 'Best wishes from God and John Smith', we should feel at once that such a phrase was blasphemous. Our acceptance of the first greeting as quite normal and proper and our horrified rejection of the second is the measure of our sense of the utter distinction between Jesus Christ and all the John Smiths that ever were or will be.

And Jesus spoke to His disciples not only of Himself and His Father but also of the Divine Comforter and Strengthener who would come from God to live with them, to teach and guide and fortify, to keep the thought of the Father and the memory of the Son alive and forceful in the human mind. The Holy Ghost or Holy Spirit, as Christians learned to call Him, is clearly personal, distinct from both the Father and the Son, and yet, it is equally clear, entirely one with Them, working only their work and conforming utterly to Their will. This scriptural experience of the Father, the Son, and the Holy Spirit is, as we have said, repeated in the spiritual experience of every Christian. We are conscious, so to speak, of the Father above us, of the Son beside us and the Spirit within us. The Father is known to us through the Son and we are kept close to the Son by the Spirit. We pray to them all, we worship and adore them all. We know that they are three distinct Persons and yet, such is the perfection of their eternal unity, that they live together the one life of the one God.

'God is Love,' says St. John. The mystery of the Holy Trinity is the mystery of Eternal and Absolute Love, the mutual love of Father, Son and Holy Spirit. Even our limited human love is experienced as a force which unites and consolidates. Jesus can speak of the perfect marriage as one in which the twain become one flesh. The absolute and unqualified divine love is one in virtue of which the three Divine Persons verily and indeed live together one Divine Life and are inevitably, because truly, spoken of as one God.

There is thus a fundamental distinction between real living unity and merely abstract mathematical oneness. Many of the mystical eastern religious cults think in terms of sheer absorption into the godhead, a process in

which the individuality and separate existence of the
person absorbed completely disappears. The Christian,
on the other hand, thinks in terms of union with God,
of living in the life of God while still in some sense remaining himself. He knows that a union which obliter-
ates one of the parties to it is a contradiction in terms.
'But we shall be one beloved,' sings the lover in the
hackneyed song, but the lovers can only become in
some sense one on condition that they remain in some
sense two. A union which destroyed entirely the personal existence of one or more of those entering into it
would not be a real union at all but a murder. 'I in thee
and thou in me,' prays the Christian, echoing the words
of Jesus as he contemplates that ultimate life of unbroken
fellowship with God which he calls heaven and in
which he recognizes his final destiny. But he knows that
such a union between himself and his Creator implies,
as of its very essence, that God remains God and that he
remains himself. This deeper insight into the meaning
of such phrases, beloved by the mystics of all ages, as
'union with God' and 'the vision of God' the Christian
owes to his belief in the doctrine of the Trinity, which
shews him what unity really is, a co-inherence of distinct personalities, a plurality of individuals living together a single common life. The Christian can think of
God as one Person, and therefore as the perfect pattern
for all personality to model itself upon, while at the same
time thinking of Him as one Society, and therefore as
the perfect pattern for all society to model itself upon.
Men usually alternate between exaggerated individualism, which turns society into chaos (e.g. the selfish and
rapacious capitalism of the nineteenth century), and an
equally exaggerated collectivism which, in the interests
of social unity, imposes upon us a bureaucratic and

totalitarian tyranny (e.g. the doctrinaire left-wing and right-wing dictatorships of our own time). It is in the life of the Trinity that we see the claims of society perfectly reconciled with the claims of personality.

Of the three persons of the Holy Trinity, the Holy Spirit is the least vividly apprehended in the conscious mind. Because His activity is carried on in the context of our own lives, we do not, because we cannot, distinguish Him sharply from ourselves. As the Christian life progresses and deepens, and as more departments of life are brought into contact and co-operation with Him, it becomes increasingly difficult for us to say precisely where our personalities end and His begins. The life of the Holy Spirit is a divine life which plunges so deeply into the depths of the human spirit that man, who sees clearly only what is external to himself or else lies on the surface of his being, is unable to form more than a confused notion of His spiritual appearance. Indeed, the acknowledgment of the Holy Spirit, although it is founded on direct experience of the gift of inner spiritual power from God, power to perform actions of which the recipients of the gift knew themselves to be previously incapable, is as much a matter of faith as of conscious perception.

The Holy Spirit is at work in the souls of all men, but not always successfully, for He is not a dictator and He demands a certain degree of co-operation from the personalities he inhabits. Sometimes this co-operation is more or less habitual or instinctive. Such men have, probably through no fault of their own, no very clear impression of the power from God that moves in the deep places of their souls, but among the ideas and ideals which are present to their conscious minds they show a **practical preference for the truest and best, with which,** and on which, the Spirit is able to work. Naturally, however, His activity is most free and fruitful where His presence is recognized and His general purposes and intentions consciously apprehended. It is under such conditions that it is possible for men to co-operate deliberately with the Spirit of God, placing themselves at His disposal, and in those acts of self-offering which are the essence of prayer adding their drop of sincere and self-sacrificing human energy to the great cleansing tide of grace which surges through their lives. It is because the Holy Spirit is thus most free to do His perfect work where His Presence is known, that it is true to say that He is at work in the Christian Church to a greater degree and with more powerful effect than anywhere else.

The Holy Catholic Church

The Church is the earthly family of God, the place where the fact of the universal divine Fatherhood is recognized and where there is made at all events a sustained effort to carry out its implications. Where there is fatherhood there must be the family. Only by sharing in the life of the family is it possible to have fellowship with the father. The Fatherhood of God implies the brotherhood of man.

It is not possible to love the Father acceptably while in a state of chronic estrangement from the brethren. When God calls us to Himself He calls us at the same time to each other. That God has created a Church for men to belong to is an essential part of the gospel. Belief in the reality of a Church, a world-wide fellowship of the faithful, created by God the Son and indwelt by the Holy Spirit for the Father's Glory, is an essential article of the Christian Faith, and hence the Creed boldly sets

F

it side by side with belief in God Himself as a matter of comparable importance. We believe in the divine Fatherhood and the human brotherhood. Without the belief in the Fatherhood, faith in the brotherhood would be sheer nonsense. Where the brotherhood is not acknowledged both in theory and practice, the reality of the divine Fatherhood is by implication denied. Where there is no churchmanship there is no true Christianity.

There is, of course, a sense in which it is true to say that God is the Father of all men, churchmen and nonchurchmen alike. God's attitude towards all men is certainly paternal but the attitude of men to God is far from being perfectly filial. The perfect Son is the eternal Son and we can only become true sons of God by learning what perfect sonship means from Christ, by sharing increasingly His attitude towards the Eternal Father and His unity with the Eternal Father. It is in that state of unity with Christ, and with each other for His sake, which we call the Church that the sons are reconciled to the Father and begin to live again their family life with Him.

The Church is described in the Bible as the Body of Christ. It is the visible agent which He now employs to make known His presence and carry on His work. It is, indeed, a kind of diffusion and extension of the Incarnation, so that, in and through the Church, Christ still continues to live an earthly life. The Church is thus not a mundane association of like-minded human beings, united by a common admiration for the personality of Jesus and a common reverence for His teaching. No early Christian ever said or thought that the life of Jesus was such a superbly good thing that the world must never be allowed to forget it, and that those who had known Him ought to form a society, to be known

as the Church, for perpetuating His memory. Christ gave
the Church to men. It is not a human contrivance. The
Church was designed by God for our salvation. It was
not created by men as an ingenious way of giving Him
glory. Churchmanship is not therefore a superfluous excellence, one way among many of serving God on
earth, and perhaps the best way for those disposed by
temperament to enjoy participation in its mode of life.
Membership of the Church, on the contrary, is a universal human duty, and to turn deliberately away from
it is to spurn God's gift, to disobey His will and to
frustrate His purpose. Because churchmanship is a duty,
non-churchmanship is a sin.

The Church is a visible society possessing all the outward characteristics of other human societies, laws and
customs peculiar to itself, abiding traditions which make
it recognizably the same Church at different times and
places. This legalistic and traditional element in the constitution and history of the Christian Church is sometimes condemned and rejected as materialistic and
mechanical; but a visible Church must necessarily have
its visible and material marks by means of which it is
recognized, just as the visible Jesus in the days of His Incarnation must necessarily have possessed His own peculiar cast of feature and the voice which His friends knew
to be like no other voice. The visible characteristics of
the Church are, so to speak, its flesh. Those who understand that God is the maker of earth as well as of heaven,
of the material as well of the spiritual, who remember
that the eternal word of God was made flesh in the Incarnation, will reject the false, and fundamentally un-
Christian, spirituality which says, in effect, that the
Church ought not to have any flesh.

Of these external marks of the Church of God, the

one which has been the occasion of most controversy is its apostolic ministry. Jesus Himself appointed the first leaders of His Church. They are known to us as the twelve apostles. From the very beginning of the spread of Christianity, they claimed and exercised the power to hand on their authority to others, to reproduce their own kind. Thus St. Matthias and St. Paul became apostles. That the leadership of the Christian Church descends to us, like the Church itself, from Christ through the apostles was clearly recognized in the early Church. 'Christ is from God,' writes St. Clement of Rome in a letter which may be dated about A.D. 95, 'And the apostles from Christ. Both therefore came in due order from the will of God . . . as they (i.e. the apostles) preached in the country and the towns, they appointed their first fruits—having proved them by the Spirit—to be bishops. . . .' Irenaeus, another early Christian writer, who flourished about the end of the second century, tells us that the St. Clement who wrote these words, 'not only saw the blessed apostles but also conferred with them, and had their preaching ringing in his ears and their tradition before his eyes'. He is therefore an excellent authority as to the belief and practice of the Church in its earliest days. To this apostolic ministry the vast majority of Christians have clung steadfastly ever since. The Roman Catholic Church, the Eastern Orthodox Church, the Churches of the Anglican Communion and several smaller bodies still acknowledge the leadership of bishops descended through the laying on of hands from the apostles of Jesus.

Most of those smaller Christian communities which have existed only since the Reformation have lost this living link with the Christianity of New Testament times. Rightly or wrongly, and usually under great provocation and with desperate sincerity, the founders of these bodies judged the situation of the ancient Church which Our Lord gave us to be so desperate that the only remedy was to institute new Churches—called after the name of Christ indeed and dedicated to His glory but certainly not founded or contemplated by Him in the days of His flesh—and to furnish them with new ministries differing both in origin and principle from that of the ancient Church. It would not be possible here even to begin to describe the varied characteristics of the innumerable forms of protestant Christianity which have sprung up in the last four hundred years. Many of them differ almost as sharply from each other as from the historic 'majority' Christianity of the Roman, Orthodox and Anglican Communions.

This historic 'majority' Christianity which has prevailed among the overwhelming majority of Christians from the earliest times until now is called the Catholic—or 'Universal'—Faith and the ancient Church which professes and practises this faith is the Catholic Church of the Apostles' Creed. It is with this faith and this Church alone that I am now concerned, not because other ways of presenting Christianity are necessarily unimportant or uninteresting, but because I have little or no special knowledge and experience of them. In any case this book would become over-long if I permitted myself to digress to any great extent from my chosen theme.

The Communion of Saints

The life of the Church, the Christian fellowship, is not lived exclusively in this world. Its unity is more than a mere unity across physical space. Its continuity is more than a mere continuity through history. The part of the Church which is visible here and now is only one province of the whole Church. We call it the Church Militant on earth, a fighting Church, continually confronted by all those forces which in a fallen world contradict its nature and seek to frustrate its aims—the jealous dislike of supernatural authority to which all natural authorities are persistently prone, the hostility of the dogmatic unbeliever, the mere worldling's indifference to the things which concern his personal salvation, the twilight of ignorance and the darkness of self-will, and, worst of all, the continual unworthiness and back-sliding of its own members.

But this fighting Church is only a part of the whole Church. The unity which Christians have in Christ is, like Christ Himself, stronger than death. There is a communion, a common life in the presence of God, enjoyed by all those in whose lives the Spirit of God is openly working in the name of Christ. In time things happen one after the other, the generations succeed each other in turn, so that some men are dead before others are born. But we must not suppose that this successiveness, because it is a law of time, is also a universal law which governs the whole realm of being. In a deep sense it is true to say that in the presence of God past, present and future stand side by side. He is God not of the dead but of the living, for all live unto Him. In the last resort we are all contemporaries. Ancient and modern touch and find fellowship in eternity. So it is that Christians remember the departed, their elder brethren, in their prayers on earth, knowing that they themselves are likewise remembered in the prayers of heaven. To believe in the Communion of Saints, in the deathless fellowship of those who know the sanctifying touch of the Spirit, is to affirm the paradox that the Church is greater than the world which apparently contains it. For this reason our Christian orders of worship and common prayer insist on regarding worship and prayer not as local activities carried on at different times and in different places, but rather as a glorification, a lifting up of all localities and times into the sphere of a single, eternal activity. It is 'with Angels and Archangels and all the company of heaven' that we worship God. We become one with God and each other not through the descent of God but through the ascent of man. We become one with God, as Our Lord's humanity was made one with His divinity, 'not by conversion of the Godhead into flesh but by taking of the manhood into God'.

The Forgiveness of Sins

This reunion of God and man, this lifting up of the manhood into companionship with the Godhead, is repeatedly frustrated by the sin of man, by his invention and retention of ways of life distinct from that for which God made him, by his relentless pursuit of purposes other than those which God ordained for him. Sin is a dissatisfying and disillusioning process. The false ways of life which man invents for himself cannot content him. The spurious purposes which he selects for himself persistently elude fulfilment. Man proposes but God disposes, frustrating us by means of the operation of the deepest laws which govern our human nature, the laws which determine the ebb and flow of interior satisfaction and disappointment. The fruit of sin is failure—the first, promptly suppressed, suspicion of failure as the mask begins to slip from the face of the superficial delight and the transitory achievement, the final irrepressible consciousness of failure when the mask is thrust decisively aside and the true countenance of what was mistaken for delight and achievement is revealed. So men boldly plan a paradise on earth and behold a world order at times disconcertingly reminiscent of hell; they propose peace and behold war; they seek world unity and behold world schism. Sin is failure—the failure of each man as a single person, of men grouped into nations and classes, of mankind regarded as one world-wide humanity. Sin separates from God, from the source of life and renewal. The memory of past sin separates from God—can it be forgiven? The triumph of present temptation separates from God—can it be resisted?

Christianity answers both these questions in the affirmative. All things are possible provided that submission to God is possible. We can do everything with Him but nothing without Him. But can we reach Him? Only by the crucifixion of pride, by surrendering the cherished illusion of personal independence and autonomy. The man who would know forgiveness of sin and the conquest of temptation must cast himself down from the lofty seat of self-government and passively submit while God becomes his Sovereign.

There is a kind of pride between man and man which is wholesome and appropriate. Most men dislike the feeling of being too dependent on other people. This dislike may be caused by a pride of the wrong kind, by a self-willed desire for a maximum of irresponsible self-regulation, but it may be the product of a legitimate fear that overmuch dependence on others obscures and relegates to the background of our consciousness our essential, abiding and total dependence on God. A topical illustration of this superficial agreement between the false pride and the true can be found in current discussions of the growing power and influence of the state in contemporary life. Old-fashioned individualists resist the tendency towards an authoritarian state because it seems to them to undermine their personal autonomy. Christians also resist this sinister tendency, but for a different reason. The individualist objects to the state becoming God because he wants every man to be, so to speak, his own God. The Christian objects because for him there is only one God, and because he knows that too great a degree of human dependence on anything that is less than God tends towards idolatry.

As between men, therefore, a certain degree and kind of pride is valid and necessary, but as between God and man all pride is deadly sin. It is indeed the sin of sins, for so long as this sin persists no other sin can be healed. The worst sins are inward and spiritual. The outward and physical sins—fornication, adultery, drunkenness, physical violence and so on—are serious enough in all conscience, but they are of an elementary character when compared with the inward and spiritual sins of outwardly good people which can damn souls to all eternity. In the perspective of the New Testament, that is, in the eye of God, the Pharisee is worse than the harlot.

Forgiveness of sin cannot be claimed as a right. It must be humbly sought as a gracious concession. This is true even in the sphere of human relationships. The offender must sue for pardon, and pardon will not be given unless and until the offence is candidly admitted and openly and sincerely regretted. When forgiveness does come, it does not minimize the gravity of the offence. To forgive sin is not to say that sin does not matter. The forgiveness of sin means that the wronged and forgiving person has absorbed and transcended the shock and hostility of the original attack, has overcome the initial frustration, and is now willing to restore the penitent aggressor to his fellowship and confidence.

It is sometimes supposed that what is called a 'sense of sin' is a morbid, almost pathological, state of mind. Psychologists have talked gloomily about the evils of the 'guilt complex', and other writers sometimes assure us that the truly modern man has no sense of sin. But the real question is one of plain fact. If we have no sins a sense of sin is clearly a morbid illusion. But if social and personal failure is one of the plain, undeniable facts of life, if it is true that we fall below the level and short of the possibilities inherent in our nature, then a sense of sin is nothing more than a frank recognition of realities as they are. A sense of reality can never be unwholesome.

The graver danger is that we may lose all consciousness of our own sins while remaining vividly aware of other people's. We all of us know what it is like to be sinned against, and although the modern world is supposed to lack any sense of sin it frequently rings with moralistic denunciations of sinners—not merely of individuals, but of whole nations and classes collectively arraigned and condemned. The complacent priggishness of a nation at war, or of class politicians demanding 'social justice' for their supporters, illustrate the moral dangers of a unilateral sense of sin. Jesus was particularly concerned that our outraged sense of other people's sins should be balanced and moderated by a penitent sense of our own. The Pharisee—the eternal Pharisee who is with us still—is pre-eminently the man without a sense of sin. Without a sense of our own sins we are unlikely to attain real charity in our judgment of sinners. Even in their guilt they remain our brothers, provided that we can recognize that we also are 'guilty men'.

Of course, there is such a thing as a pathological 'guilt complex'. It is a morbid distaste for the natural forms and necessities of life—usually, but not always, sex—which locates a vague guilt everywhere and specific sins nowhere. But this is very far from the Christian sense of sin. Christians may suffer from this malady just like other people, but it is not one to which those who cultivate a healthy sense of real sins are particularly prone. One of the most striking contemporary examples of the guilt complex is to be found in the novels of the French atheist philosopher Jean Paul Sartre. Through them all there broods a neurotic feeling that nature and the ways and institutions of ordinary life are, to use one of his favourite adjectives, 'obscene'. A pool of saliva in his mouth, the root of a tree, his own body or another's, all are 'obscene', ridiculous and unnecessary. But Sartre, of course, betrays no sense of sin in the proper sense of the word. It is clear that the guilt complex and the sense of sin must be entirely distinguished from each other.

Far from being morbid, the Christian would claim that his sense of sin is the essential prelude to an experience which is the foundation of the joy and optimistic confidence with which he faces the often intimidating and always exacting ordeal of existence—the experience of being forgiven. Those psycho-analysts who base their practice on the teaching of Freud have their own secularized substitute for the experience of divine forgiveness. 'You must not feel guilty', they say in effect, 'because you could not help it.' But this is a weak-kneed solution of the problem. It insults the patient's manhood by denying that he has any significant degree of responsibility for himself, and it is certainly not a doctrine which is likely to stimulate him to live more successfully in future. Christian forgiveness, on the contrary, tells the sinner that he need no longer feel guilty even though he was responsible for what he did and remains responsible for what he will do. It is a bracing and invigorating experience which not only pays man the compliment of acknowledging his responsibility for the past, but also strengthens and reinforces his resolve to bear the burden of responsibility in the future, by renewing and emphasizing the gospel promise that the divine companionship and the divine love will still accompany him despite all his past failures.

The Resurrection of the Body and the Life Everlasting

It is forgiveness, God's loving and immediate response to the humility of penitent man, which recreates the conditions in which fellowship between God and man is possible. This fellowship and co-operation with God is man's eternal life. The departments of our life which centre upon the transitory things of time constitute our life in time, a transitory thing in itself. But that part of our life which centres upon the eternal is itself eternal. 'This is life eternal, to know Thee the only God.' We do not have to wait for eternity. We know it now in part. We have only to wait for its expansion and fulfilment, for the ultimate realization of all its latent promise. The eternal Kingdom of God, and the eternal life that is lived in the Kingdom, can and must begin here and now —in the knowledge of God, in the love of God, in the service of God. The Christian prays first that his eyes may be opened, that he may see as much of God as God will permit, secondly, that his heart may be kindled, that he may love and desire what he sees, and thirdly, that his will may be concentrated and strengthened, that he may pursue what he loves.

This eternal life is a life to be lived by the whole man.

The Apostles' Creed does not talk, like Plato and Socrates, of the immortality of the soul, of a higher, spiritual part of man which at death gaily casts aside the baser clay with which it has so long been joined in unequal partnership. The Bible takes a high view of the body, and the Creed, as we have seen, sets earth side by side with heaven as twin children of the creative activity of God. Man is an embodied soul, and a disembodied existence would not be a genuinely human existence. If man is to survive the grave then, in some inconceivable way, the bodily condition and mode of being must survive the grave also.

The early Christians had no illusions about death. They knew quite well what happens to the bodies which we bury in graves. They were as familiar with the phenomenon of physical corruption as we are, but they had a robust faith in what we may call, with reverence, the divine common sense. God has not created embodied souls in order to frustrate for all eternity their physical needs and nature. He who provides us with the type of body suited to our present sphere of existence will no doubt replace it with the probably quite different kind of body requisite for life in that world for which this world is a preparation. St. Paul likens the burial of the old worn-out flesh and the re-embodying of the bereaved soul with its new spiritual body to the process of the sowing of the seed and the reaping of the harvest. The fruit and the flower do not particularly resemble the seed which is buried in the ground, but they are continuous with it and the one must vanish before the other can appear. St. Paul's analogy is illuminating, but it must not be regarded as more than an illustration. We do not know how we shall get our second body, but then we do not really understand how we acquired our first one. What we have yet to experience is not, and indeed could not be, more mysterious and inscrutable than the familiar yet quite incomprehensible phenomenon which we have experienced already.

Such is our Christian faith in a living, active God who has shewed Himself to man. It was neither invented nor discovered, but revealed. We know it as a reorientation and redirection of the entire life of the man who receives it, as an illumination of the intellect, as a cleansing of the heart, as a readjustment of the affections, as the death and resurrection of the will. We are not in any exclusive sense a peculiar people. This is no private knowledge. This is a knowledge that yearns to be known. This is a gospel which is not content to be accepted but demands to be proclaimed. It has been heard and must be uttered. 'The lion has roared, who can but tremble? The Lord God has spoken, who can but prophesy.' The gospel has sounded, and therefore resounds. The light shines and is reflected on the waters.

CHAPTER FOUR

THE LIFE

In the old days we rationalists believed that morality has nothing to do with religion. We prided ourselves that we were in practice every bit as good as the religious people who indulged in public worship and private prayer. Sometimes we even half suggested that we were much better than most of them. All members of organized religious bodies were strongly suspect of hypocrisy in our circle, and we delighted in reports of incidents which betrayed the moral and spiritual shortcomings of Christian individuals and groups. Church congregations were reputed to be petty and narrow-minded and given to internal combustion, whereas we regarded ourselves as broad-minded and neighbourly. The boast that without holding to a single Christian belief we remained faithful to the essence of Christian morality, with a lofty integrity and admirable consistency, was frequently on our lips. We belonged to that strict sect of ethical rationalists to which the Mr. Higgins adhered who so bewildered G. K. Chesterton:—

Now who that runs can read it,
The riddle that I write,
Of why this poor old sinner,
Should sin without delight,
But I, I cannot read it,
    (Although I run and run)
Of them that do not have the faith,
And will not have the fun.

Like Higgins we missed both the faith and the fun. We subjected ourselves to forms of moral self-discipline and personal restraint very similar to those in vogue among Christians—although not, perhaps, so exacting—but without any of that sense of fulfilling the will and purpose of a God beloved by men, of drawing nearer to the adorable Christ, which for the Christian turns discipline and restraint into a worthwhile adventure in which the splendour of the destination more than compensates for the rigour of the way.

It would be no exaggeration to say that when we assembled together for discussion we spent as much time telling each other how good we were—of course, in a broad-minded, uncomplacent way—as a group of Christians met for worship would devote to confessing their sins. And here we are confronted with an important difference between Christians and non-Christians. It is possible for the non-Christian to suppose himself a very good fellow, to indulge in the pleasant contemplation of his own virtues and achievements. But the Christian knows himself to be a sinner. He is haunted by a mental picture of Christ which shames and delights him at the same time. It is no part of his case to deny the charges which are made against him. He is concerned to proclaim God's goodness not his own. In a sense he is a witness against himself, confirming out of his own mouth the rationalist contention that Christianity is morally ineffectual.

This is not to say that we rationalists were correct in believing that on the whole we were as good as, or rather better than, the Christians. I have now spent about an equal number of years in Christian and rationalist circles and I am therefore in a fairly good position to judge which is the better camp in which to know misfortune and to stand consciously in need of selfless comradeship. I am quite sure, as a result of my experience, that on balance the comparison is in favour of the Christians, although I must admit that their superiority is not as overwhelming as it should be. I am equally certain that a comparison of this kind is unimportant and misleading, and that to build upon it a critical judgment about the relative excellence of Christian and pagan living would be to miss the whole point. The proof of the pudding lies not so much in the eating as in its long-term effects on the digestion. A comparison between the moral state of a society in which for generations ordinary people have accepted Christian beliefs, prayed Christian prayers and attempted, no doubt unsuccessfully, the exacting imitation of Christ, with one behind which there lay several generations of pagan scepticism would be more revealing, but even that would fail to get to the root of the matter.

For the essential difference between the moral life of the Christian and that of the good and conscientious pagan is to be found not so much in their respective achievements as in the sources of their inspiration. The latter has turned his back to the sun and sees always his own shadow sharply outlined before him. He can never forget himself. His is a self-reliant and self-conscious existence. Even his unselfishness is only a higher kind of self-assertion. The Christian has his face to the light and his shadow behind him. His is primarily a God-conscious and God-reliant existence. As we have already remarked, it is not a solo but a duet. To walk thus through life side by side with an absolute perfection is a strange and paradoxical experience. This infinitely unequal companionship depresses and exalts a man at the same time, at once humiliates and inspires him. It makes him at all

G

events a better man than he would have been without it, and yet at the same time prompts him to think more hardly of himself than he would have done had he never known it. More capable of virtue and yet more conscious of sin, his emotional life compounded of a greater joy and a more terrible grief than can be found in any other company, the Christian knows that his life is distinguished from other lives not by his own private excellence but by the unexpected, almost intolerably stimulating, friendship which guides and upholds it. Because it is a duet and not a solo, a large part of the Christian life is devoted not to visible moral achievements, not to generous secular activities which can spring as easily from an appetite for self-esteem or a craving for popularity and good opinion as from real and spontaneous unselfishness, but to intimate conversation with the divine Friend.

Prayer and Practice

It is this emphasis on the importance of worship and prayer which distinguishes the Christian from the moralistic conception of the good life. The mere moralist thinks of the good life, to repeat an earlier phrase, as a kind of higher self-assertion, the triumph of the will over temptation and fear. For the Christian, true human goodness begins with an act of submission to the will of God. Christianity prizes humility much more highly than virtuous paganism. Indeed, the ancient pagans of Greece and Rome did not prize it at all. We have already noticed the Christian's strange habit of debiting himself with his sins and crediting God with his virtues. What ever else there is to be said either for or against this paradoxical mental process, it cannot be denied that

in practice it lends to moral integrity a charming, unassuming quality which otherwise does not normally
accompany it. The unattractiveness of good people is a
familiar theme. 'O God,' prays the little girl at her bedside, 'please make the bad people good and the good
people nice.' Most of us would be willing to say 'Amen'
to that with considerable feeling. It is hard to see how the
merely moral type of goodness can avoid making the
kind of impression on the mind of the spectator which it
had certainly made on that of the little girl. The goodness which is the product of the higher kind of self-
assertion inevitably intensifies the good man's self-
consciousness and enhances his importance and dignity
in his own eyes. 'He is a self-made man and he worships
his Creator.' Because men cannot but worship their
Creator the whole atmosphere and flavour of their lives
is primarily determined by their convictions about His
identity.

The Christian knows himself to be a God-made man.
Even his noblest personal activities are accompanied by
a sense of sin, and his habit of going consciously into the
presence of God at regular and frequent intervals preserves his humility by repeatedly humbling him. We
become humble through being humbled, by being confronted again and again with that which we know to be
infinitely greater and better than ourselves. There is no
other pathway to humility. Sometimes hero worship
and intense admiration for a friend will suffice to humble
a man in his own eyes. But hero worship and admiration
provide but a poor anchorage for a virtue so elusive.
The more closely we approach the hero the more difficult it becomes to worship him. Man's grasp of humility
remains feeble and uncertain until he grapples it to himself in the presence of God.

The Godward Impulse

Prayer and worship, based on and guided by the conviction that God has revealed His Nature and Purpose in Jesus Christ, are thus the essential characteristics of the Christian life. Few words are more completely misunderstood than the familiar word 'prayer'. It is conventionally interpreted as though it meant a kind of spiritual bombardment of the Deity with a series of self-interested human requests, slackening somewhat during those periods when life is more or less kind to us and growing more urgent whenever she frowns. All this is mere caricature. Prayer has been better described as 'the ascent of the mind to God'; it is an offering of the self to God, the spreading out before Him of the whole content of the conscious mind, the submission of the disordered human will, confused and weakened by the endless conflict of opposite motives and mutually exclusive desires, to the perfect will of God.

The underlying psychological and spiritual urge which has impelled men of all religions and all stages of mental development and civilization to prayer is the human longing to be completely known and perfectly understood. The same urge makes the anxious man open his heart to his friend, directs the neurotic to the consulting room of the psycho-analyst and prompts the penitent to seek absolution from his confessor. But the longing which each of these valuable and effective expedients can satisfy to a certain extent is completely set at rest only in communion with God, only when the long persevering life of prayer culminates in final vision.

'Who really knows me through and through?' It is a decisive question, one which leads as surely to prayer as prayer at long last leads to God. Experience will teach the man who asks it that he will never be perfectly understood by other people, not even by those with whom he is in closest sympathy. Even his dearest friends will fail sometimes to see things as he sees them, or manifest surprise at some word or action which he feels to be necessitated by the very nature of his personality. He will discover that he in his turn fails to achieve a complete understanding of them. It is possible to have known and loved a man for a lifetime and yet to observe with a sudden shock some hitherto unsuspected facet of his character. But our self-knowledge is as partial and defective as our understanding of others. Again and again in life a man surprises even himself. The trite remark that it is good for us 'to see ourselves as others see us' is an admission that our self-knowledge is inevitably one-sided and incomplete. 'Who really knows me through and through?' No man sees and understands me whole and entire. The inner mystery of my being is not visible even to myself. I am driven back upon the fundamental truth that a created thing is perfectly understood only by its creator. The standpoint of the creator is the only one from which the whole truth can be seen. We understand best and most intimately what we have ourselves constructed. The poet is the best interpreter of his poem, the artist of his picture, the craftsman of his craft. Even so the whole truth about man is only visible to God. It is this frustration of man's desire for understanding and sympathy on the natural level that drives him to that supernatural intercourse with the God, 'to whom all hearts are open, all desires known and from whom no secrets are hid'. 'Thou that hearest the prayer, unto Thee shall all flesh come.'

St. Paul is fired by the same thought as he reflects for a moment on the far-off goal of the life of prayer and cries out, 'Then shall I know even as already I am known.' God already possesses a perfect knowledge and vision of man, and man, his appetite stimulated and desire kindled by this imperfect and one-sided intercourse, presses slowly forwards in his quest for a more adequate knowledge and vision of God.

To pray is a great adventure, a launching out into the uncharted spiritual spaces which separate God and man. It is a costly adventure, demanding, like all worth-while enterprises, self-discipline and sacrifice. It is at this point that morality and goodness become plainly relevant to the life of prayer. For a man seeking to live a God-centred life, his own personal and moral perfection is not an end in itself. It is a means to the higher end of finding fellowship with God. He does not pray in order that he may succeed in living what is called a good life. Rather he strives to live a good life in order that he may pray. Such goodness as the Christian attains is not the central aim and purpose of his existence, dominating his thoughts and energies. It is a by-product of his quest for God. That is why the goodness of godly men is less self-conscious, more graceful and unassuming, than the goodness of the conscious man of morals.

The Christian life thus falls into two parts, internal and external. Externally the Christian moral ideal covers much the same ground as that of the conscientious and serious-minded unbeliever. They are agreed in their emphasis on the importance of personal integrity and the neighbourly and civic virtues. But it is to what we may call his internal life that the Christian attaches the greater consequence.

THE INTERNAL LIFE OF THE CHRISTIAN

The life of Christ was a life of prayer and therefore the Christian life, the life which is lived in fellowship with Christ, which is guided by the example of Christ and derives its energies from Him, is characteristically a life of prayer also. Jesus was equally accustomed to the kind of prayer which a man offers side by side and in unison with other men, and to those intensely personal and private outpourings in which the man who knows that to go apart from other men is to find not loneliness but more intense and intimate companionship, achieves his full and final self-expression in the presence of God. The Christian, like Christ, must accustom himself to public and private prayer, never yielding to the subtle temptation to oppose or contrast them, to reject the one in the name of the other. We do not find in Jesus that indifference to what is sometimes called 'institutional religion' which we find in some contemporary religious people. He knew that it is not possible to achieve an isolated relationship with the Universal Father. He who would live in the presence of the Fatherhood must accept the inevitable obligations of brotherhood, however great the limitations and shortcomings of the brethren. In the days of His flesh Jesus assiduously frequented the synagogues and the Temple, the conventional places of public worship. He was well aware of the defects of His fellow-worshippers. He knew that many hypocrites, prudes and spiritually blind men were to be found among them, but He was the last to shrink from the company of sinners. A merely private, personal religion, which proudly and self-righteously refuses to have anything to do with the visible Church, is a religion which has nothing in common with the faith and practice of

Jesus. Indeed, its assumption of intellectual, moral, aesthetic or spiritual superiority to the mass of ordinary believers, its implicit suggestion that some gifted souls do not require visible and social aids and incentives to living a Christian life, has more in common with the complacency of the Pharisee than with the example set by Jesus and His little flock of often sinful, and as often penitent, friends. By joining in public worship, therefore, the Christian is following the outward example and conforming to the inward spirit of the Jesus we meet in the New Testament.

But the public worship of the Church is more intimately related to the prayer life of Jesus Christ than that. There is a profound sense in which it is true to say that Christians, by joining together in their ancient and customary devotions, are not merely imitating the prayers of Christ, but also entering into the Prayer of Christ. The Prayer of Jesus, like His earthly life and human personality, has been lifted up above all distinctions of space and time. It is not something which happened some centuries ago, which we remember with reverence and imitate as best we can. It is something which not only was, but still is and ever shall be. 'He liveth ever to make intercession for us.' The Prayer of Christ is an eternal Prayer, a comprehensive spiritual activity into which all our prayers can enter, of which all men can become a part. The Christian does not even pretend to go to God alone. He prays as he lives, 'through Jesus Christ Our Lord'. Christ alone lived and prayed, and lives and prays in perfect accord with the will and purpose of God. It is only by living in Him and with Him, by being lost in Him and found in Him, that we can rediscover the true human self and the truly human way of life. It is only 'In Christ' that man begins to

respond to the call and purpose of God. As the old peni-
tential hymn puts it:—

Look, look, O Lord, on His anointed face
And only look on us as found in Him.

The Kingdom of Heaven is not unlike the cinema
which presents to its patrons an attractive but salacious
film. 'No person under sixteen will be admitted unless
accompanied by an adult.' So runs the legend over the
door, the death knell of so many adolescent hopes. Even
so there is no entry into the Kingdom except in the
company of *the adult*, the Christ, the grown-up Brother
of the little, spoiled children of God.

Prayer in the Great Congregations

Christian worship resembles the ancient Jewish worship with which Jesus was familiar in the days of His
flesh. We still use the Psalms, the hymn-book of Israel,
and the Old Testament scriptures which crowded His
memory and came easily to His lips. We have added
to the writings which Jesus knew the writings of those
who knew Jesus, thus making up our complete Christian
Bible, but we modern Christians are like the Jews of
Our Lord's time in being the people of a Book, and to
a very considerable extent it is the same Book.

But if much of our worship belongs to an ancient
tradition of religious devotion which Jesus hallowed by
conforming to it, our highest act of worship is one
which He himself devised and ordained. Christians
have called it by many different names: The Breaking of
Bread, The Lord's Supper, The Eucharist or Thanksgiving, Holy Communion, The Divine Liturgy, The

Mass. But whatever it is called, its central feature is a repetition of the dramatic and infinitely significant gesture of Jesus after supper on the night of His betrayal. The broken bread He calls His Body and the wine in the cup His Blood. And still to-day men take them, eat and drink them, conscious that as they do so they approach more closely to the mystery and meaning of what happened on Calvary than at any other times in their lives. For some centuries now there have been differences of opinion among Christians as to what precisely takes place in the spiritual realm whenever there is a celebration of Holy Communion. What takes place in the physical realm is, of course, clear enough. There is prayer and praise, the reading of scripture and the profession of faith; the offering up of bread and wine— symbols of the wealth and fertility of the earth and the productivity of human labour—for God to do with as He will; and eating and drinking. But what takes place in the spiritual sphere and gives meaning to these visible events is less easily discerned and expressed in words.

At all times, however, including our own, the overwhelming majority of Christians have been agreed that when Jesus described the bread as His Body and the wine as His Blood, He was speaking in no merely figurative sense. He was not propounding an illuminating metaphor but revealing a grave and urgent reality. No part of the Church has ever accepted that idea of a gross and physically observable change in the elements which has been attributed, in times of wild and excessive controversy, to certain Christian communions, but that a real and decisive change of a spiritual character does take place has been, and still is, the profound conviction and inspiration of a vastly preponderant proportion of Christendom.

There have been many theories as to the manner in which this change is brought about, but this is not the place in which to elucidate and compare their subtleties. The human mind is poorly equipped to determine the ways and means of divine action. *What* God does is sometimes revealed to us, but *how* He does it remains an impenetrable mystery. There is much to be said for a reverent agnosticism about the Eucharist, which joyfully embraces and accepts the privilege of the divine presence among men without venturing to ask of Him Who comes to us how He came; which is content to know that here man can be one with Christ as Christ is one with His Father; that here God gives Himself to man so that man—in spite of his admitted imperfections—can confidently give himself to God; that here inanimate things like bread and wine and living beings like men and women are united with their Creator by a single act of obedience to His will; so that here for a moment the purpose of the earthly creation is accomplished and the destiny of man fulfilled; so that here for a moment that final reunion of all created things and beings in fellowship with God which we call the Kingdom of Heaven is anticipated and enjoyed beforehand. Holy Communion creates holy community and educates man for the life of heaven. We do not know what heaven will be like, but we believe that it will be much more like Holy Communion, with its insistence that complete human equality can only be found in obedience to God and that entire human fellowship can only be found in fellowship with God, than anything else within the limits of our present experience.

Public worship is thus for the Christian a paramount duty. Neither in prayer nor in life dare the believer in the universal fatherhood separate himself from the

brotherhood. The critic of what is sometimes most unfortunately called 'organized religion', who advocates
the pursuit of a lonely, narrowly personal path to God,
is remote indeed from the spirit of Christianity. On the
other hand it would be idle to deny that there is some
substance in his contention that public worship and
religious observance easily degenerate into mere formal-
ism. Public prayer is no more a substitute for private
prayer than private prayer for public. Like eating and
drinking, they are twin necessities. Public prayer when
prayed by people who are not accustomed to pray in
private, does tend to become little more than a habit.
People pray best together when they also pray alone. As
between the two no primacy can be awarded. God is the
Creator of both society and individuality. The innermost incommunicable essence of each human personality is known only to God and achieves self-expression
only in His presence. Similarly the social nature of man,
his inherent aptitude for society, his inability to live and
keep sane apart from his fellows, is a reality which God
willed and purposed and which must therefore play its
proper part in his religious life.

It is always misleading merely to oppose and contrast
the claims of individuality and society. Both individualism and collectivism are vicious half-truths which have
been the cause of many tragic errors. The one leads to
irresponsible anarchy, the other to tyranny and a soul-
destroying mechanization of social life. The truth is
that human personality is both individual and social,
so that no social order or way of life will permanently
content us which does not revere and serve both the
collective and private needs and aspirations of our
nature at the same time. This is as true in religion as in
politics. The Christian way is to follow the example of

Christ, and to learn to praise God, as the psalmist recommends, both 'secretly and in the great congregations'.

Prayer in Secret

It is not possible for us to consider here in detail the manner and technique of prayer. Prayer is at the same time a quest for vision and a way of self-expression. It is sustained spiritually by the grace of God, and psychologically by a thirst for the knowledge of God which is so elemental a part of man's being that it may sink down during the greater part of his life below the level of consciousness. It can be expressed by words spoken by the tongue or pass inaudibly through the mind in swift sequences of unuttered, and perhaps unutterable, thought. The great masters who grew wise in the ways of prayer through long experience have left descriptions in their writings of many different techniques and methods of conducting these interior conversations with God. The manner in which a man prays must be determined primarily by his temperament and by the degree of his spiritual maturity. An ageing saint will not pray like an enthusiastic young man who has just experienced the first drowsy, fitful stirrings of the soul. A cold philosopher of the calm and balanced, perhaps exaggeratedly rational type, will not pray like an emotional and quick-tempered woman. Probably there are as many ways of praying as there are people who pray, but most methods of prayer have much in common, and all are based on the sustaining, energizing conviction that man is made for God, so that his personality cannot flower and achieve its full fruition except in the light and warmth of the presence of God.

In an elementary book of this kind, it is perhaps most

helpful to liken conversation with God to conversation with any fellow-man. Spoken intercourse between human beings—if we ignore small talk and the merely superficial elements of 'polite conversation'—is composed of seven fundamental themes. The same is true of prayer, so that to classify the basic forms of human conversation under these seven heads is at the same time to enumerate the contents of a full and balanced act of prayer.

(1) The expression of admiration and love (Praise or Adoration).

(2) The expression of gratitude for favours received and services rendered (Thanksgiving).

(3) The expression of sorrow for specific offences committed, or perhaps for a general and comprehensive unworthiness (Penitence and Confession).

(4) The assertion of the speaker's own needs, with a request for such assistance as seems possible and necessary (Petition).

(5) The assertion of the needs of others with a request that the hearer should either assist them or co-operate with the speaker in assisting them (Intercession).

(6) The recollection of the past, particularly those elements in the past which speaker and hearer have in common or which is known to both of them (Meditation).

(7) The anticipation of the future, and the hopes and fears which it will either confirm or deny (Aspiration).

The act of prayer which comprehends all this, which begins joyously with praise and thanksgiving, and is then chastened and humbled by a vivid sense of the contrast between the perfection of God and the imperfection of the self, which perseveres through and beyond the consciousness of guilt and, with a sense of complete dependence on God, lays not the self only but the whole

human race at His feet, which treasures the memory of
what God has done and thrills at the thought of what
He will do, whether it finds expression in a sequence of
words or a sequence of thought, forms a complete whole
perfect and entire in itself, wanting nothing. It is a
unique phenomenon, perhaps more akin to the artistic
masterpiece than to other kinds of human expression. It
has a completeness and finality not unlike that of a great
symphony or poem. Prayer is indeed the supreme
vehicle of man's self-expression. It is the highest act of
the human spirit, for man is most of all himself when
what he does is most completely penetrated and sustained by the power and grace of God.

The internal life of the Christian justifies itself by its
own inherent beauty and satisfaction. It does not require
any appeal to its visible fruits. I well remember that
when I first began casually attending Christian places of
worship, I was asked by an uncle, in a spirit of quite
genuine curiosity, whether I went to church to make
myself good. Nothing is more repulsive than the idea
of a concentrated and self-conscious attempt at self-
improvement for its own sake, and I shuddered at the
very thought. I seem to remember replying that fortunately in this life some things are good in themselves
and worth doing for their own sake, without ulterior
motives, that I worshipped God as I would read Shakespeare or listen to Beethoven, because the pursuit was
one which I found intrinsically worth while. Perhaps
that is not precisely what I did say, but it is certainly
what I should have said.

Nevertheless, although Christianity is anything but an
elaborate device for improving the moral character of
human beings, it would be foolish to deny or minimize

the fact that it does bear visible and characteristic moral fruits, and that the appeal to them, although strictly and logically unnecessary, can be made with considerable force. We have already noticed that there are many unbelievers whose lives are governed by the dictates of an exacting morality. The 'good pagan' is a contemporary character with whom we are fairly familiar, but if we compare a clique of unbelievers, such as that in which I grew up, with a small fellowship of practising Christians of comparable size, such as that of which I am now a member, it is impossible to escape the conclusion that the general standard is higher and the proportion of outstandingly noble characters greater in the latter than in the former. I have already admitted that the difference is not so great as, from the Christian point of view, it should be, but from the pagan point of view it ought not to exist at all. Small as it is, it makes the external life of the Christian a subject worthy of our consideration.

THE EXTERNAL LIFE OF THE CHRISTIAN

The ancient Greek classification of the virtues which reduces them to four—wisdom, courage, temperance and justice—is one which we can accept, as the early Christians did, and adopt for convenience. It is at least as good as any other formula of the same kind.

From the Christian point of view these virtues are truly virtuous and although the Christian strives to obtain them in conscious dependence on 'the Grace of Our Lord Jesus Christ' he recognizes them when he sees them in the lives of non-Christians, and attributes them in such a context to the fact that God is at work in every human personality, in the liveliness of a man's

conscience or in his genuine devotion to all that is best in
a defective creed. The late Dr. R. R. Marrett describes
how, as a young pupil of the great Dr. Jowett, the trans-
lator of Plato, he asked him, 'Master, did humanitarian
feeling exist before the advent of Christ?' Dr. Marrett
continues, 'He appeared not to have heard, and the
silence became more painful than ever, suddenly he
ejaculated, "Yes"—just the one word—and we found
ourselves dismissed.' But there is no reason, from the
point of view of Christian belief, for the difficulty which
Dr. Jowett clearly experienced in making such an admission. The early Christian writers would certainly
have been not at all constrained by it. Christ came not to
destroy but to fulfil the law, and this is as true of the
moral idealism of pagan Greece as it is of the law given
to the Jews on Sinai. The righteousness which Christ
so perfectly fulfilled was not a novel, unheard of righteousness but an old righteousness which the best men of
many places and generations had sought ineffectively,
dreamed of in vain.

The real and important function of moral idealism in
the development of the soul is made clear by St. Paul
when he remarks that 'the Law'—the particular form in
which morality was inculcated among the Jews—was
'our schoolmaster to bring us to Christ'. The chief product of genuine moral endeavour is the sense of sin, the
sense of a desperate personal need for a power not our
own which makes for righteousness, for a saviour who
delivers us from slavery to obscure psychological forces
within us which we can neither control nor approve.
It is only a superficial morality which breeds the ugly
self-satisfaction of the Pharisee of the New Testament, or
of his brother the not-quite-so-good pagan of our own
time. The man who is really in earnest about the moral

H

struggle, who seeks the highest and best which he can
conceive with real passion and enthusiasm, who judges
himself without partiality in accordance with the most
exacting standards known to him, is left with a saving
sense of failure. Such an experience, may of course
lead him to cynicism and despair, but it may, as it frequently does, lead him to God. In the latter case the
earlier disappointment and frustration is richly compensated. The superficially moral man is no doubt well
content with his complacent consciousness of his own
excellence, but to the man who, being more profoundly
moral, becomes a self-convicted sinner there may be
revealed the infinitely more satisfying excellence of
God. Life, with a providential wisdom and justice, re-
wards each man in accordance with his capacity for
spiritual appreciation, the superficially good man with
the vision of his own goodness, the penitent sinner with
the vision of God.

Thus Christianity reaffirms the pagan virtues and suggests a new technique for acquiring them. The pagan
knew well enough what the virtues are, but when confronted with the practical question, 'How are we in
fact to become virtuous?' he could only recommend
the inquirer to try very hard. The best pagans frankly
acknowledged that this method is not conspicuously
successful. Small wonder that when Christianity came,
with its declaration that true goodness comes only by
the grace of God, all that was best in paganism respon-
ded with enthusiasm to a gospel which filled a gap
which it had known and wept over so long.

But Christianity was very much more than a new
way to practise old virtues. To the excellencies which
the pagan conscience had already received, as to the Law
which the Jews had accepted in the wilderness, it added

new moral objectives of its own. We have already
noticed its emphasis, entirely novel in the ancient world,
on the importance of humility. St. Paul supplemented
the Greek quartette of virtues with a Christian trio:
Faith, Hope and Charity. Jesus had taught His disciples
that there are some devils which can be made to depart
from the human soul only by prayer. There are some
angels which can be induced to enter it only by the same
means. Among these are the angels of Faith, Hope and
Charity. Hence these virtues have been sometimes
described as 'infused virtues'. It is useless to strive for
them. The more practical course is to pray for them. It
is these virtues that introduce the characteristically
Christian mellowness and gaiety into the sternness and
rigour which was the least pleasing feature of the best
kind of pagan living.

Faith

Faith is not so much mere belief in God's existence—
the natural reason has led many men, including the
majority of the great philosophers, to such an affirmation
as that—but rather belief in God's goodness and a willingness to trust Him absolutely, to build the whole of life
on the assumption that the revelation of Himself which
He has given us in Jesus Christ is as true in detail as it is
generous in design. Faith is thus analogous to the trust
and confidence which a man places in a friend. He
accepts his friend's statements because he believes him
to be a man of his word, and entrusts his goods to his
care because he is convinced of his honour. Trust in a
man, unlike faith in God, may be misplaced, but there is
a strong resemblance between the two.

Faith, then, is the virtue which enables a man to build

his whole life on the spiritual foundations which Christ has laid, to stake his existence on the truth of the gospel. It is as much a thing of the will as of the intellect. It fills up the dangerous gap between merely believing like a Christian and living like one.

Hope

The Christian Hope of which St. Paul speaks is that confidence in the ultimate supremacy of the will of God which assures us that victory must at long last crown the service of God. This Hope must be carefully distinguished from the natural hopeful impulses which 'spring eternal in the human heart'. Every day human nature disposes us to 'hope for the best', to desire that good times may come and bad times be avoided. This familiar emotion has its opposite in despair, the fear hardening almost into conviction that bad times cannot be avoided. Unfortunately most of us tend to drift helplessly backwards and forwards between these two emotions, clinging to our hopes as long as possible and then, when events seem to frustrate them, plunging into the depths of despair. Individual temperaments differ, of course, and those whom we call optimists are more prone to hope even in relatively bad times, while 'pessimists' are apt to despair even in circumstances in which despair is hardly appropriate. But no man is altogether a stranger to either emotion.

The supernatural Christian Hope is unrelated to either of these natural impulses; rather by it the Christian is delivered from monotonous alternation between them. The Christian Hope has nothing to do with the temperaments of individual Christians. It is an objective thing based on our knowledge of God and introduced into our minds and sustained there by the grace of God. From it is derived that unfaltering determination and unwavering confidence which characterizes, for example, great saints in their hours of trial. Theirs is no despairing 'last stand', for they know that to serve God, and to fight against the forces of evil which have intruded themselves into the world which God has made, is to serve a cause already assured of victory.

But this supernatural Christian Hope differs from the natural impulses of hope not only in having this different origin (arising out of the grace and knowledge of God and not out of our own private emotional systems) but also in content.

The natural impulses of hope expect a different fulfilment from that to which the supernatural Hope looks forward with such confidence; and if we would know the great gospel Hope which is the source of the gospel joy (the joy of which Jesus promised that no man shall take it from us) we must first learn to christianize our private hopes.

The most normal form of the natural impulse is the hope that 'all will go well' with ourselves and our nearest and dearest. But of the fulfilment of this hope the gospel gives no guarantee. It contains no promise that ease, comfort and prosperity will be the earthly inheritance of Christians. On the contrary, Jesus makes it quite clear that His followers must be ready to be baptized with the baptism with which He is baptized, to drink of the cup of which He drinks, to take up each one his cross, to be despised, rejected, hated and persecuted; in other words, that Christians must be ready to share His earthly fate. When adverse events, therefore, frustrate our natural human hope for ease and good fortune, the supernatural Hope which sustains us in our service of God remains unshaken, for the two are quite distinct.

A striking example of this contrast between natural hope and Christian Hope was provided by the tragic frustration in 1939 of the almost universal desire that Europe should avoid the catastrophe of war. We must ask ourselves whether this was necessarily a Christian Hope at all. Certainly, no Christian could conscientiously have wished that such a social order and international situation as we knew in 1939 should continue indefinitely in peace. And to-day, can we really desire that the work of erecting on the other side of the iron curtain a degraded and degrading régime of gangster oppression and inhuman intolerance should be carried on interminably without external impediment? Should we not rather say that such a serene and orderly development of the forces and purposes of profound moral disorder is neither desirable nor, in the long run, even possible? We cannot as Christians desire that the unrighteousness of a society should escape the consequences of unrighteousness. That would be to desire the banishment of divine judgment from human history. And yet, in effect, is not this what many people, even many Christian people, meant when they hoped and prayed that there would be no war in 1939—simply that their existing way of life, and hence that of the society to which they belonged, should be allowed to go on without any costly interruption?

Certainly the hope for peace was sometimes something much larger and nobler than that, a part of the wider Christian Hope for a righteousness come from God among men, incarnate so to speak, in their social, cultural, economic and political arrangements, of which peace between individuals, classes and nations would be

a result or by-product. The Kingdom on earth for
which Jesus taught us to pray in the Lord's Prayer
means, of course, more than merely a purified and reformed social order, but it includes all that such a
phrase implies. To work and pray, therefore, for such a
purification of the social order is one way, and a very
important way, of serving the cause of the Kingdom.
But hope for peace in this sense is not quenched and
frustrated by the fact of war. Indeed, no war however
terrible could possibly dissipate it, for this Hope is based
on our belief in the sovereignty of the will of God and
our acceptance of the promises made in the Gospel. 'It
is the Father's will to give us the Kingdom'—if not to-
day, then to-morrow. Hope is precisely that kind of
invincible confidence.

Charity

Charity is the specifically Christian word for love.
There are many kinds of love, of which charity is only
one, albeit the highest. In the course of conversation the
same man may declare at different times his love for such
varied objects as sausages, his friends, his children, his
parents, his wife, his country, abstract excellencies like
justice, vague collectives like humanity, or a metaphysical reality like God. Each of these can be loved, but
clearly each must be loved with a special kind of love
appropriate to its own nature.

One of the most important lessons a man has to learn
in life is never to get mixed up in his loving, for the
consequences of inappropriate loving are almost always
disastrous. There is an important Christian sense in
which a man should love all women, but, should he
appear to entertain towards the entire female sex the

kind of regard which his wife claims as her own monopoly, the result will certainly be unfortunate. In fact the kind of love which wells up naturally and spontaneously in the human heart is by nature particular and selective. It is aroused by this object and not by that, by one person and not by another. The pagan attempt to universalize human love only results in its destruction. Thus a man's natural and patriotic love for his own country is inherently better, as well as superficially more attractive, than the cosmopolitan's vague and professed attachment to all countries in general. The man who cries out that he adores his wife professes a narrower but a more profound passion than the man who discourses philosophically on his comprehensive devotion to humanity.

Unless he is a Christian, the cosmopolitan humanitarian, not knowing Charity, is forced to make this effort to universalize human love, but he destroys all its warmth and enthusiasm in the process. Experience has taught us that the superior person who loves only humanity in general rarely entertains any notably generous emotions towards anyone in particular. (Unless he turns out to be in fact a better and more natural man than he proclaims himself to be in theory.) Indeed, given the opportunity, he has often shown himself quite ready, 'for the good of humanity', to persecute and destroy human beings on the largest possible scale. For the sake of the majority he will blithely sacrifice the minority and, should he one day find himself at odds even with the majority, he is consoled by the reflection that the future happiness of unborn generations will be greatly multiplied by the misery which he inflicts on his own. The fanatical reformers and conscientious revolutionaries who have brought so much evil on the world since 1793 have taught us the severe limitations of humanitarianism. The attempt to universalize natural love, to rise from love of the particular place to love of the whole world, from love of the particular person to love of the entire human race, is one which destroys love.

Christian wisdom is at all events wise enough to know that natural love must be left alone to remain what it is, a complex of attachments to particular persons, places and things. Its characteristic narrowness is more than compensated by its depth and power and selflessness. The Christian honours and respects natural love and its characteristic vehicles of expression, patriotism, the life of the family, the devotion to the very soil of a particular locality so noticeable among peasant peoples, and so on. The world of natural love is an unbalanced world, but nothing is to be gained by spreading out love so thinly over everything that it becomes transparent. The old world of love can only be balanced by calling into being the new world of Charity.

Charity (*agape* in Greek) is primarily the kind of love with which God loves man, a love which is not prompted or merited by anything lovable in man, but one which overflows so to speak from the depths of the divine being. God loves man not because man is lovable but because He is love. In the presence of this love the the Christian knows that he is confronting an ultimate mystery. The analogy of fatherhood perhaps provides the most likely clue to the mystery. The father loves his children, even the worst and most unrewarding of them, in the last resort simply because they are his. God perhaps loves His creation simply because He is its Creator. This Gospel message of God's unmerited and unmeritable love for man awakes an echo in the heart of the man who believes it, a responsive love for God, infinitely feebler than its original, yet having something of the same disinterested qualities. 'Thou shalt love the Lord thy God. . . . This is the first and great commandment.' The charity of God towards man must fulfil itself by begetting and nurturing into an increasingly lively existence the charity of man towards God. 'We love Him because He first loved us.' Only when this first commandment has been fulfilled does obedience to the second commandment become possible. 'Thou shalt love thy neighbour as thyself.' Once charity has brought us to God's side we begin to see the human race from His point of view; it becomes possible for us little by little to share His attitude towards it. To see men as God sees them, as Jesus saw them from the immense spiritual altitude of the Cross, that is the secret of charity.

The one word *charity* is thus used to describe three distinct but intimately related attitudes; the attitude of God towards all men declared in the gospel; the attitude towards God of those who hear and respond to the gospel; the attitude towards their fellow-men which the latter learn and acquire as a result of their mystical friendship with God. Charity is thus not a readaptation of the natural love which all men experience towards particular persons, places and things, still less is it a substitute for natural love. It is an addition or supplement to our natural capacities, existing side by side with them, balancing their narrowness and particularity with its own universalism.

Thus charity does not destroy love. It disciplines it and gives it a sense of proportion that love often lacks when left to itself, but it does not destroy it. Unregulated love begets idolatry. The idolater is a man who exalts some greatly beloved, or greatly feared, created thing into the place of the Creator. He builds his whole life round it, subordinating every other consideration to the thought of its well-being or its wishes. It dominates his whole philosophy. The false God may be an idol of stick or stone, as among the heathen. It may be wealth, or social ambition, or family life, nation or political party. But charity will at least remind a man that no gift of God, however good and lovable, can rightly be loved so immoderately that in effect it usurps God's central place in the direction of our lives and energies. Charity is thus, from one point of view, the sense of proportion which disciplines our loving. It operates by making and keeping us conscious of One Who is more lovable than any of those whom we naturally love. Even our most selfless affections are subjected to His judgment and must obediently stop short this side of idolatry. The Christian must love his neighbour *as* himself—no less, for he knows that his neighbour is as dearly loved by God as he is—no more, for he knows that he is himself as dear to God as his neighbour. But to his love for God the commandment sets no boundary, nor does it place beside this total obligation any measure or equivalent. 'Thou shalt love the Lord thy God with *all . . .*'

The Christian life is lived in three separate, although interpenetrating, spheres. There is the sphere of personal life in the narrower and more intimate sense of the term, within which we enjoy intercourse with those with whom we are personally acquainted. There is the sphere of public life, in which a man has to deal with and take into account that vastly preponderating proportion of the human race with which he neither has nor can have any immediate contact. The politician scheming for the welfare of the masses, the general, manœuvring to attain his military objectives with a minimum of casualties, the ordinary citizen trying to make up his mind about the next election, these are typical examples of men at all events attempting to adopt a moral attitude towards their unknown neighbours. Lastly there is the sphere of Church life. Here again the Christian has to deal with a world-wide society the great majority of whose members he can never know, although to these particular unknowns he is closely linked by a common faith and by kindred spiritual habits and practices.

Into each of these three spheres the Christian must inevitably go, and in each of them he must for a time abide. The problems of adjusting himself to their respective and sometimes competing claims will often be a source of embarrassment and perplexity. Nevertheless, it remains true that our sevenfold scheme of natural and supernatural virtues—wisdom, courage, temperance, justice, faith, hope, and charity—is the classical and lucid formula which most adequately describes the kind of person he will attempt and at least tend to be, and the moral valuations which will influence his conduct when it is most deliberate and responsible, in whatever sphere of existence he may for the moment be operating.

CHAPTER FIVE

ALL THIS—AND POLITICS TOO!

At the present time many thoughtful people are obsessed with politics. Political disorder intensifies political speculation and discussion. In the same way nothing makes a man so conscious of his digestion as indigestion. The tendency to be more concerned with things that are going badly than with those that are going well is natural and indeed inevitable, but it may destroy our faculty of seeing things in perspective. The acute dyspeptic may be led to suppose that nothing in life matters so much as his digestion. The conscientious and observant citizen of the present time may be induced by a similar error to underestimate the nonpolitical factors in life. In such a mood he will tend to judge a religion by its contribution to politics. Thus the leftist is apt to let his judgment of Christianity be determined by its capacity and willingness to persuade its adherents to join his favourite political party and advocate his pet political reforms. Similarly the right wing politician sometimes seems to regard Christianity and the Christian Church as a means of inculcating loyalty and obedience to the existing government and social order. Each desires to exploit Christianity in the interest of his own political purposes, and each is tempted to allow his judgment of religion and the Church to be determined by the degree to which they show themselves willing to submit to his will.

Almost any parish priest can tell of men who have left

his church because, to use the kind of expression which they employ, 'he was afraid to speak out' about social and political questions and 'give a lead', in other words, because he would not say precisely what they wanted him to say and follow tamely in the direction in which they had already decided to go. On the other hand, he can probably recollect others who have left his congregation for precisely the opposite reason. 'Because he would keep mixing politics with religion', in other words, because he was more critical of the existing social set-up than its beneficiaries and dupes would tolerate.

The relation between religion and politics is a perennial theme of discussion and dispute. Pre-Reformation Christianity was quite clear that the two cannot be dissociated. Political actions, after all, are human actions, determined on by some, acquiesced in by others and perhaps resisted by yet a third group. To determine, to do, to acquiesce, to resist—these are all human actions, which can either serve or frustrate the true purposes which the earthly life of man is designed to fulfil, which can be either good or bad, which can be either in or out of line with the will of God. The claim that religion has nothing to do with politics is in effect a claim that certain classes of human actions—political actions, that is the actions of men grouped in societies for the pursuit of wealth and power—are exempt from moral and spiritual criticism.

Clearly this is a claim which the Christian must in principle reject. It is not, in fact, possible to declare the Christian gospel without in a very real sense 'interfering in politics'. To proclaim the gospel is to make—sometimes explicitly, sometimes by implication—assertions about the nature of man and the value and destiny of human existence which will inevitably suggest thoughts criticial and sceptical of the social order in any realm which falls short of the Kingdom of God. Both in Nazi Germany before 1945 and in the Soviet empire at the present time the Churches and their leaders have been and are repeatedly charged with interference in politics. In justice it is only fair to say that the totalitarians are probably right from their own point of view. A Christianity compatible with their conception of a good social order could only be secured by drastically rewriting the scriptures and the Church liturgies, and by obliterating from the Christian memory two thousand years of the prophetic tradition of preaching and prayer. This sounds absurd, but something like such a drastic re-editing of the Christian Faith was actually attempted by the Nazis, and a not dissimilar, although much more modest and humane, reconstruction of Christianity, so that it will no longer jar upon the prejudices and limitations of the typical western contemporary mind, is advocated by our own modernists.

Obviously the theological criticism of the twentieth century, and the prophetic diagnosis of its maladies, is too vast a subject to be treated in a single chapter of a book primarily concerned with other matters. But the extent and depth of the contemporary interest in the relations between political and religious thinking is now so great that the subject cannot be altogether ignored even here. '

Political conditions in other countries have favoured the growth of specifically Christian parties. No responsible person, so far as I know, seriously advocates a development of that kind in this country. On the contrary, the strategy of Christian political action in Britain depends on the presence of Christians of ability and integrity in the councils of all political parties, so that serious Christian political thinking may flow into and through all party channels. Such a strategy requires in addition groups of free-lance Christian political thinkers and writers, working in detachment from all party ties and loyalties, and slowly influencing the established parties through their Christian members. It is not too much to claim that something of this kind has begun to happen on a very modest scale.

But I have no intention here of attempting any sort of contribution to such momentous discussions. The concern of this book is with the fundamentals of Christian life and thought, and so I propose to confine myself to a brief description and exposition of five fundamental biblical ideas which, as it seems to me, must necessarily regulate and direct all Christian political thinking.

1. *The Creation*

The Christian account of the origin of human life in a deliberate, creative act of God carries with it the very important implication that life is no accident.

All things are the embodiments of deliberate purpose. If we were indeed driven, as those who put their entire trust in the natural sciences seem to be, to the conclusion that we have no alternative but to accept the brute fact that the universe exists, and is the kind of universe which we partly know and increasingly discover it to be, as an ultimate datum to which the mind must resign itself, without any hope of being able ever to explain it in terms of rational necessity or design, then we shall be driven also to the conclusion that life has no inherent purpose of its own and that men must devise their own purposes for themselves.

Much of the semi-religious, semi-ethical literature

which has been produced in recent years in such large quantities by the more humane kind of scientific writer bears witness to this necessity. In effect, we are told, the progress of natural science has exploded the old religious and theological view that the purpose of life is the purpose of its Creator. But since life cannot be lived successfully in practice without any purpose at all, we must fill the void left by the disappearance of religion from the modern consciousness by devising new purposes with which to give unity and direction to contemporary living.

But such writers set themselves an impossible task. It is useless to foist a mere outward show of purpose on something which is inherently purposeless. If life has not an obstinate and ineradicable purpose of its own, prior to its coming to us and independently of our possessing it, it is too late and futile for us to start trying to improvise a purpose for it when we reach an age of conscious reflection.

The idea of the Creation, on the other hand, implies that the purpose of life is given by life itself and derives from the same source, that successful living requires that those to whom the privilege of life is entrusted should grasp the essentials of that purpose with their minds and consent to it with their wills. Clearly, we are drawing an essential distinction between the Purpose of life (with a capital P), and the multiplicity of purposes (small p) of which men more or less approve in a more or less superficial manner, and which they pursue more or less consistently. Life itself embodies a Purpose independent of and infinitely more stable than the wide variety of subjective purposes which compete for our recognition and succeed each other in our conscious minds. To acknowledge and co-operate with the Pur-

I

pose is wisdom; to squander human energy in the service of crudely improvised alternatives is, in the literal sense, vanity.

The purpose of life is the purpose of life's Creator. If this Christian account of the matter is incorrect, the only valid alternative is the paralysing conclusion that life has no purpose at all. But the idea of creation implies more than this. The purpose of our life is one which we are designed and equipped by our Creator to pursue and fulfil. The biblical idea of creation means that man has not only an inescapable destiny but, behind and beneath his relatively superficial self-adaptations to changing and different physical and social circumstances, an unchanging psychological core to his nature. The interpreters of the approaching—as it is presumed—'scientific' social order, with their semi-ethical, semi-religious bias, their very significant and conscientious search for something which cannot be found in the more ruthlessly scientific accounts of our existence, seem to suppose that man's nature is as fluid and as much under his control as his purposes. They assume that just as a man can and must ask himself the question, 'What purposes shall I devise for myself and pursue?' so he must also ask himself the further question, 'What kind of being do I propose to become?'

For the Christian both these questions are futile. The biblical idea implies that the purpose of life is what its Creator meant it to be and cannot become anything else, that man is what his Creator made him and cannot by taking thought add or subtract one cubit to or from his stature. The purpose of our being, and the human nature equipped and designed for its pursuit, come to us with life itself and from the same source; and the nature only functions harmoniously and fruitfully in the service of the purpose. It is true that it displays a capacity for change, for free and often original responses to different situations, for adapting itself to novel stimuli. But behind this outward show of change the inward core of personality is composed of permanent and indestructible elements, one purpose, created like itself, insistently claiming its allegiance, and the very elements of its own being blindly and restlessly clamouring for the kind of existence which their inherent destiny would dictate to them, and persistently refusing to be at rest in any other. Thus the first question which the Christian must ask about any proposed way of human life, of any ethical, social and political design for human living, is a crucial one. 'Can it accommodate man's true nature without subjecting it to distorting pressures? Can it facilitate his fulfilment of his destiny? Is it a way of life or social system adapted to man's true nature, and to the service of the ultimate purpose which he embodies, or does it propose instead a futile attempt to adapt his nature to meet its own artificial requirements?'

2. Man's Duty to God

In the last resort man's only safeguard against totalitarianism is his conviction that his moral life is not wholly absorbed in what we call service, in his performance of his many duties towards his neighbours. What do we mean by 'totalitarianism'? The popular use of the word is so loose and ambiguous that the question is one of some importance. 'We must substitute the ethics of social responsibility for the outworn religious dogmas,' said a member of the Trades Union Congress during a debate on education some years ago. It was really a totalitarian cry, although the speaker was doubtless unconscious of its implications. It could be paralleled again and again out of the mouths of Nazi leaders, for the Nazis had much more in common with liberal secularists and anti-clericals of the old school than the latter usually care to admit. They all share the conviction that man's only duty is to his neighbour. It is true that the Nazis would not have given the same answer to the question, 'And who is my neighbour?' as the liberal humanist. For the Nazi the German had moral duties only to Germans—just as the Jew of old did not feel himself so responsible morally toward Gentiles as towards his fellow-Jews, and the ancient Greek could not conceive that he was bound to the barbarian by obligations comparable to those which linked him to his fellow Hellenes. For the modern liberal humanist, who is after all a product of Christianity, the area within which moral obligation is experienced and regarded as binding upon the conscience is a much wider one, comprehending the entire human race.

Group morality in its most familiar form conceives this area more narrowly. It is that state of ethical development in which a man acknowledges moral duties only towards the other members of his own group—his family, clan, caste, nation or race. At this stage he may acknowledge no duties towards the outsider at all or, while assuming a rather more positive ethical attitude than that, he may regard those responsibilities external to his group which he does recognize as infinitely inferior both in degree and intensity to the obligations which hold good within it. Clearly the area within which moral obligation is experienced, and constitutes a more or less effective force, may be either greater than, or less than, or coincide with the area within which men are politically and socially organized into a governmental unit. Thus a man passing through a phase of moral development which makes him unconscious of any other duties than those which bind him to other members of his clan may find himself, like a Scottish Highlander in the seventeenth century, suddenly brought within the framework of a modern nation state. Inevitably the result will be a clash between what the government will regard as his duty to the nation as a whole, and what he will regard as his duty to his own clan. The liberal humanist, on the other hand, may on occasion regard his duty to humanity as a whole as more imperative than his duty towards his own country. For him the area of moral responsibility is wider than the area of political authority. Lastly, a man may regard his whole moral life as dominated by his duty towards his country and its government. He will participate without question in criminal and aggressive wars, he will betray his own father if he thinks him disloyal to the régime, he will break, without sense of shame or guilt, any moral law known to the conscience of man at the behest of his country's leaders or in what he regards as the national interest. It is this last stage that we call the totalitarian stage, and our discussion has led us to a point at which we are able to define 'totalitarianism'.

Totalitarianism is the coincidence of moral and political frontiers. It is what happens to man when the area within which he experiences moral obligation is the same as the area within which his political life is organized by constituted authority. Thus where men are organized tribally, the tribal ethic is a totalitarian ethic; where they are organized in nation states, the nationalist ethic is a totalitarian ethic. Should at any future date a world state or any central world authority emerge out of our present international chaos, then the world-

wide humanist ethic would become totalitarian in its
turn. Group morality does not cease to be group morality simply because the group becomes very large, or because it succeeds in swallowing up all other groups. The
essence of group morality is its refusal to allow that any
member of the group has any duties which transcend its
own life and any significance or importance apart from
his significance and importance to and for itself.

The Christian's conception of man's over-riding duty
towards God, 'the first and great commandment', is his
protection against the present lure and impending menace of world totalitarianism. The moral life of man does
not consist merely in his performance of his duty towards his neighbour, in 'service', as the jargon of so
many modern youth movements seems to imply. Man's
duty towards his neighbour is an important yet subordinate department of his moral life. Christ's command,
'Thou shalt love thy neighbour as thyself' means not
only, 'Thou shalt love thy neighbour very much—as
much as thyself,' but also, 'Thou shalt not love thy
neighbour too much—not more than thyself.'

In the last resort there are only three conceptions of
the moral life: selfish individualism, which teaches that
a man belongs to himself, and that his primary duty is
towards himself; altruistic or social idealism, which
teaches that a man belongs to his community, however
widely or narrowly conceived, and that his first duty is
towards his fellows; and the Christian belief that man
belongs to God, that he exists primarily for neither
communal purposes nor his own, but as the creature of
the divine purpose, so that his supreme duty is neither to
himself nor to his fellows but to the Creator of his selfhood and theirs.

The Christian would agree that there are important

truths in both individualism and social idealism; a man
has a real duty to himself, that is to the particular self
with its characteristic gifts and capacities which God has
entrusted to his care; and he has also a real duty to his
neighbours, who like him have been entrusted by God
with immortal selves to preserve and develop. Just as
excessive individualism produces anarchy and injustice,
so excessive, uncriticized social idealism tends towards
totalitarianism, the insistence that a man must live and
move and have his being within the life of his community, the denial that there is anything in his nature which
transcends, which is more important than, the life of his
community. This insistence and this denial would not
cease to be totalitarian in its effects merely because the
community in question had become a world community. Indeed, it is the emergence of a world totalitarianism of this kind which seems to me to be the danger
which we shall have to face once we have succeeded in
putting down the class totalitarianism of the Soviets as
effectively as we have already destroyed the racial totalitarianism of the Nazis. We must always beware of good
and enthusiastically well intentioned men who doubt or
deny the reality of God. They have a fatal tendency to
make a mortal God of their community and a fanatical
religion of their moral idealism.

I agree, of course, that the enlightened, worldwide
outlook of the modern liberal is anti-totalitarian *for the
moment*, but I discern in it the germ of a future world
totalitarianism. So long as the world is composed of a
plurality of independent nation states his passionate insistence on our moral obligations to all mankind—his
basically New Testament conviction that for the enlightened conscience there is neither Jew nor Gentile,
neither Greek nor barbarian, neither slave nor free man

—exerts a wholesome influence and, where it evokes any positive response, effectively prevents political authority from making or even attempting to make, any sort of total claim on our lives and consciences. But should the humanist ever succeed in setting up the world state of his dreams, his ethic would at once become in fact the totalitarian ethic which it is potentially even now.

We may see all through history the operation of a process which tends continually to transform what began as an anti-totalitarian protest into a wider and more comprehensive totalitarianism. The revolutionary moral idealist asserts, often with courage and self-sacrifice, that the area of moral obligation is wider than the area of social organization, that men have duties towards other men outside their own group. In so far as his point of view prevails the area of social organization is widened in order to accommodate his teaching, from the family to the clan, from the clan to the tribe, from the tribe to the nation and so on—and the moment the social organization catches up with the ethic the latter becomes totalitarian. The only real safeguard against totalitarianism, at any stage of moral and political development, is the assertion that man has real and supremely important duties which are owed not to other men at all—but to Him who is infinitely greater and more important than even mankind as a whole, so that our duties to Him are not only different and more numerous than our duties to our neighbours but also more urgent and absolute.

I know that some of the more Christianly minded humanists would attempt to evade this direct contrast by the simple expedient of identifying our duties to our neighbours with our duty to God. 'What God wants of us', they would say, 'is the zealous performance of our duties to our fellows. Inasmuch as we do good to the least of our neighbours we do good to God Himself.'

A half-truth is worse than a lie because it is less easily exposed, and this is a particularly dangerous half-truth. Clearly, there can be no true service of God which ignores our obligations to our fellow-men. The man who pretends to love God while hating his brother is a liar. But we must also remember that our neighbour is not God, nor are we, and that he can no more make an absolute claim on us that we on him, that, more important still, mankind as a whole is not God, and cannot therefore make an absolute claim on either or both of us. A man may be his brother's keeper, but he is certainly not his brother's owner. The conviction that in the last resort each man belongs to God alone, and that God has an absolute claim on his services, is the foundation of human liberty.

All this amounts to saying that society and social organization are subordinate to the highest human purposes. It is not given to social convention or statute law to make atonement between the will of God and the soul of man. The social order has, nevertheless, a certain relevance to man's pursuit of his highest and most ultimate purposes. It may encourage the most wholesome elements in his environment, and free him from major distractions by minimizing the number and intensity of political and economic conflicts. A healthy minded, just society would be a more suitable operational base from which to set out on the quest for God than, for example, the afflicted, hysterical, preoccupying world in which we now are, so like, as the wit said in the last war, a lunatic asylum run by its inmates.

3. *The Remnant*

These reflections make it very clear that, from the standpoint of the Bible and Christian experience, few theories are more palpably false than that which interprets moral goodness by what a modern writer has called the 'principle of sociality'. The doctrine that goodness consists in loyal conformity to the customs of the societies to which we belong, in a steadfast cultivation of good neighbourliness, has been maintained by many thinkers at different times and in different ways, but it is certainly not maintained in the Bible.

There we are confronted with what appear to be forlorn minorities in the midst of a nation which has fallen far short of its own vision, with a battered remnant which survives the catastrophe that overtakes the nation as a whole, with isolated individuals lifting up the voice of truth in a wilderness of falsehood. In the Old Testament Israel is the people of God not because the majority of her citizens are conspicuously godly, but because running through her history is the fine thread of prophecy, always strained yet never snapped. It is the glory of Israel that the Word of God is repeatedly spoken to her by her noblest sons, and the shame of Israel that she will not listen.

In the New Testament we are again confronted with the creative minority. The voice of the few is once more the voice of the future and the voice of the many the voice of the past. In the decisive hour of crisis and judgment, when Israel stands face to face with the Messiah of whom its prophets had prophesied, and for whose coming its more numerous men of prayer had prayed with simple and unmarked sincerity, and neither knows nor loves him, Jesus becomes Himself the remnant. The future belongs to the lonely Man on the cross and not to the great mob of 'common men', the ninety-nine-out-of-a-hundred, the 'damned, compact majority', which howls for His blood. In Christian history also, from the days of the little company in the upper room until now, the life and soul of the Church has lurked in a creative minority of utterly devoted souls rather than in the often not more than half converted ecclesiastical majority.

It would be easy, of course, to overstate this principle. When Ibsen's Dr. Stockmann remarked, 'Majorities are always wrong; minorities are always right', he was no doubt exaggerating. It is possible for minorities to sink below as well as rise above the community standard. In a well ordered society professional thieves are as much in a minority as saints. Nevertheless if majorities usually contrive to avoid what is grossest in life, it is also true that what is highest escapes them with equal persistence. Minorities are sometimes right but majorities never, and a wise majority will cherish its minorities as a man in the dark will value his torch.

Of course, the principle of the supremacy of minorities is not peculiar to the Bible, nor to Christianity. No artist would determine the beauty of a picture merely by consulting the views of the sightseers who throng the art gallery. No scientist would decide on the merits of a novel scientific theory by the simple process of taking a vote. In the realm of every particular human interest or science there will be found a natural aristocracy of those who know, who possess the requisite training and capacity for responsible judgment, and the much more numerous company of those who do not. The most important activities in life are minority activities. A living religious faith, a selfless devotion to beauty, a disinterested desire for truth, these are all minority qualities, and the minorities which possess them enrich the lives of the less gifted and inspired majority by giving free and independent rein to their own characteristic spiritual urges.

This assertion of the minoritarian principle is not by any means an attack on democracy—very much to the contrary! But it will almost certainly lead those who are impressed by it to interpret the word 'democracy' very differently from the way in which it is now conventionally understood. We may hold that the minoritarian principle constitutes the very essence of true democracy, that democratic political institutions are essentially an elaborate device for enabling minorities to lift up their voices and for keeping aggressive majorities in check, but we must face the fact that this has ceased to be the thought uppermost in the mind of the politician or journalist as he works that hard-worked word a little more hardly still.

4. *The Fall*

This is not a theological treatise and here I can do no more than summarize a conception which must necessarily exercise a decisive influence on any Christian thinking which concerns itself with politics.

It is common ground between Christians and many non-Christians that the good life for human beings must be one which is precisely fitted to our nature, one which will permit the harmonious exercise of all our native gifts and capacities. Our idea of what will constitute the good life for man is thus dependent on our understanding of human nature. But how are we to achieve any adequate understanding of human nature? 'By looking at human beings, by a careful analysis of

their behaviour, past and present, individual and collective,' reply the historian, the psychologist and the sociologist with one voice. At first sight this appears to be a
very reasonable proposal, but unhappily the results of
such a method of procedure, instead of providing us
with a picture of human nature which will serve as the
foundation of a truly human ethic, of a conception of
what would constitute the good life for man, rather
makes us despair of finding any solution to our problem
at all. For the picture which it provides is one of all-pervading conflict. It is not merely that history is so largely
a record of past conflict and sociology, so preponderantly
an analysis of present conflict. Psychology, despite its
immaturity and the chronic disagreements of its most
distinguished professors, indicates clearly that the source
of these large-scale public conflicts is the persistent conflict within the private mind of thought with thought,
of emotion with emotion, of desire with desire, of private inclination with public obligation, of the immediate impulse with calculated self-interest, of the authori-
tative conscience with the rebellious ambition, of the
morally scrupulous consciousness with the amoral content of the unconscious mind impinging persistently
upon its frontiers. It is difficult to see how there can be
any harmonious way of life, any peaceful and co-opera-
tive expression of varied gifts and aptitudes for such self-
contradictory and self-contradicting beings as we appear
to be.

The Christian diagnosis and solution of this problem is
expressed in the doctrine of the Fall. It is the most paradoxical of all Christian beliefs, and of such profundity
as almost to elude both comprehension and expression.
In the present context its most important implication is
its suggestion that man has become in history what he is

not by nature; that the life of man as we live it and observe it is not an undistorted reflection, as might be expected, of the real underlying truth about man. Human
nature is only partly expressed in human life, which also
partly conceals and partly caricatures it. Human nature
can thus be thought of in two ways, in terms of what it
has become—and this is how the historians, psychologists and sociologists understand it, and how we ourselves
understand and interpret human life lived within and
around us—or in terms of that underlying and concealed nature, repressed and frustrated but not abolished
by sin, which for Christians is revealed in the human
perfection of Jesus Christ. This is the distinction between
sinful human nature—human nature as it has become
through sin—and redeemed or restored human nature—
human nature brought back to the way of life for which
it was created, designed and equipped, and in which
alone it can find secure peace and happiness.

Clearly this basic axiom that the good life for man is
one which fits his nature, and which permits it to enjoy
perfect and harmonious self-expression, can now be
understood in two senses, according to which of the two
interpretations we give to the ambiguous phrase 'human
nature'. Are we to select sinful or redeemed human
nature as the basis of our social and ethical calculations?

The Christian would say that sinful human nature is
incapable of harmony either personal or social. There
can be no world safe for sinners to sin in. But a world
safe for sinners to sin in seems to be the goal of most
modern and contemporary political reform and of not
a little psychoanalytic practice, and the burden of most
proposals to readjust our morals. Those who are most
zealous for social justice are not on the whole particu-

larly concerned for a deepening of personal and private morality. They talk of the importance of good faith and disinterestedness in public life, but are often comparatively indifferent to fidelity in marriage, self-control outside marriage and the unselfish fulfilment of parental responsibilities. Indeed many of our most vocal reformers seem to desire a social order in which the private and domestic virtues will be superfluous. The absorption of so many political idealists in public morality, and their blindness to the importance of personal ethics, runs parallel to the equally perverse preoccupation of many good Christians with individual and private morality. The former believe that a good society would in the long run produce good men, while the latter are confident that a society of good men would necessarily produce a just social order. Both are wrong. We have as little warrant for supposing that personal goodness is the automatic product of social righteousness as for the opposite notion that public health is the necessary consequence of private probity. There can be no priority as between absolute essentials. Public and private goodness are correlative terms. We can no more have one without the other than we can have the left without the right or the back without the front. They must be sought and found together, or not at all. So long as sin continues there will be an element of corruption and imperfection in the depths of society which will repeatedly succeed in ruffling its surface. So long as sin continues, there will always be something to win and something to defend, unachieved perfections to be attained and novel threats to existing excellencies to be bravely and sacrificially overcome. So long as sin continues, in other words, both the conservative and revolutionary attitudes towards the social order and its problems will continue to be justified, radicalism by the manifest imperfections of the *status quo* and conservatism by the persistent insecurity of valid human achievements in a fallen world.

Political and ethical planning, therefore, is better based on an understanding of the real, underlying and partly concealed nature of man than on mere observation of what man through sin has become. Let us base our scheme for human living upon what we believe man really is by nature and has it in him to become in fact. *De facto* sinful human nature comprehensively understood, and not as interpreted by various psychological schools—which produce an appearance of personal unity by selecting certain elements of personality for emphasis at the expense of others—provides no indication of the direction in which social harmony or stability is to be sought, or of the method by which it is to be found and maintained.

According to the Christian doctrine the visible truth about Christ is the submerged and concealed truth about every man. He is 'the Man'. His is the real humanity. For the conception of the Fall properly understood sets before us no merely temporal contrast. It is not that man was perfect *once* but has become imperfect *now*. That would be a superficial interpretation indeed. The contrast is more immediate in character and more tragic in its consequences. Man is perfect by nature and imperfect in visible and conscious achievement. He was made for one kind of life and he has immersed himself in another, with the result that his *de facto* existence cannot content or satisfy him. He cannot live in heaven because he is a sinner and he cannot be abidingly happy outside heaven because he is a child of God. In philosophical language, his *becoming* contradicts his *being*. His natural capacities were designed for one purpose, and by an act of crude and unsuccessful improvisation have been roughly adapted to another.

All political thought and planning, whether consciously or unconsciously, is based on some interpretation of man. Christian political thinking will take for its point of departure this specifically Christian insight into the fundamental human conflict, and will envisage a society designed to accommodate man's being rather than to facilitate his becoming. There can be no world safe for sinners to sin in, but a society consciously Christian in its assumptions about the nature of man might well be safer even for sinners than our present lethal community.

The Christian will have no use for utopias, which either ignore sin, or seek to accommodate it, or superficially presume its automatic disappearance in response to a reformation of our social circumstances. Nor, on the other hand, will he be impressed by the cynical realism which would accept and reconcile itself to sin, adapting political theory to human imperfection as though it were possible to escape the consequences of sin by flattering it to its face. A Christian realism will ignore neither the underlying persistence of man's true being nor the force and momentum of his present becoming. The conviction that man's lot will remain relatively unhappy, and his social order relatively unjust and unstable, so long as sin continues, will be balanced by the belief that man's true nature persists through suppression and continues to operate *incognito*, so to speak, so that, *by the grace of God*, a happy return to it is a *permanent possibility*. This is the truth that underlies the Gospel proclamation that the 'Kingdom of God is at hand'. 'The Kingdom of God' is always 'at hand', but utopia, a kingdom for fallen men established by political action

K

alone, exists nowhere except in the imagination of the utopians.

The utopian is literally 'presumptuous', not only in presuming the possibility of utopia but even more in presuming the invulnerability, the perpetual security, of utopia once established. In all projects for perpetual reform—such as 'no more war' movements—there is an element of presumption and conceit. It is not for us to know the times and the seasons. It is not for us to dictate political settlements to the centuries yet to come. Hitler once declared that his régime would last a thousand years. It is wiser to remember that in a fallen world all good things are persistently evasive and insecure, not easily reached, grasped only with difficulty and always uncertainly held. What has been fought for and attained in one generation must be fought for all over again in each succeeding generation if it is to be retained. What has hitherto been fought for and lost remains worth fighting for and must be fought for still, and perhaps lost again and again. In the world of moral and spiritual experience, of which politics properly understood is one particular province, there is no certainty except the certainty of perpetual struggle, and no secure prize except the satisfaction of having never surrendered.

This theological doctrine of the Fall has been one of incalculable political importance in the history of our civilization. From it the Christian thinkers have evolved that conception of constitutional government and the rule of law which has become the basic political ideal of democratic society. A constitution is, after all, only an elaborate political device for securing a division and dispersal of power among various individuals and groups. Similarly the aim of law is to subordinate power to generally approved purposes and ideas. No doubt these devices have their political disadvantages. Hedging power about with checks and balances and constitutional limitations often makes it difficult for even right and desirable actions to be carried out swiftly and efficiently. Indeed, if only we could find some inherently righteous unfallen men, beyond the power of temptation and above all suspicion of any·conceivable corruption, there would be much to be said for giving them absolute control of our destinies. But the doctrine of the Fall implies that there are no such men, that no man or a particular class or group can safely be trusted with too much power. In such circumstances the wiser course is to disperse and distribute power as widely as possible, to balance one form of power against another, above all to make power the servant of fundamental rules of justice guaranteeing the basic human rights and freedoms which power itself is powerless to set aside.

Historically speaking indeed this conception has been the chief contribution of Christian thought to political philosophy. We can see it gradually beginning to take shape in the writings of the great Christian philosophers of the middle ages. In modern democracy there is a tendency to turn away from this doctrine in certain important respects. The idea of the 'absolute sovereignty' of parliament, for example, seems to set a certain important form of political power above rather than below the law. But it remains true that the basic democratic ideal is that of a state limited and circumscribed in its functions and powers. This is a conception to which those who believe in the doctrine of the Fall will resolutely cling, recognizing in it the only alternative, in the last resort, to degrading tyranny and oppression.

5. The Kingdom

The Kingdom of God is one of the most important of New Testament conceptions. It refers not primarily to a place but to a state of things in which the purpose of God is triumphant. The Lord's Prayer immediately relates the coming of God's Kingdom to the performance of God's will. Wherever and whenever the will of God is done, there the Kingdom of God is already come. Thus Jesus can claim that the Kingdom is already present in His person, 'in the midst' of those who stand round about Him, and promise that the witnesses of His approaching resurrection, and the great evangelical outburst of Pentecost, shall see for themselves the powers of the Kingdom visibly victorious. The essence of the conception is thus the obedience of the creatures to the Creator's will.

But the Kingdom of God implies more than the final triumph of the divine will. It is a humane as well as a theological conception. It implies man's self-fulfilment as well as divine supremacy. The Kingdom is the state of affairs for which man is made and in which, consequently, he is most true to himself. Christianity is, in its own unique way, a humanistic religion. It believes in man profoundly and passionately, but qualifies such a faith with its recognition that man is not really man except in God, until he has embraced and reconciled himself with his true nature and destiny in God's Kingdom.

The idea of the Kingdom of God is, for the Christian, the standard against which all forms of human community must be measured and judged. Such a critical procedure leads to an intense and comprehensive but quite unusual kind of social criticism. For the Kingdom of God is an end which renders those who seek it more instead of less scrupulous about the means they employ. Most English people feel that contemporary political fanaticisms, like Communism and Fascism, have more in common with religion than with politics as we know it. A sound instinct tells us that mere prudent social calculation would never of itself generate passions so violent as these.

It is certainly true that in our time many political doctrines and parties have succeeded in eliciting a religious response from their followers, usually with deplorable results. But not even a political dogma which is adhered to with religious devotion can be so absolute in its judgment on society as a real religion, religious not only in the quality of the response it arouses but also in the sense that the stimulus which it provides is not a prevision of some future human perfection but an immediate vision of the present perfection of God. By contrast with such a vision as this even our fancied perfections are seen to be imperfect, and the goal towards which the secular idealist believes himself to be progressing appears to be little better than his despised and rejected point of departure.

The political struggle seen from within appears to be a conflict between conservative and revolutionary tendencies, between those who are benefited by and therefore approve of an existing social situation, and those who are more or less victimized by and therefore disapprove of it. No doubt there is also to be found on either side a minority of honest, selfless souls whose intellectual judgment is independent of their estimate of their own present and future fortunes.

Seen from without, however, the political struggle presents a very different picture. From this external point of view it would appear to be fratricidal struggle

between two different forms of conservatism, which
we may call static and dynamic. The tendency of the
static conservative is to regard the social system as something *in being*, as a more or less completed whole and,
approving of it, to resist adventurous and perhaps foolhardy attempts to change it. The dynamic conservative,
however, recognizes that society as we know it is in a
state of *becoming*, that it is more accurately described in
terms of its prevailing tendencies, of the path which it
has pursued during the recent past and is still pursuing,
than in terms of its existing and relatively fixed institutions. What he approves of is not society as it is but the
direction in which society is moving. He is usually dissatisfied with its pace, which he regards as too slow, but
not with its goal. What he demands is the full realization
of all the logical consequences of principles which society
as a whole has already conceded. Thus in a prevailingly
individualistic age he cried out for more individualism
and for a speeding up of the individualizing process.
Similarly, in a collectivist age he is loud for more collectivism, and the sooner the better. The progress of
which we hear so much from excited progressives is
thus little more than the process of implementing the
consequences of the last intellectual revolution to sweep
society. 'Progressivism' is the demand that this last
revolution should enjoy a one hundred per cent triumph.

    This analysis enables us to perceive why it is that the
progressivist, or dynamic conservative, as I prefer to
call him, is always more effective in argument than in
history. He succeeds in argument because he appeals to
principles—equality, for example—which his society
has already in effect conceded, and which his more
cautious, static conservative opponents themselves accept. In history he is seen to be less effective than in argu-

ment because history never permits that complete and logical triumph of a particular point of view which he demands. Long before the consequences of the last intellectual revolution have been completely implemented, or even deduced and promulgated, the next intellectual revolution has arrived, and our progressivist, a pathetic spectacle now, who once marched proudly forward with the advance guard of the race finds himself suddenly and uncomprehendingly fighting stubborn rearguard actions.

To express the essence of this distinction in a single bold contrast: the static conservative is the man who says, in effect, 'What is, ought to be, and ought therefore to continue to be,' whereas the dynamic conservative affirms that, 'What is happening, ought to be happening and ought, therefore, to go on happening—only more quickly'. To this extent, at least, all modern 'leftism' has become Marxian. It does not conceive itself as courageously defying history and the general trend of events on grounds of moral conviction, but rather as humbly submitting to and co-operating with them. The essential doctrine of Marx was not that world socialism is desirable—many others had desired it before him—but that, whether desirable or not, it is *inevitable*, the destiny which the wise man accepts and which guarantees victory to him who makes himself its instrument. History as it is, the general trend of events, the 'march of time', has thus become for the 'progressivist' what 'divine Providence' is for the Christian.

From our present point of view, therefore, the contemporary political struggle between right and left, between conservatives and radicals, is less significant and absorbing than the antagonists on both sides sincerely suppose. Certainly the dynamic conservatives are nearer to the truth in interpreting society in terms of becoming rather than in terms of being, but their attempted sub-ordination of events to logic betrays a poor sense of history, whereas the static conservative's indifference to the rigorous implications of principles which he has him-self conceded is often justified by the bewildering way in which to-day's despised relic of a rejected past be-comes the exciting and significant discovery of to-morrow. If he hangs on long enough to his apparently outmoded point of view history may well return to him again, and yesterday's 'reactionary' find himself hailed as to-day's 'progressive'. It has happened like that before, and may well so happen again.

I do not wish to suggest that the choice between left and right has no significance at all, but it is clear that from the point of view of those who are as critical of the direction in which society is moving as they are dissatis-fied with its present constitution, the difference between left and right, interpreted from their standpoint as a difference between dynamic and static conservatism, has very much less significance than is usually attributed to it. The truth is that only a political philosophy which criticizes the kingdoms of men from the standpoint of the Kingdom of God can be absolutely radical. In secular politics radicalism is usually motivated and sustained by some form of utopianism, a belief in a final perfect kingdom of man attainable in history, which is only a secularized version of the idea of the Kingdom of God. We have seen reason to reject all utopias, but at least a utopia makes a root and branch criticism of existing society possible. The mere contrasting of the actuality of the present situation with its visible potentialities, of the present state of things with that future state which even the superficial observer can see to be emerging out

of it, can provide no genuine radicalism and usurps the
name of revolution.

Clearly a political analysis based upon such presuppositions as these is likely to lead to unfamiliar conclusions. The Christian must be ready to follow where the
Christian argument leads. That it should contradict prevailing intellectual tendencies is not at all surprising.
Such a contradiction is no novelty and perhaps corresponds to an inherent dialectical necessity. 'The cross
stands while the world revolves', or, to employ a similar
but more immediately relevant analogy, the cross
stands while the world swings about it like a pendulum.
The social witness of the Church in any particular situation must concern itself primarily with correcting the
current exaggerations. In the over-individualistic nineteenth century the Christian social witness expressed itself through the Christian socialism of men like Kingsley
and Maurice, who reminded their contemporaries, not
altogether in vain, of their overriding responsibilities
to the social order and to each other. A hundred years
ago the working classes were the proper objects of
Christian compassion, the obvious victims of the prevailing social injustices. But that has ceased to be true.
Now the middle-class way of life, based on an ethic of
self-help and personal responsibility—and quite as noble
in its own way as the traditional working-class way of
life, based on an ethic of mutual aid and mass solidarity
—is being rendered almost unlivable by savage taxation.
We cannot stand by unmoved while one aggressive
social group seeks to destroy another. In an age of increasing economic collectivism and political totalitarianism the restatement of a Christian individualism is our
proper task. In biblical and Christian history the prophet

is always and necessarily in opposition. In an unbalanced world he is all things in turn, a socialist among individualists and an individualist among socialists. He is condemned always to be estranged from the reigning spirit of his age. To some extent, however, he can atone for and overcome his enforced intellectual isolation by concentrating on the unsolved problems of his time. If he cannot share the prevailing prejudices he can perhaps re-establish contact with the mood of the age by striving to answer its most characteristic questions.

CHAPTER SIX

DEFENCE—AND COUNTER-ATTACK

Such, in brief, is the Christian Faith which I have received from others, and so I have been accustomed for some years to understand and present it. As compared with any modern system of unbelief known to me, it is at once broader and more profound. Its scheme of life is more complicated than that of materialism or positivism because it is one in which there are more realities to be reckoned with. On the other hand it is, for the same reason, a more interesting and satisfying one intellectually speaking. Its problems are more diverse and numerous. Unlike so many paper theories of life, it is as complex and profound as life itself. It is more penetrating and searching because it recognizes the reality and importance of levels of experience which do not lie so well within the range of our everyday consciousness, and are not so easily discussed, as those which receive the undivided attention of secularists of all species.

Nevertheless, the fact remains that a not inconsiderable minority of our contemporaries do not accept this faith, and the great majority of them, not bothering sufficiently about such things to know whether they believe it or not, certainly make no attempt to practise it. The historic lands of Christendom are places in which the larger proportion of the population cannot be called Christian in any serious sense of the word, and this has been true for at least two hundred years. To face the fact of unbelief, and interpret its prevalence in our modern world, is the plain duty of any man who ventures to speak for Christianity to this generation. The reader has a right to demand that I should not shirk it here.

Nevertheless, I do not wish to approach this subject in quite the conventional manner of Christian 'apologetics', and this for two reasons. In the first place, I do not believe that there is any distinct way of reasoning and body of conviction which can be labelled 'modern thought' or the 'spirit of the age' and set over against Christianity. There is, in fact, no agreed system of 'modern thought', no accepted contemporary alternative to Christianity. If the term 'modern thought' refers to anything real, it is a name for the process of modern thinking, and modern thinking is a very animated debate between strongly contrasted philosophies and points of view which shews not the slightest sign of coming to any conclusion or of reaching any measure of agreement in any foreseeable future. One of the most vocal and effective contributors to this debate is Christianity itself. Christian thinking in the modern world is a form of modern thought, taking its full and lively part in the intellectual rough and tumble of the time.

Modern Christian thinkers are just as modern as their pagan contemporaries. C. S. Lewis, Jacques Maritain and Reinhold Niebuhr are modern in the same sense, and for the same reason, as Bertrand Russell, Aldous Huxley and J. D. Bernal are modern. They are just as much concerned with contemporary problems and they participate with equal enthusiasm in our interminable debates. It might perhaps be suggested that the Christians are less modern than the unbelievers because they have made themselves the mouthpieces in their own age of an ancient orthodoxy. But the unbelievers, after all, are merely the contemporary exponents of heresies which are, if anything, even more antique. The truth is that the modern debate is still recognizably the same debate as the ancient one. It is sometimes concerned with new problems, but it does not see or discuss them from any fundamentally new points of view. Modern thought is a phase of that untiring development of western thought which has been taking place continuously since the seventh century B.C. Christianity has been making important and often decisive contributions to that process for the last two thousand years, and still continues to do so.

There is then no debate which can properly be described or conceived as one between Christianity and modern thought. The Christian contribution to modern thought, on the contrary, is a rational analysis which refutes the prevalent notion that a conscientious intellectual cannot be a Christian, by shewing it to be based on certain errors of judgment and superfluous assumptions which the conscientious intellectual will instantly abandon upon recognizing them for what they are.

My second reason for refusing to inflict on the reader an essay in conventional religious apologetics is my inability to believe that these dialectical subtleties will really get to the root of the situation. The average non-churchgoer does not reluctantly refrain from worship because he has just read Darwin or Marx and lost his rational faith. Even the intellectual who offers reasoned objections to Christian belief may, in fact, be much more decisively influenced than he would care to admit by those social and psychological forces which have so estranged the men and women of our time and place from God. To become conscious of the historical, psychological and sociological currents which motivate and sustain modern doubt and unbelief is the best way of becoming strong enough to resist them. In what follows, therefore, I shall be as much concerned with the unconscious causes of unbelief as with the conscious and explicit beliefs of the unbelievers.

For the unbelievers, curiously enough, are psychologically quite capable of belief, and in fact commonly believe all sorts of things. Whatever the modern discussion about Christianity may be, it is certainly not a debate between those who are temperamentally inclined towards 'simple faith' and those whose more robust intellects find doubt and open-minded inquiry more congenial. The Christian may quite possibly be a hard-headed 'realist' who is sceptical about almost everything except the Apostles' Creed. The unbeliever, on the other hand, may be a marxist, or a scientific humanist with a 'beautiful faith', so comforting, that 'science' will shortly create a golden age of happiness and plenty for all. In either case the modern Christian finds himself face to face with a capacity for simple, childlike faith, a willingness to swallow a rigmarole of abstract—and visibly unlikely—dogmatism, a proneness to find consolation in airy-fairy dreams, which leaves him gasping with incredulous surprise. No, if the capacity for 'simple faith' is the proper test of spiritual maturity, then the Christian must humbly acknowledge that he cannot even distantly rival the communists, fascists, utopian socialists and scientific humanists of our time.

It must be clear that the great philosophical issues which I am going to discuss in the rest of this chapter really need a whole book to themselves—indeed, many books. My method of presentation will have to be selective and summary. I shall pick out certain aspects of the subject which seem to me particularly important, and then sum up the main conclusions to which I have been led by such reflection as I have been able to devote to them.

The anti-Christian ideologies which have been presented to the European public in such continuous profusion ever since the first quarter of the eighteenth century seem to me to rest on one or more of three fundamental errors or misunderstandings: a misunderstanding of history, a misunderstanding of science and reason and a misunderstanding of civilization and humanism. Normally it is in the name of historical fact or probability, or in the name of scientific integrity, or in the name of reason or in the name of man himself that we are exhorted to forsake or avoid the Christian Church and gospel. I shall try not only to describe and expose these misunderstandings but also to suggest that in our modern, increasingly non-Christian world the traditionally reverenced ideals of historical, scientific and rational integrity, and the essential truths and values of humanism, are as gravely challenged as Christianity itself, and that, as the present situation develops, the task of defending them will tend more and more to be undertaken by Christian thinkers and the Christian Church.

Modern Unbelief as a Misunderstanding of History

The case against Christianity may be argued from the point of view of history either by saying that the Christian attitude is incompatible with the methods and presuppositions of the best kind of modern historical thinking, or by saying that the characteristic Christian beliefs are refuted by the appeal to the relevant historical evidences.

The former of these two ways of arguing is perhaps the more impressive. It is widely supposed that the historian necessarily assumes that all historical events are fundamentally of the same order, that there is a family relationship and resemblance between them, that they are all of one piece. No particular event, or course of events, can possibly be unique. If such is the case, the Christian claim that God has revealed Himself in a unique way in and through certain courses of events— the history of Israel and the life of Jesus—would appear to be incompatible with the historian's way of thinking. A less subtle argument might be based on the evolutionary and progressive prejudices of so much modern thought. From this point of view it would be said that the truth must be sought in the future rather than the past, that it is part of the very nature of progressive historical development always to be moving onwards towards its great climax, so that, from the point of view of modern thought, it is little short of scandalous to suppose that history's 'finest hour' lies somewhere far back in the past.

This second form of the argument is so superficial and unconvincing that it may perhaps be convenient to sweep it out of the way before giving more careful consideration to its fellow. We must face the fact that history is not a single evolutionary process, a homogeneous course of events moving in a single line from some one absolute beginning either towards some one absolute end or at least into some one absolutely endless future. History is, in fact, *the histories* of many different cultures and civilizations which have been born and waxed and waned and died. Such at all events it has been in the past, and it is at least probable that so it will continue in the future.

The idea of a single course of history, the notion that a process of development is now going on which will continue to the end of the world, is itself borrowed from the Bible, but it was always a mistake to apply it to the secular history of the world as a whole. Fifteen hundred years ago, when the power of Rome was visibly collapsing in western Europe, St. Augustine, in the first of the great reflective philosophical books which have tried to moralize about history as a whole, argued that this process of continuous development through and beyond the mere rise and fall of civilizations applied only to spiritual and religious development, the 'City of God' as distinct from the secular 'City of Man'.

In our own day Arnold Toynbee, in his great *Study of History*, based, of course, on a much wider acquaintance with historical facts than St. Augustine could command, has in effect reasserted the same doctrine in modern language. Churches are tougher than empires. Great religious systems are more durable than the secular political and economic systems which appear so much more imposing and powerful in the heyday of their influence. This may seem a paradox, but the probability appears to be that it is only our religious development which really has an assured future. Christians in particular have always looked to the future as much as to the past. Jesus for the Christian, as we have seen, is not a dead hero but a living Lord Who will come again at the end of the world, and the Christian creed points towards this final consummation of the ages as even more supremely the climax of history than the Incarnation itself. We may sum up by saying that the evolutionary conception of the course of history as a process of continuous development, far from being incompatible with Christianity, is only true of Christian history, so that, if Christianity is not true, the evolutionary conception of history has no validity at all.

L

But we may now turn to the more profound and challenging form of the argument. Is it really true that history abhors the unique? I am going to suggest, on the contrary, that history presupposes the unique as the very foundation of its method. History, and this is where it differs from the natural sciences, is a search for a particular kind of knowledge about particular persons, places, times and events. Unlike science it does not seek to discover what is true in general about a large number of different instances and occasions, but concentrates its attention on some particular person or episode, trying to understand what was peculiar to him or it. Natural science seeks truth about things in general; history truth about things in particular. Thus, in a sense, history is always nearer to the truth than science. Science deals only with the general aspects of things, with what they have in common considered in abstraction from what each one is in reality. The general is necessarily abstract, for the concrete reality is the world of particulars, of things which are in fact 'all different' however much they may resemble each other. In our world resemblances are relatively superficial and differences relatively profound. Above all, this is true in the realm of history and personal intercourse. To say that a man is a 'typical' member of some human group or other implies only that the speaker does not know him very well. We are always vividly aware of the personal peculiarities of those with whom we are intimately acquainted. The bank clerk is never 'just an ordinary bank clerk' to his friends; the Irishman is never 'a typical Irishman' to his wife. She knows better.

It appears, then, that the real assumption of the historian is that all persons and historical events are unique. That is why we cannot discover what happened at a particular time or place by a course of general reasoning or research which will shew us what must or ought to have happened, but only by making very particular inquiries into what actually did happen. History cannot be reconstructed from first principles. There have, of course been some historians who have attempted to deduce what must have happened from some preconceived general principle or doctrine of history, and then turned to the evidence only to confirm the general principle by showing that it did in fact happen. Whenever we are influenced by a 'philosophy of history' there is a danger of this kind of mistake, but in the modern world by far the worst offenders are the marxist writers, whose attachment to their basic dogma of the economic interpretation of history has rendered them incapable of writing serious history, or even of interpreting current events in an open-minded and unbiassed fashion.

This does not mean that there is no place for more general reflection in history. On the contrary, the results of historical investigation will often point towards certain wider general conclusions but, and this is the important thing to notice, the results of different historical researches into different epochs and events will point to conclusions of a different character, and contribute to the unravelling of quite distinct problems. In other words, although history will always speak to us, it will not always say the same thing, because it will not always speak to us about the same thing. Thus the story of Napoleon may prompt general reflections on the nemesis of militarism. The economic history of Europe and the new world in the nineteenth century illustrates, more clearly perhaps than that of any previous period, the influence of economic pressures and changes on political and social development. Biblical history, in the same way, speaks to us primarily about God. All historical events are thus unique and all history has a certain revealing quality. The historian as such labours only to discover what precisely happened at some particular time and place, but once the events are clearly ascertained they often point beyond themselves to broader generalizations.

Thus the particular historical episodes in and through which, according to Christian experiences and belief, God revealed Himself, are not really exceptions to the general historical rule after all. They are unique, but then all historical events are unique. They point to certain general conclusions about the character of God and the destiny of man, but then almost all historical experience points towards some sort of general conclusion about something or other. The rule of procedure is the same for the historian whether he is investigating the life of Jesus or the life of Napoleon. First of all, if he is a working historian, he must sift his evidences and discover and delineate his particular facts. He must try to make clear what was peculiar to the particular course of events which he is investigating. It is no part of his task, at all events at this stage, to tell us that these facts are very much like other facts. If that is his conclusion, he has failed. What we want to know from him is precisely how these particular facts differed from all other facts, even from those which bear some superficial resemblance to them. When he has done that, and if he aspires to be an interpreter of history as well as a working historian—and not all good working historians are or need be successful interpreters of history—he may consider any more general conclusions which are indicated by his particular set of facts.

Now this brings us to the point at which the non-Christian historian may shift his ground and, instead of arguing that Christian belief is incompatible with the historical method and presuppositions, he may begin to tell us that his scrutiny of the surviving historical evidences does not support the Christian account of that particular set of historical facts which Christianity regards as the vehicle of the divine revelation. In other words, he may begin to call in question the trustworthiness of biblical history. After all, for our knowledge of the history of Israel and the life of Jesus we have very little to rely on apart from the Bible itself. May it not be that those documents which traditional reverence has hallowed as 'the Holy Scriptures' were coloured and perhaps deliberately falsified by the theological beliefs and prejudices of those who wrote them?

Such a question inevitably arises, and the Christian dare not set it aside. He has deliberately appealed to the historical facts, and he has no right to complain of even the most drastic and critical scrutiny of the evidence. Any attempt to prevent historians from investigating the trustworthiness of the biblical records would not only, in the modern world, have been doomed to failure; it would also have implied a most reprehensible lack of faith. In fact, however, Christian historians have themselves taken a leading part in the process. It is not too much to say that the general course of the investigation is more and more pointing towards a triumphant vindication of the Christian attitude to the Bible. Archeological evidence increasingly confirms the trustworthiness of the general outline of the Old Testament narrative. The widespread radical tendency of the nineteenth century to relegate almost all the documents of the New Testament to the second century A.D. has broken down beneath the accumulating weight of reassuring evidence.

Thus, to note but one example, a century ago radical

New Testament scholarship dismissed the Gospel of
St. John as a late composition written towards the end
of the second century A.D. But during the last twenty
years scholars have discovered a fragment of a copy of
this gospel and quotations from it in a harmony of the
four gospels which both date from the first half of the
second century. Meanwhile archeological evidence increasingly supports the view that the author was well
acquainted with the topography of Jerusalem before its
destruction by the Romans. Now the world of scholarship finds itself compelled to consider very seriously the
view of Torrey that the fourth gospel is a translation
into Greek of an Aramaic document written about
A.D. 70. Yet another historian of high repute holds
that the narrative portions of this gospel were written
as early as A.D. 40.

But perhaps even more important than this striking
rehabilitation of the New Testament as a primary
source of historical evidence, is the complete absence of
any evidence whatever pointing towards some alternative account of what happened and capable of giving
some other explanation of the rise and power of the
primitive Church. The fact is that the non-Christian
historian rejects the Christian account of the origins of
Christianity, not because of any lack of evidence suggesting its trustworthiness, still less because of the presence of any evidence suggesting its falsity, but because
for subjective reasons of his own which we need not
analyse here he finds it incredible. In other words, he
rejects the Christian account and interpretation of the
life of Jesus not as a historian but as a man. Such a procedure is indeed very human, but not at all historical.
Of course, if the career of Jesus really was what Christians believe it to have been, it was utterly and starkly

unique. But, as we have seen, the historian who really understands his own methods and presuppositions ought never to reject the unique as such. It is precisely because all historical events are unique in some way or other that he has to study history in his own historical way, and not by the methods of sampling, experiment and generalization characteristic of the natural sciences.

The historian is never justified in rejecting an alleged event, for which there is at least some finite evidence worthy of serious consideration, merely on the ground that science shews it to be impossible, or that it is 'not the kind of thing that seems to happen nowadays'. If it happened it must of course have been possible, but whether our present stock of scientific knowledge is capable of telling us precisely how it was possible is, so far as the historian is concerned, neither here nor there. At this point the basic principles of historical and scientific research are in fundamental agreement. In both history and science fact is always prior to theory. If the theory does not fit the facts, then the theory must be modified or even rejected, but on no account may the facts be denied. It is said that Cuvier, the famous zoologist, once had a dream in which the devil came to him and threatened to eat him. 'Oh, you can't do that,' replied the dreamer. 'Why not?' asked the devil. 'Because you have a cloven hoof, and all cloven-footed creatures are herbivorous.' This only goes to shew how unscientific even great scientists can be in their sleep. He should, on the contrary, and in the interests of science, have encouraged the devil to essay the experiment of trying a bite. For if the devil really could have eaten him there would have been something wrong with his theory after all. The true scientific faith is faith in the scientific method, not a belief in the finality of any particular scientific conclusions. Indeed, over-confidence in any scientific theory is, paradoxically enough, incompatible with the genuine scientific outlook.

As an alternative to the argument that biblical history is untrustworthy, anti-Christian propaganda has made great play with the *canard* that as a matter of historical fact Church history has been scandalous. *Écrasez l'infâme* cried Voltaire, and since his time unbelief has persistently presented itself as anti-clericalism, as a reading of the history of our civilization which presents the organized Church as the villain of the piece. We are familiar enough with this scandalmongering anti-Christian propaganda, in which the Church is saddled with responsibility for almost every European misfortune from the downfall of the Roman Empire and the decay of classical civilization to the victory of General Franco. The dreary details of this stale narrative are equally well known—the corruption of late medieval monasticism, the opposition to the early progress of the scientific movement, the horrors of religious persecution and warfare, the hostility of the Church to modern social reforms, and so on.

This picture is misleading not so much because of what it falsifies as because of what it ignores. For there is another side to the story. Indeed, it must be obvious that this conventional anti-clerical presentation of history entirely fails to account for the persistence and vitality of the Church. Anti-clericalism has, in fact, always tried to get over this particular difficulty by pretending that the Church has lost its vitality and is unlikely to persist much longer. Thus somewhere about 1750 Voltaire declared that the Church would not live to see 1800. The house in which he ventured on this somewhat rash prophecy became in the twentieth century the Parisian office of the British and Foreign Bible Society.

'The report of my death', wrote Mark Twain to a daily newspaper which had published his obituary notice, 'has been greatly exaggerated.' The death of organized Christianity is often heralded in equally premature and baseless fashion. One of the most surprising of the discoveries which I made on drawing close to the life of the Church was the creative intellectual and spiritual vitality of a community which I had been taught to regard as moribund. Indeed, the self-critical boldness of its thinkers and the self-sacrificial labours of its missionaries have made the twentieth century one of the greatest epochs of Church history. While the secular world has been relapsing into the intellectual and moral barbarism of fascism and communism and the 'planned society', while the liberal democrats have been floundering in a helpless inability to interpret and express the great ethical and social values for which they stand in abstraction from the Christianity out of which they sprang and to which they really belong, the Church has been renewing its life in a new theological understanding of its character and world mission, in a new sense of possessing a greater antiquity and a more assured future than the doomed secular forces with which it finds itself confronted in our disintegrating social order. This is as true of protestant as of catholic Christianity. Those who know the life of the Church at first hand—and know also enough history to disabuse their minds of any illusion that 'God is on the side of the big battalions'—cannot, I think, entertain the slightest doubt of the epoch-making future that stirs within it. Whatever else may be true or false of the impending centuries, I would venture the confident prophecy that the Church will be there to make its creative contribution. I cannot see any other contemporary forces for which I would care to make the same claim. 'The gates of hell shall not prevail against it.' But they are undoubtedly making an energetic and sustained effort to do so at the present time. The sad thing is that so many honourable and intelligent men have been cajoled into assisting the powers of darkness to manipulate them. For that tragedy the shortcomings of many generations of professing Christians are at least in part responsible.

For, make no mistake about it, a great deal of Church history really is scandalous, and it is no part of the Christian Faith or of the Christian propaganda—if I may use the rather unpleasant phrase—to deny the fact. From the first Jesus chose to keep company with the publicans and the sinners, and He has never abandoned the practice. The Church militant is not a perfect society, nor a company of elect souls displaying their choice virtues in a highly rarified moral atmosphere. What an insufferable place it would be if it were! The man who makes up his mind to accept the social and spiritual discipline of church membership must expect, like Jesus, to find himself the companion of all sorts and conditions of sinners, not only moral perverts but also, and even more unattractive, tasteless philistines and unintelligent bigots. More than that, he must discover that sin looks much worse in the Church than it does in the world. The abomination of desolation never looks quite so abominable as when we see it standing where it ought not.

Of course, the defects and failures of Christians have been greatly exaggerated by the almost pathological hatred of Christianity which has agitated so many modern breasts, an echo of the hatred which Jesus Himself aroused in so many of His contemporaries and compatriots. Nevertheless, the failings themselves are undeniable enough and, if Christianity is true, then the sins of Christians really are worse than the sins of other people. Inevitably more is expected of those to whom more has been given. But if Christianity is not true there is surely less reason to make such a fuss about the sins of the Christians. After all, they have not invented any new sins. The worst that can be said about them is that they sometimes commit the same sins as other people. Even the most violent and vindictive attack on the historical record of the Church amounts to no more than the assertion that the Church has often behaved in a very worldly fashion. If Christianity is true this is indeed very scandalous, but if Christianity is false it is neither surprising nor particularly reprehensible. The Church has occasionally persecuted its enemies, frustrated the growth of knowledge and impeded legitimate and desirable social change. Shocking indeed, but hardly an ecclesiastical monopoly! On the contrary, although the Christian must shamefully acknowledge that his Church has done all these things—if only because the frank and open confession of sin is part of the Christian way of life—yet his duty to the truth compels him to add that it has done so much more rarely and on a much smaller scale than the great secular organizations which have functioned side by side with the Church in our civilization. Its record in all these respects is disgraceful enough, but greatly superior to that of most political régimes and parties. The Church has been in continuous activity for two thousand years. The communist party has only just observed the centenary of its first manifesto, but it has almost certainly persecuted more opponents to the death in one century than the Church in twenty. It is probably true that in the whole of its history ecclesiastical persecution has claimed fewer victims than Hitler in twelve years. There is certainly no episode in that history which compares as a sadistic outburst with the French revolutionary terror of 1793. To take one random example: the Inquisition was set up in the Portuguese Indian colony of Goa in 1500 and dissolved in 1850, but during this lengthy period it passed and carried out only one hundred and fifty death sentences. What a trifle that must seem to a modern political persecutor on the grand scale, like Robespierre, Hitler or Stalin!

The Church's record only looks so bad when we judge it by its own standards. When we compare the Church with other historical organizations its record begins to look very good indeed. Through long periods of its history it has avoided persecution and intolerance. It has normally enthusiastically taken over and used its influence to protect the values of secular civilization—the Greek philosophy of the ancient world, for example—and we may well live to see it championing the cause of liberal democracy and the true scientific values when the 'progressive' minds have accepted the totalitarian politics of the planned society and a merely utilitarian conception of the function of science.

The truth is that most of the familiar attacks on the historical record of the Church conceal an implicit compliment to Christianity, although the writers, of course, would never admit it. The implication is that more should be expected of the Church than of other organizations, that Christians are somehow more to blame than other people when they commit the common sins. The Christian must humbly say 'amen' to such a judgment as that. *But it is a verdict which only makes sense on the assumption that Christianity is true.* Judged by ordinary humanistic standards, the Church has, on balance, wrought magnificently for mankind, has done probably more good than any other single historical organization. Nevertheless, judged by the standards of the gospel, the Church's record is indeed a bad one. It is this latter verdict which the Christian must sadly, but not despairingly, accept. The unbeliever, however, will be more consistent with his own point of view if he assumes an attitude of generous and ungrudging admiration.

One of our difficulties in trying to arrive at any kind of decisive moral judgment about the Church's record is the absence from history of what we may call a 'pure' Church. A man is never just a Christian or solely an ecclesiastic. He is also a member of this or that profession at this or that time or place, inheriting particular social traditions and moved by particular personal and group interests. It is never possible to say with any certainty precisely how much of his conduct must be ascribed to his religion, and how much to other motives and influences operative in his life. Thus we are all familiar with the stories of the harrying and persecution of pioneers of the modern scientific movement like Copernicus and Galileo. The conventional way of telling the story attributes such attacks to purely religious motives. It is certainly true that the assailants were usually ecclesiastics, but it is only fair to remember that they were usually university professors as well. In those days, for historical reasons which reflect no discredit on anybody, almost all teaching posts were held by clergymen. Our modern predominantly lay society was only in process of slow creation. Clerk and cleric amounted to the same thing. The question which arises is this: How far was the attack on science due to genuinely religious motives, and how far to the professional fears and jealousy of the older

Aristotelian teachers, who saw in the rise of the new science a threat to their prestige and livelihood? Obviously the question is not one to which any clear answer is possible. The motives of these men were mixed, as ours so often are. But we may at least notice—a detail which the conventional, anti-clerical version of the story commonly omits—that many of these persecuted pioneers, including Galileo, received a considerable amount of ecclesiastical, and even papal, patronage, support and protection against the worst excesses of the outraged university professors.

Again, it is only fair to ask how far some of the well advertised errors of the Church have been all too human reactions on the part of churchmen against the scurvy way in which the world has treated them. Left-wing political groups loudly deplore the tendency of the Church in the last two centuries to oppose social reform movements and to fraternize with reactionary social forces. But how far has this been due to the doctrinaire anti-religionism of so many left-wing political movements, and their mania for indulging in vindictive religious persecutions once they have achieved power? In the early stages of the French Revolution the reformers received very considerable support from the representatives of the clergy. Indeed, in 1789 they could not possibly have achieved their first bloodless victories without it. But the moment the revolutionary régime was safely in the saddle it launched a violent anti-religious offensive —the first of the great left-wing religious persecutions which have made so foul a mark on modern European history. Is it altogether surprising if such ingratitude, with its clear evidence of an irrational anti-Church complex which no experience could dissipate or modify, produced in Church circles a chronic suspicion of the political left which has tended to estrange them ever since?

Nevertheless, the Christian writer must not permit his honest conviction that the Church has a surprisingly good case before men conceal, or even appear to conceal, his candid admission that before God it has no sort of case at all. In the modern world there are too many pseudo-historians who turn history into the raw material of mere propaganda. I have no wish to add to their number. It cannot be pretended that by the manipulation of historical evidences it is possible to shew that the Church, or even some selected branch of the Church, has always been right. In the nineteenth century nationalistic historians shewed us nations which had always been right—even before they could possibly have existed—and nowadays we are most of us sick of the monotonous way in which, according to the dreary communist writers, the Soviet Union has always been absolutely right about everything. With all its faults the Church of God is too noble a thing for such lickspittle service as that!

Nowadays, indeed, t is particularly important that the Christian propagandist should try to set an example of honesty and integrity in the use of historical evidence. The widespread exploitation of history in the interests of nationalist and political propaganda has now reached such a pitch that it constitutes a major threat to the integrity and trustworthiness of historical thought. It is sickening to notice how a change of the political régime in any part of the world is followed almost immediately by a drastic revision of the historical textbooks used in schools. No doubt the books that are swept away richly deserve their oblivion, but can we suppose that those which replace them are any more objective? The new regime shares with the old the assumption that it is the function of history to foster the sympathies and loyalties which it regards as socially desirable. The political control of education, inevitable once it has become a state monopoly, has proved a cultural disaster.

Is a really honest propaganda possible under modern conditions? It is certainly very rare. I should like to feel able to claim that the Christian propaganda is always and everywhere just that, but I hesitate to do so. It is wiser in the long run to claim too little rather than too much. But I will say with some confidence that it is nearer to the ideal of a rigidly honest propaganda than any other with which I am at present acquainted.

Modern Unbelief as a Misunderstanding of Science and Reason

The use of the term 'rationalism' as a party label for those whose outlook is primarily influenced by a humble admiration of the triumphs of physical science, and an enthusiastic and sometimes extravagant faith in further triumphs yet to come, is a misleading and confusing practice. Properly speaking, rationalism is a confidence in the power of unaided reasoning to deduce from the very concept of reality all that must necessarily be true concerning it. The rationalist works not in the laboratory but in the armchair. There can be no doubt that his method has had its major triumphs, the elaboration of the great deductive mathematical and logical systems, the examination of the presuppositions of our various sciences, the illuminating pursuit of the implications of our common beliefs down to their most ultimate consequences. We must not despise the armchair as an intellectual point of view. Not everything can be seen from it, but what can be seen may be seen very clearly by the right kind of observer. Nevertheless, the modern scientific movement is based on the presupposition that, so far as matters of fact at least are concerned, the proper way of knowledge is the way of observation, scrutinizing and describing real things, where possible taking them to pieces, experimenting with them, above all measuring them. This is called the empirical method and it should be clearly distinguished from rationalism. Of course, the empirical scientist if he is wise will not despise pure reason altogether. It has provided him with the most important of all his tools, mathematics—'the language of nature', as Galileo called it—and it can deduce for him not only the consequences of his hypotheses and discoveries, but also the latent implications, and, more important, the inherent limitations, of his method and presuppositions. Nevertheless, for him the primary function of reason is the scrutiny of facts. In his view reason works most efficiently and effectively when it is checked and disciplined by the necessity of constantly deferring to the evidence.

The thought of ancient Greece was primarily rationalistic. We can see in Greek culture, indeed, the first beginnings of the scientific attitude, and for a time it was 'touch and go', as we say, whether the Greek mind would come down on the side of empirical science or of soaring, rationalistic metaphysics. In the end, however, it chose the latter. This was not in the existing circumstances necessarily a bad thing, and it is perhaps significant that it was two of the best and wisest of the Greeks, Socrates and Plato, who most consciously and deliberately turned their backs on the empirical attitude. But it is significant that when the scientific mood reawoke many centuries later, it was able to make progress and flourish from the very first because it found itself in a more

M

favourable and sympathetic intellectual atmosphere. What had occurred during the intervening centuries to cause this change in the climate of thought? There is only one possible answer. The intellectual revolution which followed the introduction of Christianity into the Roman world, and through it into the later civilization of medieval and modern Europe.

Obviously this was a momentous, world-shattering event whose consequences might well exhaust a whole encyclopaedia. Here I am only concerned with the methodological implications of the emergence of the new science of Christian theology. This was a study of the divine nature and human destiny as we find them revealed in the historical figure and record of Jesus Christ. It was in the realm of theology that the essential points of view of both modern history and modern natural science were first clearly established and explicitly justified. In the first place, theology was a rational examination of a particular life and personality, of a particular course of events, which sought to ascertain and formulate not what it had in common with other lives and events but what was peculiar to itself. Thus history first became conscious of its own inherent character and aims. But if theology was historical in its method, it was also empirical. It sought ultimate truth about being and human destiny not through the armchair reflections of the pure reason but through the careful scrutiny and analysis of the particular set of facts recorded in the New Testament, supplemented, checked and verified by the accumulating personal experience of Christians trying to live the Christian life in the context of the Christian community.

Of course, like modern scientists, the theologians and the Christian philosophers reverenced and employed the reason. It provided them with their principal intellectual tool—formal logic—and it helped them to deduce the consequences of their theories and to comprehend and affirm the presuppositions of their method. But the very nature of theological thinking implied the priority of fact and experience over thought even in the sphere of religious and metaphysical knowledge, which the pure reason had been disposed to claim as above all others incontestably its own.

The empirical character of theology is made quite clear by writers like St. Augustine and St. Anselm. Theology is defined as 'the Faith seeking to understand itself', and it is laid down as the basic methodological rule of the science that faith must precede understanding (i.e. that the living experience of being a practising Christian and an active member of the Christian community is the indispensible prelude to any quest for an understanding of the meaning of Christianity). Christianity can no more be understood apart from Christian experience than a branch of natural science can be taught and learned without observation and experiment. The testimony of even so extreme a Christian rationalist as St. Thomas Aquinas really amounts to the same thing. In his view the pure reason, employed in the old armchair manner of the great Greek metaphysicians, is capable of yielding a certain number of important conclusions which go far to vindicate what we may call the generally religious character of the universe and human life. Nevertheless most Christian beliefs, including all the more characteristic and important ones, are the product not of pure reasoning but of an empirical study of the facts of Christian life and revelation. It is the function of reason to shew that the truths perceived by the pure reason are compatible with the conclusions of empirical theology, and to refute the purely rationalistic arm-chair criticism of these conclusions put forward by non-Christian philosophers. The most important upshot of his work was thus a brilliant delineation and vindication of the methods of empirical theology, which was by implication a justification of all empirical science before its time. Whatever the late-medieval ecclesiastics thought of the new natural sciences when they began to flourish and be widely cultivated, it is undeniable that the early and mid-medieval ecclesiastical thinkers had already prepared the way for them, and indeed provided them with a ready-made justification.

Aquinas himself, of course, remained satisfied with what he knew of ancient Greek science, and never foresaw the extension of his attitude towards the religious knowledge gained through revelation to the realm of natural knowledge. Nevertheless, they are fundamentally the same. Indeed, the empirical, scientific doctrine really amounts to treating all experience as Christians treat the facts in which, as they believe, the divine revelation is embedded. In science the relevant facts have the same kind of priority and authority over our theorizing as the events which provide the Bible with its epic theme have in Christian theology.

The claim that there is a profound incompatibility between the empirical temper and procedure of natural science and that of theology is thus almost the reverse of the truth. Whether or not theology is, as was supposed in the middle ages, the 'Queen of the Sciences', she is certainly the firstborn and the pioneer among the empirical studies.

But perhaps the well advertised 'conflict between religion and science' is in the field of results rather than in that of the methods and presuppositions of science. This is the more familiar interpretation. It is widely supposed that specific scientific discoveries are in conflict with other equally specific Christian teachings. This prevalent error is due partly to the wide vogue of biblical fundamentalism, and other forms of unintelligent theology, especially in countries with a protestant tradition—where fundamentalism is sometimes even supposed to be the essence of orthodoxy—and partly also to the modern habit of making very speculative and precarious philosophical applications of scientific notions and labelling the result 'the scientific outlook' or 'scientific philosophy'. Thus the great success and fruitfulness of the hypothesis of evolution in biology has influenced some philosophers—Bergson, for example—to depict the ultimate reality as an evolving, striving spirit. Such a bold, imaginative flight of fancy may indeed provide real intellectual stimulus, but it cannot for one moment validly claim to be a 'scientific view'. The so-called 'conflict between religion and science' is thus no more than the hybrid offspring of bad theology and pseudo-scientific philosophical speculation. The so-called 'scientific outlooks' and 'scientific views of the world' which are so fashionable nowadays have, in fact, nothing scientific about them. These strange compounds of metaphysics and personal ethics may indeed employ scientific concepts in their imaginative constructions, but they in fact address themselves to answering the sort of questions which real science never asks, for the excellent reason that the scientific method was not devised and is not adapted to answer them.

There is no better way of characterizing and distinguishing between the forms of propositions and systems of thought and inquiry than by considering the different types of question which they endeavour and purport to answer. Thus in history and literature and everyday life we have to answer questions which demand particular and personal answers like, 'Who? . . .' or 'Which? . . .' or 'Why did he? . . .' or 'What did he? . . .' or 'When did he? . . .' Science on the other hand tries to answer questions about whole groups of things in general regarded as indistinguishable from each other —not absolutely, of course, but for the purpose of the inquiry. The typical forms of the scientific question are, 'How do x things or processes operate?' and 'Into what elemental components can y things or processes be analysed?' It is difficult to see how our answers to questions of such a radically distinct character and intention can contradict each other. There may seem to be a possibility of conflict where there is historical evidence for asserting that an event took place which on scientific grounds would be dismissed as impossible—as, for example, in the case of the resurrection. But we have already seen that to declare any particular event impossible is a profoundly 'unscientific' thing to do. Indeed, it betrays the fundamental spirit of scientific inquiry, for to declare an event impossible is to subordinate facts to theory, whereas it is of the essence of science that it subordinates theory to facts.

From the point of view of Christianity, and of what I have called the 'dramatic' view of life, the questions which religion and philosophy answer are of the same kind as those with which we have to deal in history, literature and personal life. The Christian gospel does not confront us with a theory of the nature of 'the divine' in general, but with certain definite assertions about the particular way in which God has dealt with us, and deals with us, in and through Jesus Christ. Once we have thoroughly grasped this principle of the radical distinction between these different forms of thought and spheres of intellectual and human concern, we shall see clearly enough that no conflict between their distinctive testimonies can conceivably arise.

There are those, of course, who declare, on one pretext or another, that only the 'scientific' type of question is capable of being answered, at all events by beings with minds constituted as ours appear to be. But in life as we know it many other questions arise than those which science knows how to answer, and many other problems have to be dealt with beside those which science can teach us to handle. If only scientific knowledge is valid how can we account for the development of the human intellect and culture in its early pre-scientific stages? In its extreme form, indeed, this positivistic philosophy—for it is philosophy and never science— would render the past inexplicable and the present intolerable. The human reason has accomplished too much in the past, and has to shoulder too many great responsibilities in the present, of a non-scientific character for us to suppose that only when it operates in the sciences is its work really valid and fruitful.

The real clashes between the scientific and religious attitudes take place on the personal and social levels of life. They are clashes within and between men. For the historical, dramatic, personal attitude towards God and our fellow-men and the scientific attitude towards things are not two mere alternatives between which we may choose. We have all of us to adopt them both on different occasions. The most positivistic of scientists will know hope, ambition and frustration, may fall in love, marry and become an affectionate parent, must die sooner or later, and live meanwhile like the rest of us perched precariously on the razor edge that separates life from death. He cannot take his scientific attitude with him as he wrestles with the intimate, personal problems of his existence. There is a crude and hoary old undergraduate joke which tells of a mechanistic biologist who lectured with such enthusiasm on the theme that men and women are no more than un-usually complicated machines that he even convinced himself, and on returning home lubricated his wife with an oil can instead of kissing her! It serves at least to illust-rate the importance of keeping clear the distinction be-tween our scientific and dramatic categories of thought.

On the other hand even the most unscientifically minded man finds himself in the modern world sur-rounded by and using the products of a scientific age. He drives a car, travels long distances by rail, enjoys music and drama on the radio, and when embarking on some outdoor excursion turns quite eagerly to the weather forecast in *The Times*. In a large scale elabor-ately planned social order like our own, even our rela-tionships with other human beings are by no means exclusively and directly personal. Life repeatedly manœuvres us into treating other men as mere means to our own ends, into the necessity of taking thought for men in the mass rather than for each man as a person. The tension between the scientific, generalizing attitude and the intimate, personal and dramatic religious atti-tude stretches and strains within the depths of the private consciousness of every one of us. The man of good will aspires to benefit his fellows, and finds himself planning for them impersonally in the mass as though they were no more than so much welfare fodder. A scientist may endeavour to regulate his career by the most rigorous and obecjtive scientific standards, and yet find himself hurrying to publish the fruits of his research in order to impress the girl with whom he is in love, or intriguing to get his income increased for the sake of his children. This kind of conflict is not a struggle between men organized into opposing groups, but a conflict within men compelled by life to employ different systems and categories of thought on different occasions and for different purposes. Such a tension is only resolved if and when we clearly perceive that these distinct systems of thought are not really antithetical after all, but mutually complementary. All of us, religious and irreligious alike, have a deep-seated psychological interest in seeing this particular tension between scientific and religious attitudes resolved and exorcised as completely as possible.

But there is another form of the conflict which really is, or at least bids fair to become, a controversy, or even a battle, between contending human groups. In the modern world science has become a form of power as well as a form of knowledge. In the middle ages that strange visionary genius Roger Bacon foresaw clearly that it would be so, and pleaded that the Pope should make himself the patron of science so that this new form of power might be his to command. At the beginning of the seventeenth century Francis Bacon was aware of the same possibility. Yet the fact remains that until quite recently the overwhelming majority of scientists have interpreted science as primarily a disinterested search for truth.

It is only during the last generation or so that by no means negligible groups of scientific workers have begun to entertain the thought that in a planned and technological social order they are themselves promising candidates for supreme power. Of course, their dawning egotism, like all egotism, conceals itself beneath a smoke-screen of idealism. They think and talk, deceiving themselves no doubt as much as other people, of the great benefits which the rule of a scientific *élite* would confer on mankind. But beneath it all we can recognize the stirring of the old Adam who has stirred so often and so destructively in the hearts of previous *élites*. It is the same old Adam who ruined the great civilizing work of the medieval Church, and is even now despoiling the labours of the political leaders of the modern nation state. A science which forgets that it is a quest for truth, in the thrill of realizing that it has become a form of power, is not only a menace to civilization but also to the essential values of science.

In opposing and witnessing against the project of a 'scientific' social order, which proposes to attain the fullness of physical welfare by concentrating on such a goal to the exclusion of every other, the Church will be fighting not only for religion but also for man, for civilization and for science itself. Yet it is a battle which the Church will do well to fight humbly, without forgetting its own past errors. The priest has perhaps at least the right to say to the scientist, 'We once spoiled our great contribution to life, in the moment of maximum opportunity, by making it minister to our private will to power. Do not you do the same with yours.'

Modern Unbelief as a Misunderstanding of Civilization and Humanism

But far more profound—both in itself and in its influence on the religious situation of modern man—than any speculative misinterpretations of history, reason and science is the widespread, half-unconscious, resentful suspicion that God is the enemy of man's higher aspirations and achievements, that religion is the antagonist of civilization, so that only by avoiding the contagion of strong religious convictions can it flourish and progress. God humbles man in his own eyes, and the contemplation of His works and majesty surely dwarfs all man's achievements. When men are in a mood to idolize their power and nourish their self-esteem by cultivating a sense of their own prowess, irreligion becomes one of the indispensible vehicles of their self-assertion.

In one form or another the defiance of God by man in the name and for the sake of progress, civilization, knowledge and power is one of the favourite themes of post-Renaissance literature. We see it in the legends of Faust and Don Juan, in the heroism of Satan in Milton's *Paradise Lost* and in Shelley's *Prometheus*. In philosophy the same conception appears in Machiavelli's prince and Nietzsche's superman, and also, as it seems to me, in Sartre and the contemporary atheistical existentialists. Only if there is no God, or, an even more exciting possibility, if the God who is can be heroically defied, can man be truly and absolutely himself.

We do not understand the real thrill of evil, and the fascination which it has exercised over so many post-Renaissance minds and cultural tendencies, so long as we think of it as a merely selfish desire to enjoy the pleasant fruits of sin. Above everything else evil is a means of asserting man's will to power. What this kind of sinner enjoys and desires is not the sin itself and its consequences but the sense of possessing the power to defy every moral and religious law known to him. Thus Shelley's Cenci rapes his daughter not because he desires her but because this seems to him the most evil deed he can conceive, and therefore the most heroic action he can perform. Even so, in the myth of the fall in the book of Genesis, Eve eats the forbidden fruit not because it is pleasant to taste but for the sake of the thrill of disobedience. Through such an act of power and self-assertion, she is led to suppose, men and women will become like gods.

In the modern world this fundamental spiritual *motif* has been reinforced by other important intellectual and social tendencies. Foremost among these is what I may call the 'myth of modernity'. This is really an eighteenth-century myth, although it still lingers on as an indefensible and quite unhistorical anachronism. According to this view man, after a long period of savagery and superstitition, has progressed at last into an age of enlightenment in which the truth can be clearly seen. The phrase 'the modern view' becomes synonymous with the true, or at least the truer or nearly true, view. The past has nothing to teach us, except perhaps in the sense of warning us against relapsing into its errors, whereas enlightened modern man has a great deal to teach the future, a golden age whose foundations he has generously and securely laid.

Perhaps the most celebrated expression of this totally false historical perspective is to be found in Gibbon's *Decline and Fall of the Roman Empire*. According to Gibbon there had been a previous 'enlightened' age, the classical civilization of Greece and Rome, rising to a pinnacle of achievement, as he supposed, in the time of the Antonine emperors. But Christianity, alas, had crept into the Empire from the barbarous east and had drowned this first pioneering experiment in genuine civilization beneath a tidal wave of superstition. 'I have described the triumph of barbarism and religion.' This was one way of expressing the post-Renaissance prejudice that the millennium which intervened between the collapse of Rome and the Renaissance was a 'dark age' of human degeneration which witnessed no important cultural developments. We now know that this view of the period was absolutely false. In fact the middle ages saw the transmission through the Church of the values of classical civilization to the new populations of Europe, the successful defence of the West against the challenge of Moslem and Mongol, a brilliant intellectual outburst certainly without peer and perhaps without parallel in the whole history of European philosophy, the slow building up of intellectual attitudes which prepared the way for the development of modern science, unforgettable artistic achievements, the foundation of the universities, and vitally important political experiments from which the modern world has derived the basic democratic and constitutional conception of the 'rule of law'. This was, in fact, one of the greatest and most creative periods in the whole history of civilizing endeavour.

But Gibbon was equally mistaken about the age of the Antonines. Far from rising to the peak of its achievement in that epoch, classical civilization was by then already in a late stage of decay. Its great creative period had, in fact, begun to come to an end, four centuries before Jesus was born, in the Peloponnesian War, in which the Greek city states fought each other to death—rather as the European nations are doing in the twentieth century—and prepared the way for the great empires which indeed spread classical civilization far and wide, but spread it thin. Plato was quite consciously a philosopher thinking and teaching in an age of crisis and convulsion. Aristotle was the last great interpreter of the political ideals of the city state, and also the tutor of Alexander the Great. In fact the coming of Christianity gave the classical civilization new life and inspiration and prepared a surviving institution, the Catholic

Church, through which its values were preserved and handed down to the modern world.

The truth is that all civilizations erect themselves and begin to flourish on a religious basis. This is as true of the classical civilization of Greece and Rome as of our own west-European culture. An outburst of brilliant worldly scepticism is usually a sign of the beginning of cultural decay. Plato and Socrates had to fight the sophists, just as the Church in the modern world has had to do battle with the positivists and agnostics, and in both cases the struggle is a fight for the very soul and future of civilization.

The religious character of civilization is perhaps best illustrated and emphasized by an inquiry into the religious origins of all the great forms and vehicles of cultural activity. Thus drama, music, dancing, poetry, and the higher development of the visual arts all originate as aspects of religious ritual and ceremonial. Science and philosophy are of priestly origin. It now seems that the early development of the state as both an object of reverence and a source of public welfare is part of man's religious history. The earliest kings were above all priest kings, descended from the gods and regarded as the fathers of their peoples. Liberal individualism rejected this paternalistic conception of the state, but the development of socialism and the conception of the welfare state has brought us back to it again. The mood of civilization is only secular in the hour of its decline. In its creative moments its inspiration and the source of its energy is always religious. Both modern anthropology and modern comparative history supply overwhelming evidence of the truth and importance of this generalization.

Nevertheless, it is undeniable that seldom in human

history has the sophisticated reaction of the later stages of a civilization against its religious origins occurred with the violence characteristic of European unbelief since the eighteenth century. Among us the conflict between religion and unbelief has been complicated and intensified by the purely social and economic rivalries and hostilities which were fanned and fostered during our period of transition from a clerical to a lay society. In the middle ages cultural leadership was almost entirely in the hands of clergymen. Sensitive and refined spirits could find no refuge and no congenial sphere of life outside the Church. Education and thought, the developing techniques of bureaucratic government and social administration, art and the Latin literature of the time were almost entirely clerical activities. Bishops and abbots functioned as statesmen, diplomats and lawyers. The unity of western civilization—how enviable and precious it seems to us now in retrospect!—was itself primarily an ecclesiastical unity. Lay schools of law and medicine flourished in Italy, but elsewhere in western Europe the intelligentsia was almost entirely clerical.

This situation was due to the necessities of the time and reflects no discredit on the clerical *élite*—on the contrary, it emphasizes the magnificence of their tremendous achievement—but it was fraught with the gravest consequences for the Church in the modern world. In the Church itself it bequeathed to us that tradition of exclusively clerical leadership in religious life and work, side by side with a relatively inactive laity, which is now clearly seen to be the Church's greatest contemporary handicap. Ecclesiastical leaders often complain that as compared with former ages there are now too few clergymen, but the truth is that in former ages there were too many of them, and the proper remedy for our present weakness is not more clergy but more instructed, active and responsible laymen. Above all the Church needs a new generation of first class lay theologians to take a leading part in its deliberations and decisions.

More serious still is the extent to which the relations of the Church and the modern world have been embittered by the tendency of the cultural *élites* of our predominantly lay society to regard clergymen as defeated but still potentially dangerous rivals, or even as rivals not yet altogether overcome. The conventional attitude towards the middle ages reflected in Gibbon is quite clearly an ideology born of an ambitious, although in itself quite justifiable, lay protest against the institutions of a clerical society. It subtly suggests that European civilization during its period of clerical leadership was hardly worthy of the name civilization at all. As history this verdict was as unjust as it was ungenerous. But we understand it better if we interpret it not as serious history but as a useful weapon in the intellectual warfare which accompanied a profound social change. Nevertheless, in consequence of this development the word 'lay' became in effect synonymous with the word 'secular', and so fostered the belief that our modern civilization is necessarily secular and irreligious in its basis. The chronic divisions of Christendom since the Reformation have reinforced the same prejudice, for how, it was plausibly asked, can we escape from the horrors of religious rivalry and warfare except by becoming less religious?

Meanwhile the economic and industrial development of the modern western world has provided us with a living environment less and less favourable to the conscious enjoyment of any kind of religious experience.

Our world is an elaborate and delicate political and economic structure composed primarily of impersonal relationships and processes. The Christian experiences life, on the other hand, not as an impersonal process in which he is himself of small account, but as an exciting drama of redemption in which he is one of the central characters. The gospel thus attributes a significance to the human person which is belied by his working experience of life. In other words, in our society the assumptions and suppositions of secular life contradict the assumptions and presuppositions of the Christian gospel. The modern world has created a point of view from which Christianity does not appear to be a true interpretation of life as we live it.

We can, of course, reject the characteristically modern point of view, we can criticize and rise above it, but we can quite understand that for large numbers of ordinary people such an imaginative and intellectual detachment from contemporary forms of thought and experience is a psychological impossibility. This is indeed a serious matter. In our world the pressure of social conditions is tending to mould a new type of man to whom the Christian gospel cannot be preached. In his own eyes he is a being caught up in impersonal processes, not one who participates actively in exciting personal dramas. Nor is he necessarily dissatisfied with such a role. The institutions of the welfare state conspire to suggest that such a life need not be physically uncomfortable, and may become pleasantly irresponsible; for those odd people who have a taste for power and authority, and think it worth its disciplines and duties, can safely be trusted to look after his welfare. Not to matter very much can be humiliating; but also comforting, for after all nothing very much is demanded of the unimportant.

N

Of course, there will always be those who will react against these depersonalizing tendencies of a mass society. By no means all of us care for the thought of sitting back passively while the social order conforms us to its image. It may even be that the vitality will gradually ebb out of the kind of mass society which we have been so long and painfully creating, that it will collapse and pass out of history because it has nothing more to contribute to history. It may well be that the hand of the Lord is even now raised against us in just judgment. Until the whole play is enacted to the final curtain we cannot tell, but so far as it has gone the drama of modern civilization looks undeniably more like tragedy than comedy. Have we yet reached the stage at which it is permissible to suggest that a happy ending would be a crude and inartistic anti-climax? I am no prophet and so I content myself with throwing out the question.

But so long as our kind of society persists the Church will still be compelled to struggle against a strongly flowing tide of contrary influences. In the earlier phases of western history there were in effect two ways of becoming a Christian. Many people were Christians by tradition. They absorbed Christianity from their environment. It is easy to depreciate this way of coming by a religious faith, but there are probably a considerable proportion of simple and relatively unintelligent, unimaginative people, whom God loves and wants, who cannot come by such a faith in any other way. And, of course, there are still many Christians who have received their faith and joyfully accepted it from their parents and friends.

But always there have been others who came to Christianity through the hard way of personal conversion, as the result of an intense and often agonizing inward moral, spiritual and intellectual experience which breaks their self-sufficiency and leaves them with no alternative but to assent to the gospel with their entire being .We may call this the existential as opposed to the traditional way to Christ. It is because I travelled myself by this hard existential road that I do not think I have the right to be critical of what has seemed to some to be too easy a way of finding the faith. Indeed, in some moods I feel disposed to envy those who have known Christ almost literally from the cradle. But for most of us now it is the hard way or none at all. What we may call the psychological mechanism of tradition is almost everywhere breaking down, with terrible consequences for that very large proportion of the human race which is not equipped by nature to travel spiritually and intellectually by any other route.

This breakdown of the psychological mechanisms which normally transmit traditions and so give society continuity and cohesion, is a characteristic phenomenon of the modern world. Freud had a useful name for it— indeed, he had a name for almost everything! He called it the 'oedipus complex'. Oedipus was a character in Greek tragedy who murdered his father. The oedipus complex is the survival, in the unconscious mind, of the infant's jealous dislike of his father, and resentment of his father's authority, which sometimes expresses itself in a conscious rejection of the father's values, of the social and religious traditions by which the father lives.

We are familiar enough with such symptoms through our interminable discussions—in the newspapers, among educationists, at religious conferences, etc.—of what is called the restlessness and unsettlement of modern youth, the widespread indifference of the young to our basic moral traditions, their tendency to irreligion and

extreme varieties of left-wing politics. We should be
quite wrong to suppose that young people are everywhere and always like this. On the contrary, there is
plenty of evidence to shew that at most stages in the
growth of most societies this kind of problem hardly
arises at all. Normally the psychological mechanisms
which transmit tradition operate with tolerable efficiency. Otherwise indeed peaceful and cumulative social
development would be impossible.

We know, of course, that there are purely social factors which militâte against the transmission of tradition.
Where there is a high degree of human mobility, and
people are frequently called upon to leave their homes
and families, the grip of tradition tends to relax. Again,
where the tempo of social change is very rapid, so that
the young feel more at home in contemporary society than
their elders, the so-called 'wisdom of experience' is increasingly discounted. But these social factors are hardly
sufficient of themselves to account for the depth and
extent of the youth problem in our society. If Freud is
right there is something pathological about it.

A great deal of modern irreligion is in fact neurotic
in origin. There is a bitterness and hatred in much anti-
religious propaganda, prompting violent and slanderous
diatribes in some places and issuing in cruel and bloody
persecutions in others, which defies any normal and
wholesome explanation. Where there is a neurotic
condition we usually expect overt hysterical symptoms,
and in this case we have not far to look for them. The
modern world's substitute for religion is not mere
irreligion but hysterical and violent politics. The alternative to Christ for great multitudes of our contemporaries is the political leader, some infamous thug like
Hitler or Stalin, who makes himself the fomenter and

instrument of mass passion. His hands are red with blood, as the Aztec idols were smeared with the gore of human sacrifice. But the blood only heightens his prestige, because it speaks to his devotees not of his brutality but of his power. Yes, the modern world has its political religions, in the last resort the only alternatives to Christianity possible for western man. They offer the believer a real faith, however crude and ridiculous, and a genuine hope, however unintelligent and illusory, but, alas, not charity.

The Christian psychologist can only interpret this tragic mental condition as the consequence of the contemporary frustration and repression of man's spiritual nature and its spontaneous promptings and needs. Modern intellectual prejudices and social conditions have conspired together to stunt and narrow the self-consciousness of the great majority of modern men. They no longer consciously recognize their own religious needs for what they are. But thus neglected and ignored man's spiritual nature does not atrophy and decay, as many well-meaning religious writers have feared. On the contrary, it continues to work actively in the unconscious mind, penetrating the conscious life in heavily disguised but often tragically effective forms. If indeed, as all Christians believe, man is made for God, we should expect a period of widespread indifference to religious experiences and behaviour to be also a period of prevalent neurosis.

The neurotic substitute for religion is not always, of course, found in politics, but wherever the thwarted religiousness turns for consolation it always introduces an unhealthy fanaticism into a natural sphere and form of activity which is probably not in itself unhealthy at all—sport or art or the cinema or romantic love or philanthropy or social reform. Nevertheless, it is through the ruthless and violent politics, sometimes 'left' and sometimes 'right', of the revolutionary tradition—with its crazy blend of sadism and idealism, humanism and cruelty—that the greatest evils of modern times have entered our lives. In a novel published in 1847 Benjamin Disraeli, later Prime Minister of England, ventured upon a somewhat high-flown generalization which, as we can now see, had in it some of the prophetic insight of his great Hebrew ancestors: 'Man is made to adore and to obey: but if you will not command him; if you give him nothing to worship; he will fashion his own divinities and find a chieftain in his own passions.'

This, then, is the end-product of anti-religious propaganda and polite scepticism: not an intelligent and refined agnosticism but the mass creeds of the men who march in step, idolizing nation or race or class, feeding the insatiable will to power of the managerial *élites* who lead and manipulate them. I believe that in the long run only the Christians will know how to stand up to this new generation of political dervishes, matching conviction with conviction and opposing pathological hatreds with the bottomless sanity of the gospel of love. Already the polite sceptical intellectuals—pitifully because unintentionally guilty of a situation they do not really understand—are disappearing from view in the smoke of the gigantic conflict now moving with increasing speed from one unparalleled climax to another. I suspect that there will none of them be there when at last the totalitarians and the Christians meet at Philippi.

True Humanism

This degeneration of a godless, or politely sceptical,

humanism—which in the hands of its most charming and graceful expositors attracts most of us, at least in certain of our moods—into a ruthless political totalitarianism underlies also the present threat, which we have already noticed, to the integrity of history, reason and science. It is the totalitarian state which is above all turning history into propaganda—although it is true that nineteenth century liberal nationalism took the first fatal steps in that direction, and there is also a whiggish 'democratic' version of history which is closer to propaganda than to objective record. Similarly, it is above all the totalitarian state which is turning scientific research into a means to sub-scientific social and political ends. The democratic and capitalist societies have certainly subsidized and endowed science handsomely for their own non-scientific purposes, but it is the totalitarian planned society which tempts scientific workers not merely with the substance of financial prosperity but with the much more alluring prospect of power.

The truth is that the sceptical and secular liberal philosophy of life professed for so long by a large proportion of our intellectuals is proving too weak to serve as a foundation for the genuine liberal values—toleration, free discussion, the disinterested search for truth for its own sake. The great mass of men have yet to understand and appreciate such values. To them many cultural pursuits appear socially irrelevant, and they value science not as knowledge but as power. The liberal values are not likely to be upheld or even tolerated for long by the masters of a totalitarian state or the leaders of a mass democracy. The only hope for such values lies in a return to a religious humanism.

For a Christian the religious basis of humanism and the liberal values is clear enough. Man really does matter supremely, not so much because of what he now is or has, but because of God's attitude towards him. Rough-hew his nature and destiny how he will, he remains the object of a divine love and the embodiment of a divine purpose. If he is not the lord of creation he is nevertheless the fulfilment of its deepest and most ultimate ends. All things are made for him precisely because he himself is made for God. Again, for the Christian all truth is God's truth. What we call, from the human side, man's discovery of truth is at the same time a further instalment of God's revelation of Himself to us, and it is this consideration which gives all truth an absolute and inherent value of its own, independently of its usefulness in secular practice.

This is the only kind of humanism which can save us now. Nor is it altogether or merely a matter of faith. There is empirical evidence for holding that this kind of humanism is indeed the *true* humanism. We have already glanced at it. The well attested fact of the religious origins of the forms of civilized living, and our painful contemporary experience of the neurotic character of our substitutes for religion, indicate quite clearly civilization's desperate need for religious inspiration and control. Berdyaev once remarked that, 'Without God man is not man,' and Kierkegaard says somewhere that, 'It is the God-relationship that makes a man a man.' We are now facing a situation in which there is a real danger that man will cease to be man, or cease at least to be treated as such, and become instead a mere pawn in the totalitarian game, cannon fodder when the will to power of our ruling *élites* expresses itself in war, organizational and welfare fodder when their ruthless egotism glorifies and idealizes itself in imposing and impersonal peace-time civic structures.

We are familiar enough with the hackneyed remark that ours is an age of crisis. Christianity is above all a creed for the crisis, because it is a religion which has at its very roots the perception that in fact all times are times of crisis. It is indeed a faith which was literally made for such a time as this. It is precisely because we see so clearly to-day, whether or not we are Christians, that 'now is the crisis of this world' that we have our golden opportunity to perceive also that now is the appropriate and predestined moment for 'the Son of Man to be lifted up'.

CHAPTER SEVEN

THE PROLOGUE TURNS UP AGAIN AS EPILOGUE

This book is nearly over, and it must now be clear that I have substantially kept my initial promise. Quite obviously this has not been a book about me, although I candidly admit that I may perhaps have overdone that peeping out from the wings at times. Nevertheless, I have not the heart, or the time, to go over it all again, removing the lingering traces of a foolish egotism. What egotism the Holy Spirit has not yet purged out of me had better shew. I cannot conceal it from God; why then should I try to deceive the reader?

But I am glad that I have had the opportunity of writing this book. It has enabled me to write briefly about many fascinating themes of which I shall never have either the time or the specialized knowledge and ability to write at length. Above all it has given me a chance to say, with a certain amount of elaboration and emphasis, what seems to me the most important thing that any man can ever say, the sentence which I should like to utter if I were told that I only had time for one more. *God is in Christ and the world's only hope is in God.*

But at least I have not presented myself as the prophet of a new religion, or a scissors and paste man painstakingly constructing a new syncretism. The faith of which I have spoken has not only the disadvantage of being my faith, but also the priceless advantage of being the faith of Saul of Tarsus, Augustine of Hippo, Thomas Aquinas,

Pascal, Francis of Assisi, Vincent de Paul, Kierkegaard, Dostoievski, Newton, Pasteur, Mr. Gladstone and William Temple, and many more whose names are also written in the books of earth, and countless millions more, of course, whose names are written only in the books of heaven. I would rather have a faith which I can share with such men as these than any private, synthetic pseudo-religion of my own devising. To add my own small testimony to its unfailing and unflagging moral energy, its inexhaustible intellectual stimulus, dancing and dazzling in the light of thought, its endless aesthetic delight, is the best and proudest thing that I can ever do.

And also the most joyous. The years of my existence, forty of them now, have been years of crisis and turmoil, and my primarily sociological interests have kept me perhaps more than usually sensitive to the gravity and peril of our situation, but I think my friends would say that I never leave off laughing for long at a time. God will not let me. I am reminded of the story of the depraved gangster who was converted by the Salvation Army. He was given the big drum to play in the band, but instead of striking it only on the appropriate occasions he belaboured it in season and out of season with all his might and main. When rebuked he replied, 'I can't help it, I can't help it. I feel so damn good I should like to burst the bloody thing!' It is not my custom to express myself in quite the gangster's way, but I am thankful that life has so dealt with me that I know quite well what he meant. Has life dealt in that way with you?

And yet, as I write these last few paragraphs, I am seized with a serious inward misgiving. Is one more discussion of the meaning and truth of Christianity quite what the world now needs? It was Kierkegaard who remarked that the real question which confronts modern man is not, 'Is Christianity true? Ought I to be a Christian?' but, 'Can I be a Christian?' So long as we ask only the former question, we deceive ourselves by implying that we *could* be Christians if we really thought we *should*. Are we justified in such an assumption? No doubt we could try, but we should probably find, like so many of those who have tried before us, that we should not be particularly successful. But perhaps this kind of failure is better than most other kinds of success.

Nevertheless the challenge of Kierkegaard's remark is worth pondering again and again. We cannot become Christians by inclining to think, on balance, that Christianity is probably true. When the argument ends the serious and lifelong business of becoming a Christian begins. The world will not be saved, and nor will we, by writing books or reading them. Though the book is written and read and reviewed and criticized and done with, the real question abides for both writer and reader alike.

And Jesus said, 'Are you able to drink of the cup that I drink of? and to be baptized with the baptism that I am baptized with?'

And they said, 'We are able.'

What shall we say?

BOOK TWO

GRACEFUL REASON

FOREWORD

The Rev. Dr. J. V. Langmead Casserley is rapidly becoming one of the most important teachers at work in the Protestant Episcopal Church. It was little more than a year ago that he came to the United States from England. I cannot recall anyone from our sister Communion, the Church of England, who has made such a distinguished and respected place for himself so quickly in our midst. He was known, when his election as the Mary Crooke Hoffman Professor of Dogmatic Theology at the General Theological Seminary was announced in 1952, to a small group of Episcopalians who had read and appreciated his earlier books. Today, his reputation as a brilliant, witty, and profound theological thinker and lecturer is strongly established.

It is always a tribute of more than considerable proportions when a profound theologian begins to be in wide demand as a speaker to clerical and lay groups. The popular mind, unfortunately, has been conditioned to expect theology to be dull and irrelevant, because more often than we like to think, it has been the personality of the theologian that has been dull. The quick response which the Church public in this section of America has given to Dr. Casserley is, on the one hand, convincing evidence that people want to get theological meat to chew on, and on the other hand, that when the right man comes along they will listen with intelligent understanding and appreciation. All of us who have watched this small miracle take place have fairly burst with decorous Episcopal delight that Dr. Casserley belongs to the Anglican Communion and at least for a few years, we trust, to the American Episcopal Church.

In addition to seminary teaching, extensive preaching, and lecturing at conferences of various sorts, Dr. Casserley now brings out an excellent book. This is no mean accomplishment, because when one has become endeared to the American Church public as quickly and as solidly as Dr. Casserley has, there is precious little time left to do much writing.

The book is about the delicate and touchy problem of the place and importance of Natural Theology. It is significant because the question of the proper relationship between theology and philosophy comes very close to being the formidable fence over which honest advocates of differing theological viewpoints eye one another with the greatest suspicion today. Dr. Tillich understood this very well when he wrote the first volume of his *Systematic Theology*. Dr. Casserley is grateful to Dr. Tillich for pointing his finger at the area of greatest theological sensitivity, but he does not believe that the cure which is suggested will bring the needed healing. He believes that there is place for a roomier mutual collaboration between the philosopher and the theologian than Dr. Tillich's suggested method affords. This book will deserve and get much study and discussion on this point alone from the technical experts in both fields of thought.

Yet, it would be a great shame if *Graceful Reason* were read only by the highbrow set, even if the ideas which they wrestle with on their particular Mount Olympus do in time trickle down to shape the pedestrian minds of all of the rest of us. Without losing one ounce of intellectual force, Dr. Casserley has a way of writing which any reasonably educated man can quickly grasp. As one who has to interpret theology daily to the man in the street, I find all that he writes useful grist for my humble mill.

The street where my mill does its grinding happens to be Wall Street, where the shepherd cares little if his sheep are often mistakenly called wolves by some, and bulls or bears by others. One mental characteristic, however, predominates on this street. People here are realists and they are in a hurry. When they ask questions, they expect relevant and practical answers. I am grateful to the author of this book, not only for coming down to Old Trinity frequently to speak directly to our congregations, but also for supplying me through his clear writing with some more food for my zoo-like part of the vineyard. I believe that when you read what he has set down here, you will be grateful, too.

JOHN HEUSS

Epiphany, 1954

CONTENTS

CONTENTS

CONTENTS

INTRODUCTION

Every system of theology, or essay in theological thinking, is compelled in some way or other to relate itself and its findings or contentions to philosophy. Although theology is very different from philosophy there is a considerable overlap or convergence of interest which links them together. Many, although by no means all, of the questions discussed by philosophers, and particularly by the very great philosophers—questions about the meaning and purpose of human existence, about ultimate reality and absolute truth, and whether and how man can know them—are also questions necessarily discussed, from their own point of view, by theologians. Thus, the theologian can never entirely ignore philosophy. He can take up a negative or sceptical attitude toward it, but a negative or sceptical attitude toward philosophy is itself a form of philosophy, although in the opinion of most of the very greatest philosophers not a very competent or satisfying form.

INTRODUCTION

In most of the classical systems of theology the department of the subject which overlaps with philosophy, and in which the theologian makes his own philosophical position clear, is usually called natural theology. The traditional view, found in the writings of almost all Catholic theologians and not a few Protestants, is that philosophy at its best, the greatest philosophers in their highest moments, is characterized by a recognizable movement in what we may call a Godward direction. Some hold that philosophy can even conclusively demonstrate the existence of God, while others content themselves with the more moderate view that philosophy can at least indicate that the existence of God is a much more probable conclusion than any known alternative. Those theologians who are impressed by this widespread Godward movement in philosophy usually hold that it constitutes an important form of evidence which the Christian ought not to ignore. They argue that the Christian revelation indeed fulfils and goes far beyond the highest expectations of philosophy, but add that it does not overthrow them altogether.

Since the time of Emmanuel Kant, the great German critical philosopher, however, many Protestant theologians have taken the view that the final product of philosophical thought is a scepticism about the capacity of human reason to reach any kind of ultimate truth about the universe and the meaning of existence, and have concluded that the Christian theologian cannot rely upon or make any use of philosophy at all. Such theologians usually claim that they reject all forms of natural theology. Nevertheless, even they are compelled to relate their theological thinking to phi-

xvi

losophy and to provide it with some kind of philosophical foundation—in this case, of course, a sceptical one.

It is no exaggeration to say that the fundamental distinction between theologians and schools of theological thinking today is that between those who believe that some kind of metaphysics is possible and valid within its limits and those who deny the possibility of any kind of metaphysics at all. The question of the validity of metaphysical philosophy is not, however, for most theologians a purely philosophical one. Each of these two contrasted positions has its own theological interpretation. Those who deny the competence and value of philosophy usually hold an extreme view of the Fall of man according to which that primordial tragedy had the effect, among its many other tragic consequences, of completely cutting off the human intellect from all ultimate reality and truth. Those, on the other hand, who tend to believe that some kind of metaphysical thinking is valid and possible take a slightly more moderate view of the Fall. They argue that it cruelly injured and viciously distorted all human activities, including rational thought, but they hold that the image of God in man still persists, so that here and there in human existence we can still observe and experience its reality. It is not easy, they say, for fallen man to use his intellect with complete honesty and integrity of method and purpose, but it is not altogether impossible, and sometimes it actually happens. Nevertheless, both those theologians who believe in some kind of natural theology and those who reject all kinds of natural theology have at least this in common: they both see the need for providing their theological thinking with some kind of philosophical foundation. Such a foundation is provided as much by a philosophical scepticism as by a formulated natural theology, and there can be no doubt that from the point of view of rounding off and completing a theological system, both philosophical scepticism on the one hand and the traditional natural theology on the other are about equally efficient.

Dr. Paul Tillich in the first volume of his *Systematic Theology* has proposed what is in effect a new way of trying to relate theology and philosophy via natural theology. For him it is the task of natural theology to ask the questions and the task of revealed theology to provide the answers. This way of relating the verdicts and illuminations of revealed or "supranatural" theology, as he terms it, to the rational questions which result from our attempt to analyze our own experience, he calls "the method of correlation."

The method of correlation is an interesting and often important conception which will, I believe, contribute in many ways to the development of the logical structure of theological thought and discussion in the future. But I do not believe it is strong enough to bear the whole burden of the relationship between theology and philosophy. Natural theology cannot be defined, as Dr. Tillich seems to imply, simply in terms of a method of correlation. "The method of correlation," he says, "solves this historical and systematic riddle [that is, the problem of natural theology and its relation to Christian revelation] by resolving natural theology into the analysis of existence and by resolving supranatural theology into the answers given to the questions implied in existence." [1]

The limitations of the method are brought out clearly enough when we see that the analysis of existence produces not only questions which call for a theological answer but also insights and verdicts which require a theological interpretation, a very different thing. Conversely, revealed or supranatural theology itself, not only supplies us with answers to our existential questions, but also raises questions which call for a philosophical and often an existential answer.

The true relationship between philosophy and theology is one of more equal collaboration in which questions are raised by both sides and answers are required of both sides. It would seem to me, therefore, that Dr. Tillich's interesting and important method of correlation does not really solve the problem of whether in the long run we should relate philosophy and theology on the basis of a sceptical and critical philosophy which dares affirm no metaphysical proposition or whether we should relate them on the basis of a philosophy which, however cautiously, still ventures to believe in the possibility of valid metaphysical insights and discoveries.

But a natural theology has one advantage that philosophical scepticism does not possess. It provides the Christian thinker with a point of contact or convergence with non-Christian thought which, from the apologetic point of view, may be of the greatest philosophical importance.

[1] Paul Tillich, *Systematic Theology* (Chicago: University of Chicago, 1951), I, 65-66.

It seems to me that the greatest danger at the present time is the development of a situation in which the Christian thinker and the non-Christian thinker have nothing whatever to say to each other because there is nothing about which they are agreed and no theme in which they share a common interest.

Those of us who are interested in the possibility of keeping alive an intelligible discussion between the Church and the world—and surely all Christians must be vitally interested in such a possibility—cannot ignore or take a negative attitude toward the questions raised by natural theology.

In this book I have attempted to discuss the problem of natural theology almost entirely from this second point of view. I have said very little about the role and logical place of natural theology in systematic Christian theology. Instead, I have concentrated on describing some of the varieties of natural theology and on evaluating them primarily from the point of view of their usefulness in the field of Christian propaganda and rational apologetics. But the question of natural theology is not only of an intellectual or even practical importance; it is also one with which we find certain very real ecumenical overtones connected.

The Anglican, as he looks out upon the surrounding theological world, sees that the whole problem of the nature and status of natural theology is one of those issues about which Christians are divided. This division, however fundamental in itself, is symptomatic of much more profound divisions. As I understand it, it belongs to the very office of an Anglican (it is part of the inherent function of an Anglican within Christendom) to address himself particularly, in an irenical and peacemaking mood, to any of those great controversies in which he sees Christians who stand, so to speak, to the right or the left of him hotly engaged. Always to stand in the middle of violent contestants and speak a word of peace is of course a dangerous vocation, but it seems inherent in what we may call the Anglican situation —or better, perhaps, the Anglican predicament! In any case, it is in this mood that I approach the present problem.

When I discuss theological issues with leading and gifted Roman Catholic theologians, I am impressed with the strength of the case for some sort of natural theology. Turning, on the other hand, to theologians of the Reformed persuasions, I am similarly impressed by many of the criticisms which they make of natural theology in what I may venture to call "its received Roman Catholic form."

As an Anglican, I feel that it is my duty to attempt some kind of restatement in an endeavor to meet some of the criticisms (though we shall probably have to confess that it is not possible, and perhaps not even necessary, to meet them all) and to bridge the gap. As I say, it is inherent in the Anglican situation that we should spend the whole of our existence toilsomely building bridges, and then standing in the middle of them, facing in both directions. The reader will agree that from the physiological point of view this is an extremely exacting operation! Nevertheless, it is to such an office that the Holy Spirit of God has called us in the Anglican communion, and by our Anglican allegiance we are committed to it. This is indeed no small vocation, and certainly not one for which we need apologize to any man.

This book is based on the Reinecker Lectures given early

in 1953 to students of the Episcopal Theological Seminary at Alexandria, Virginia. I have expanded the lectures somewhat in order to give them a more literary form, and I have added a fair amount of new material, but I hope that something of their original purpose and intention has survived the process. The lectures were given to students and not to or for expert philosophers and theologians. No doubt some of the students were, and some of them may become, expert philosophers or theologians, but I have had to deal with students so long that they no longer trail any clouds of intellectual glory for me. Most of them are ordinary people who happen to be studying, so that there need be very little difference between a lecture or a book intended for a student audience and a lecture or a book intended for any audience of generally well-educated people motivated by a genuine interest in the kind of question which the lecture or book discusses.

In other words, because the lectures were originally given to students, this book which has grown out of them is essentially a book for the general reader, and it is as such that I venture to hope that it will be received by such a public as it attracts and enjoys.

CHAPTER ONE

A DESCRIPTION OF NATURAL THEOLOGY

What is Natural Theology?

There can be no simple answer. Natural theology is not a specific and unchanging form of doctrine which can be written down, discussed, and criticized once and for all. On the contrary, it is a particular kind of Christian intellectual activity which has assumed many different forms in the past and may, for all we know, assume new forms in the future of which at present we can have no conception. As new points of view arise and establish themselves in philosophy and the sciences, they present new opportunities to the natural theologian, so that not only is his task never finished, but it has always to be started all over again.

Nevertheless, I think it possible to discern and describe at least four different ways of approaching and understanding natural theology, none of them adequate by itself, because usually any particular essay in natural theology is compounded and blended of various elements drawn from each type of approach. But it will be useful to describe briefly these four different ways of understanding natural theology as a prelude to the discussion of the whole subject which follows.

First, by natural theology we may mean any intellectual movement of the mind which is conceived to lie in a Godward direction, proceeding from some point or from many points in the immediate life and experience of man. It is thought that man undertakes such a movement of his mind because it is natural to man, because he is a specific kind of being—a being with an intellectual destiny orientated Godward, roughhew it how he may. From this point of view, some sort of Godward movement of the mind is natural to man because man, even fallen man, is a man made for God. It may be held that in proportion as his thinking has integrity and a genuine humanity, it will inevitably tend to take this generally Godward direction. Natural theology may be the development and verification of such an assumption as this.

Second, by natural theology we may mean some sort of argument, based on naturalistic premises, for the validity of religious behavior in general, for the existence of God or for the existence of a spiritual realm. I suppose the best-known arguments for the existence of God are of the cosmological kind—that immense variety or family of arguments which are basically of the form "because the world exists, God exists." No doubt this is the best-known kind of natural theology, so much so that many people think it is the only possible kind, but it is important for us to recognize at the outset that there are in fact many kinds of natural theology of which this is only one, although certainly the most familiar.

Third, we may mean something quite different from either of the above. Natural theology may mean to us a theology of nature. This will not be an argument from nature to God, but an attempt to show that the theological categories of thought are adequate to the interpretation of nature and the natural sciences. This is a much less familiar conception, but I am quite certain that it is a theme which cannot be omitted in any attempt, however brief, to survey the scope and variety of natural theology.

The fourth approach is one peculiarly dear to the Anglican mind and the Anglican heart. It is the specifically Anglican form, a form classically expounded by one of the very greatest of the theologians of the Anglican tradition, Bishop Butler (though not by him alone). Here, natural theology takes the form of the tracing of an analogy between what I will call natural and evangelical experience. In Bishop Butler's *Analogy of Religion,* of course, we find this argument immediately related to eighteenth century controversies which are dead and gone. But that does not mean that the essential insights of the book are outmoded, though it may and does mean that it is now necessary for us to rethink and restate the argument in relation to twentieth century controversies of which Bishop Butler was necessarily ignorant.

As I have said, we should not suppose that this argument is peculiar to Bishop Butler alone. We find, for example, an excellent statement of the germ of it in a book published two years before his. It will interest American readers to know that it was written while the author was residing for a short time in the United States. The book was the *Alciphron* by Bishop George Berkeley, possibly the greatest contribution to Anglican divinity ever written in this country. Berkeley writes: "It will be sufficient, if such analogy appears between the dispensations of grace and nature, as may make it probable (although much should be unaccountable in both) to suppose them derived from the same Author, and the workmanship of one and the same Hand." [1]

This doctrine of the analogy between the realm of grace and the realm of nature (between religious and physical experience) must be very carefully distinguished from the doctrine of analogical predication which we find in Thomas Aquinas and other medieval writers. The doctrine of analogical predication asks and attempts to answer the question how it is that we are able to use affirmative human language about God and yet avoid the danger of crude, or even refined, anthropomorphism. The answer is given in terms of a theory which traces and affirms analogies between God and His creatures, while at the same time steadfastly rejecting any kind of identity.

Although these are different theories, we would be mistaken in supposing that there is no connection at all between the two. In fact, we find in Berkeley's *Alciphron,* also, a passage in which the author gives as lucid a summary statement of the scholastic doctrine of analogical predication as can be found in the English language. Because of

---

[1] Arthur A. Luce and Thomas E. Jessop, ed., *Works of George Berkeley* (Edinburgh: Nelson), III, 281. Used by permission of the publisher.

the intrinsic worth of this passage and because of the interesting way in which it betrays the familiarity of an eighteenth century Anglican bishop with medieval philosophy, I venture to quote a part of it.

Thomas Aquinas expresseth his sense of this point in the following manner. All perfections, saith he, derived from God to the creatures are in a certain higher sense, or (as schoolmen term it) eminently in God. Whenever, therefore, a name borrowed from any perfection in the creature is attributed to God, we must exclude from its signification every thing that belongs to the imperfect manner, wherein that attribute is found in the creature. Whence he concludes that knowledge in God is not a habit, but a pure act. And again, the same Doctor observes that our intellect gets its notions of all sorts of perfections from the creatures and that as it apprehends those perfections, so it signifies them by names. Therefore, saith he, in attributing these names to God, we are to consider two things; first, the perfections themselves, as goodness, life and the like, which are properly in God; and secondly, the manner which is peculiar to the creature, and cannot, strictly and properly speaking, be said to agree to the Creator. And although Suarez, with other schoolmen, teacheth, that the mind of man conceiveth knowledge and will to be in God as faculties or operations, by analogy only to created beings; yet he gives it plainly as his opinion, that when knowledge is said not to be in God, it must be understood in a sense including imperfection, such as discursive knowledge, or the like imperfect kind found in the creatures: and that, none of those imperfections in the knowledge of men or angels belonging to the formal notion of knowledge, or to knowledge as such, it will not thence follow that knowledge, in its proper formal sense, may not be attributed to God: and of knowledge taken in general for the clear evident understanding of all truth, he expressly affirms that it is in God, and that this was never denied by any philosopher who believed in God. It was, indeed, a current opinion in the schools, that even

5

being itself should be attributed analogically to God and the creatures. That is, they held that God, the supreme, independent, self-originate cause and source of all beings, must not be supposed to exist in the same sense with created beings, not that he exists less truly, properly, or formally, than they, but only because he exists in a more eminent and perfect manner.[2]

Thus, the doctrine of analogical predication, the doctrine that analogy is the proper means of religious communication, depends upon and presupposes a doctrine of analogy between natural and what I have called evangelical experience in the realities themselves.

It is possible for us to use analogy in our communications with one another only if reality itself is characterized by certain broad and profound analogical trends. In other words, we can draw analogies validly only if there are some real analogies to be drawn. So this particular form of the doctrine—an advance, as it seems to me, upon anything we find in Thomas himself except in the form of a mere hint—may validly be regarded as the specifically Anglican contribution to natural theology, the one which is peculiarly rooted in our own great intellectual traditions.

A Basis for Apologetics

Accompanying all forms of natural theology is the suggestion that a natural theology is normally and properly something conceived and elaborated by a Christian in faith. A natural theology is not first and primarily a ladder on which one climbs to faith but, on the contrary, something which the Christian, thinking in the tradition of faith, labors to construct for two reasons.

[2] *Ibid.*, 168 ff.

6

The first of these reasons is intellectual in character. He devises a natural theology in order to fill an indispensable niche in any adequate theological system. The second is of a practical, pastoral, and evangelical character. He elaborates a natural theology in order to establish a basis for carrying on conversation with a non-Christian or a sub-Christian man.

Although a natural theology is normally formulated by a Christian in faith, standing upon the faith, nevertheless, in its essential nature it is animated and motivated by a desire for conversation with those who lie outside the faith. Thus, it seizes gladly and avidly upon any point of convergence which it can find as it looks at the life and the thought of those who stand outside the Church (in the widest sense of the word).

But natural theology has also a positive function in relation to the life and thought of the faithful Christian himself. The Christian is never only or merely a Christian. He is also man: a vegetative animal living with nature; a social animal clashing and collaborating with his fellowman; an aesthetic creature, prizing and delighting in a conscious response to such of the beauties of life as he is capable of appreciating; a worker participating in some of the activities which constitute the life of his society. If he is a truly faithful Christian, no doubt his interests in Christianity will be the primary interest of his life; but even if he is a theologian, it will almost certainly not be his only interest. Indeed, in a theologian such a narrow concentration of interest would be deplorable.

Every Christian, in other words, shares some interests

with non-Christians. For his own sake, therefore, as well as theirs, he must find some positive and constructive way of relating such interests to his Christian faith. If he cannot relate his interests—philosophical, scientific, artistic, literary, political, or social—to his Christianity he will never succeed in becoming a complete and integrated Christian. He will live a mixed life, part Christian, part secular, spiritually torn asunder by motives and forms of conduct which he does not know how to harmonize with each other.

Precisely because the Christian man is also the natural man, he requires the guidance of a natural theology in order to remain at the same time one man, one Christian man completely devoted to the service of God within the context of his natural life, one natural man giving himself up entirely to the fulfilment of the purpose of the Creator of his nature. To use a piece of modern philosophical jargon, because the Christian man is also the natural man a natural theology is for him an existential necessity.

A Question of Fact

We may ask ourselves, do such points of convergence as those to which we have alluded exist? Indeed, there are some theologians who deny that they *can* exist. But, it seems to me, the question whether such points of convergence exist is primarily the empirical question: do we in fact encounter such points of convergence? and not the purely *a priori* question, *can* there be such points of convergence?

Some Biblical theologians try to show that there cannot be a natural theology simply by quoting appropriate pas-

8

sages of Scripture—and also, like so many Biblical theologians, by not quoting inappropriate passages of Scripture! But the question whether a natural theology exists is primarily a question of fact; do we discover points of convergence, not by reading the Bible, but by reading all sorts of other books? And surely the answer to that, by any honest mind that does read other books, can only be that in some sense we do.

Just as the Christian looking round about him in the world in which he lives, or studying history or the biographies of great men, often discovers in the lives of non-Christian men and women instances of conduct and high character which he cannot fail but admire, and cannot but admire precisely because he is a Christian, so will he often find in the writings of non-Christian thinkers affirmations and points of view with which, precisely because he is a Christian, he cannot but agree. Sometimes such writers will even say things which will lead him to a more profound understanding of the meaning of his own faith than he had before. Christian thought has never throughout its history been an isolated or introverted form of intellectualism, ignoring all but specifically Christian writings and specifically Christian thinkers.

The earliest Christian writers during the second century were influenced by the stoics and middle-platonists: Augustine by the neo-platonists; Thomas Aquinas by an epoch-making rediscovery of the text of Aristotle; and contemporary Christian philosophers by Darwin, the twentieth century physicists, and anti-Christian writers like Marx and Freud.

It seems to me undeniable that the living points of convergence, upon which natural theology seizes, exist today just as they have existed in the past. As long as such points of convergence exist, natural theology remains both a possible and a necessary activity.

A Warning and a Qualification

If the existence of these points of convergence is so obvious and undeniable, why is it that a considerable number of theologians refuse to allow that natural theology has any kind of validity at all? Partly no doubt, it is due to the belief of so many contemporary Protestant theologians that Christian theology ought to be not merely primarily Biblical in its inspiration and appeal but also exclusively Biblical in its foundation and method. For myself, I can find no ground either in the Bible itself or in the history of Christian thought or in what we may call Christian common sense for so rigidly exclusive a Biblicism as this. The issue first clearly arose and was formulated at the Council of Nicaea, when any narrow and exclusive Biblicism was decisively, and to my mind rightly, set aside.

However, this is not the kind of objection to natural theology which seems to me sufficiently important for discussion here. A better reason for distrusting natural theology is the suspicion that if there is a natural theology there must also be a natural religion which corresponds to it. This illusion, that the validity of natural theology implies the possibility of a merely natural religion, is the great mistake, in particular, of some of the natural theologians of the eighteenth century, and it seems to me that a distrust of natural theology is quite legitimate unless and until this particular illusion is clearly seen for what it is and set aside.

Natural theology, as I understand it, is necessarily a department of Christian theology, a phase of Christian intellectualism. It cannot compose or correspond to a religion because after all it consists of no more than a series of inferences, whereas a real living religion is not a series of inferences but a confrontation with reality. A living religion is something which happens, not when and because man infers (however valid his inferences may be), but when and because God acts and speaks. The great makers and architects of systems of natural theology, Thomas Aquinas, for example, see this clearly enough. For them the culminating point of natural theology is when it demonstrates the need for revelation. It shows the emptiness of a niche which philosophy can perceive but which it cannot fill. From this point of view natural theology has a relationship to the Christian revelation akin to that of the relationship of Hebrew prophecy to the great self-revealing acts of God in the life, death, and Resurrection of Jesus Christ.

Natural theology may indicate the need for revelation, and it may bring the philosophical man to a point where he is ready to listen to revelation, but it cannot act as a substitute for revelation. The relationship between the inferences of natural theology and the Christian revelation which confirms them, we will consider later on. It will be enough at this stage for us to see clearly that the possibility of a natural theology in no way implies the possibility of a natural religion. This being so, the one really important reason for the prevalent distrust of natural theology among contemporary theologians can safely be set aside.

Two Definitions

This section contains two brief essays in definition. We shall be concerned with the definition of two terms: "general revelation" and "nature."

The use of the terms general revelation and natural theology. A considerable number of recent theologians, while either denying or ignoring traditional natural theology, make a great play with what they call "general revelation." What is the relationship between general revelation and natural theology? Is it just another name for the same thing; is it a new name for some novel reinterpretation of the same thing; or is it an entirely independent concept?

The basic idea seems to be that nature does not so much prove or imply the existence of God (so that we can argue from nature to God) as declare or attest or make manifest the existence of God, so that we must say that in some sense all nature and experience speak to us of God.

"The heavens declare the glory of God, and the firmament showeth His handiwork," said the psalmist. One of the greatest scholastic philosophers and theologians, Bonaventura, laid great stress on the way in which nature directly manifests the glory of God, and many passages in Calvin reflect the same idea. Among Anglican theologians, Bishop Berkeley's conception of a natural, visual language, through which God speaks to us as step by step we experience the world around us, really amounts to very much the same thing as the modern conception of general revelation and even provides it with a philosophical basis which the doctrine sometimes lacks in the writings of contemporary theologians.

Quite clearly, all theologians, even those who believe in natural theology, will agree that the heavens do indeed declare the glory of God. There is no necessary contradiction or distinction between saying that nature proves or implies the divine existence and saying that nature manifests the divine glory. Indeed, it is easy to see that these two statements simply look at and report the same phenomenon from opposite sides. Nature can only make manifest the divine glory if it also proves or attests the divine existence. Conversely, if it proves or attests the divine existence, it also proclaims the divine glory. When we say that nature proclaims the divine glory, this can only be so because God is ultimately responsible for the existence of nature and because all reality which is other than God is God's handiwork. But if all existence which is not God is creaturely existence, then clearly all existence which is not God rationally implies the supreme reality of its Creator.

Natural theology looks at and formulates this fact in a philosophical way; general revelation contemplates and delights in it in a devotional way. Neither natural theology nor general revelation are possible apart from the other. No doubt, from the point of view of our spiritual and devotional life, general revelation is the more important of the two; but from the intellectual point of view, natural theology is prior to general revelation.

The heavens can only declare the glory of God if we already know that God exists. Once we know that God exists and is responsible for the existence of nature, then we see clearly enough that nature makes manifest His glory. The great natural theologians like Thomas Aquinas do indeed, without using the term, expound a doctrine of general revelation. For them, the fact that the creation makes manifest the glory of the Creator is the foundation of their whole doctrine of the analogy of being, which makes it possible for us to discover, within our experience of the creation, analogies or clues to the mystery of the being of God.

Thus, the concept of general revelation is quite useless to those theologians who wish to ignore or deny natural theology. Far from being an alternative that enables us to dispense with natural theology, it directly implies it. Indeed, it implies also that doctrine of the analogy of being which is disliked, almost as much as natural theology itself, by most of those theologians who reject natural theology. Personally, I do not think that the term general revelation has proved a very helpful one in contemporary theological discussion. I do not propose to use it at all in this book. In so far as I do use it, I prefer to reserve it for those occasions on which I discuss the question of whether or not any degree of divine revelation can be found in non-Christian religions. The term "natural theology," on the other hand, is one I shall employ when I am considering whether any degree of approximation to theological truths can conceivably be observed in the course of the development of general philosophy. In that way we can arrive at a rough-and-ready way—not, I am afraid, very profound or fundamental—of distinguishing between the two.

A definition of the word nature. As with many of the

great classic words of human thought, the word "nature," in the modern world, has become ambiguous. Now it seems to mean either everything in general or nothing in particular. "Everything in general" is nearly always, in practice, identical with "nothing in particular." Usually, the word nature is used as a collective noun to describe all the things that compose the non-human creation; it might have been better to have reserved some word such as *cosmos* for that purpose. Possibly the word nature can be made to include both the human and the nonhuman creation, in which case it becomes a collective noun identical with the noun creation (creation referring to the *creata,* the things created, and not to the activity of creating them). This may seem to be a more valid and a more Christian way of using the term nature. I prefer, however, to reserve the word *creation,* or the phrase *the realm of the creatures,* for this purpose.

In Greek philosophy and in classical Christian thought and theology, however, the nature of anything is its characteristic pattern of process. Thus, it is "in the nature of man" to grow out of childhood into an adult creature. *Nature* thus signifies the characteristic pattern of the type or species, its peculiar form or mode of growth and development.

From this point of view, we know there can be deviations from the natural as a result of many different combinations of circumstances. Thus, for example, man may deviate from the human *natura* through sin. The Fall means a catastrophic, primordial deviation from nature. Nature itself is both a descriptive and a normative term at one and the same time; it does describe a norm and it does purport, in

15

the vast majority of cases, to describe a norm that is in fact observed.

But the essential meaning of the doctrine of the Fall consists in the statement that the peculiarity of the human norm (the human *natura*) is that, although it is the norm, it is not in fact always obeyed—perhaps because the human norm, unlike most natural norms, is not automatically or spontaneously observed but requires conscious, willing adhesion. It is part of the catastrophe in which man finds himself that he is not himself, that he is estranged from himself: being estranged from God, he is therefore estranged from both the origin and the end of his own being.

This takes us back to our first approach to natural theology. A natural theology is a kind of theology which is natural to man. This does not mean that it is the kind of theology which man nearly always or necessarily thinks; for, under sin and because of the Fall, man is not always natural, by any means. Nevertheless, this kind of theology is natural to man in the sense that the human mind approximates it in proportion as its thinking rises toward the ideal of complete rational integrity and undistorted humanity.

For the Christian philosopher the term "natural" carries with it another very important connotation. For him the realm of the natural, the whole created order, is the realm of that which can only be empirically known. The realm of the natural is, as the classical Christian philosophers and natural theologians say, contingent: it does not *have* to be; it simply *happens* to be. It is dependent upon the creative will of God, who quite conceivably might have created otherwise, or might even not have created at all.

Natural or created facts cannot be discovered and known by any process of purely rational analysis. They have to be observed and described; they can only be discovered in and through experience of them, in which they manifest and reveal themselves. To say this is to emphasize the closeness of the connection which exists between the Christian conception of nature, based on the Biblical doctrine of Creation, and the emergence of the natural sciences in and out of the expanding life of Christian civilization, as a revelation of its hitherto latent implications. This recognition that knowledge of natural facts cannot be obtained by purely rational analysis (*i.e.* that empirical knowledge is not *apriori*) will also be seen to have great significance for us in the later stages of our discussions in this book.

The Cosmological Argument

As I have said, for most people the norm of natural theology is the second of the four approaches, "an argument based on naturalistic premises." And this argument, classically called the cosmological or teleological argument, is any variant of the general idea, "because the world exists, God exists."

There are many forms of this argument, and it can be expressed very crudely, for example, as: "Somebody had to make everything else, so I suppose somebody had to make the world." (Conceivably, this is just permissible, occasionally, in the Sunday school class, and I think most Sunday School classes get it at some time or other!) But obviously the argument does not have to be in this crude form; it can be a mechanistic argument for a Supreme Mechanic, or a

17

technological argument for a Supreme Architect. In the works of quite recent writers such as Sir James Jeans and Sir Arthur Eddington, it has been a mathematician's argument for a Supreme Mathematician (and that is also the form which it assumed centuries ago in Plato's *Timaeus*). Or it can be, as in Whitehead, a metaphysician's argument for a final and ultimate creative principle that regulates the interplay between the potential and the actual.

There can also be aesthetic forms of the cosmological argument. This may on one hand consider reality as primarily a work of art and the nonhuman-creation as something closely analogous to the visual and plastic arts (the analogy being betrayed by the fundamental similarity that exists between our aesthetic response to nature as a spectacle and our aesthetic response to visual art as a spectacle); or, on the other hand, it may trace an analogy between the human life and works of drama and fiction, betrayed when we use some such phrase as "the drama of history." (Very often we find people who say that they prefer good history or biography to novels because they are even more extraordinary.) For example, in Dorothy Sayers' *The Mind of the Maker* and in other similar books we find such an aesthetic form of the cosmological argument.

Its Existential Form

There is also what I would call an existential form of the cosmological argument, going back at least to Augustine, and finding a very profound re-expression in the often sadly heretical philosophy of Johannes Scotus Erigena in the ninth century. In its existential form, the fundamental contingency (the dependence) of the real, as we know it, upon that which transcends it is discovered particularly and most vividly of all in man's experience of self-conscious existence.

I lay some stress on the analogy between the form of the argument, "because the world exists, God exists," and the existential argument, "because I exist and suffer and agonize and go through all that I do, and know myself to be dependent and contingent, therefore God exists," since I think it is true that a very considerable number of people in the twentieth century fail to see that what they call an existential approach to theology is fundamentally as naturalistic as Thomas Aquinas' cosmological approach to theology. In each case the Christian thinker is beginning with, and using as a bridge to his adumbration of the meaning of the Gospel and the Christian faith, a number of considerations drawn from man's experience of existing in the world.

The cosmological kind of natural theology may stress the world, and the existential kind of natural theology may stress human existence, but they have one basic postulate in common: they both claim, through their analysis of that phase of our experience with which they are preoccupied, to discover the fundamental "give-away" fact of the contingency of the real. A Thomist may look at the world and say, "Aha! The world is contingent!" An existentialist may look at himself within the world and say, "Aha! I am contingent, and I have a shrewd suspicion that other people are contingent, too!" But if the existentialist theologian adds, "How much profounder am I than the Thomist with his merely natural theology!" he is mistaken. He is using the word natural only in the sense of cosmic, but more accurately, as we have seen, nature includes both human existence and the cosmos. Or, alternatively, both man and the cosmos are characterized by their own specific natures.

We are now in a position to see the significance of at least some part of our brief digression on the meaning of nature. It indicates that the existentialist approach to theology, so fashionable among contemporary theologians, and above all among those contemporary theologians who make the greatest parade of rejecting all natural theology, is itself a form of natural theology. We only make the mistake of supposing that an existentialist theology is not natural theology, and is even opposed in spirit to natural theology, because we have formed the bad habit of using the word nature as a collective noun for all the subhuman things which compose the cosmos.

Once we understand the word nature properly, we see clearly enough that a theology or philosophy which takes for its point of departure man's self-conscious experience of his own existence is just as naturalistic in its premises as one which takes for its point of departure our observation and knowledge of the cosmos which environs us. There is much to be said for the view that this existentialist approach to theology is the form of natural theology most appropriate to the climate of opinion which predominates in the twentieth century, just as the cosmological approach found in Thomas Aquinas was the form of natural theology most appropriate to the climate of opinion in the thirteenth century. But this does not mean that any fundamental distinction can, or should be, drawn between them, still less that each is opposed to the other in its essential spirit.

We must always remember that natural theology is in some sense a missionary as well as a purely intellectual enterprise. Hence, the natural theologian must always be peculiarly sensitive to the climate or climates of opinion predominating in his own time. Thus, when we read the *Summa Contra Gentiles*, we must never lose sight of the fact that Thomas was a kind of missionary to the Aristotelians, traversing not physical distances in order to get to the other side of the globe, like the more familiar kind of missionary, but traveling vast metaphysical distances in order to get to the mind and speak to the condition of his students and colleagues.

Today many Christian theologians are similarly impressed with the rise and vogue of the many highly diverse forms of philosophy which we describe as existentialist, and they are right to see that even in its most radically anti-religious form it has a deep significance for Christian thought. Nevertheless, they are wrong to assume that there is any fundamental departure in either the conclusions or the spirit of their thinking from that characteristic of Thomas and the cosmological theologians.

Inference and Revelation

We will postpone for the moment any consideration of the intellectual value of such arguments; but before closing this first chapter, I would like to reconsider briefly its first form: the doctrine of an inherent ordination of man, even

21

intellectually, toward God. I believe that it is at this point that many of our difficulties and misunderstandings begin. Hence, this is the point at which it is necessary, by a certain amount of re-definition, to begin to clear up these misunderstandings.

"Both-and" or "Either-or"

Broadly speaking, when two beings thinking in the same tradition (as, for example, two Christian theologians) differ from each other there are always two possible explanations: first, that they only think they differ with each other because they do not quite understand each other. I believe that we should always assume at first that this is what is happening. At all events, I am sure it is the irenical Anglican way to begin with such an assumption! The other possibility is that they really do differ. But let us not acquiesce in that conclusion until we are driven to do so by stern ineluctable facts. Let us start on the more hopeful assumption that something can be done in the way of re-definition, re-explanation, and re-thinking.

In some respects it does seem to me that the whole mind and bent of Anglicanism is rather synthetic or Hegelian. Many so-called dialectical theologians seem to delight in multiplying "either-or" situations, by impaling the reader on the horns of one dilemma after another. But the Anglican mind always dislikes arbitrary "either A or B" situations, and tends to say, "surely, we can have both A^1 and B^1." I say both A^1 and B^1 and not both A and B because a true synthesis does more than merely lump together its two terms in a bare paradox. Instead, it transforms and enriches the meaning of each term in the very process of reconciling it to the other. A true synthesis is neither a compromise nor a self-contradiction, but a profounder apprehension.

Kierkegaard criticized Hegel by saying that there are certain either-or situations in life which cannot be bridged or transcended in the Hegelian way. I do not doubt that Kierkegaard was right. But I think there is something to be said for assuming that we may be in a both-and situation first, and only reluctantly agreeing that we are in an either-or situation when we are ultimately constrained by the facts. That seems to me a very good form of intellectual procedure. When we leap to the either-or situation it is just possible that behind the severity of our judgment there lies a very real intellectual laziness, or possibly sometimes a very real intellectual uncharity.

On the other hand, in order to show that the laugh can sometimes be against the Anglican, we may remind ourselves of the story of the very, very modernist Anglican bishop who was asked whether or not he believed in God. He replied, "I dislike these hard and fast distinctions."

This suggests that there are certain ultimate limitations to the Anglican mode of intellectual procedure. It suggests also that Kierkegaard was right in the end. All I am proposing is that we should not assume that he was necessarily right at the beginning.

My own conviction is that in the realm of philosophy and theology—where honest and gifted and not seldom intellectually inspired men differ from one another and wrestle not against one another for the mastery, but with one another for the truth—both-and situations arise much more

23

frequently than either-or situations, although it may well be that the latter, precisely because they are so rare, are, when we do meet with them, more profound and more fundamental to our whole way of life and thought.

If this is so, the proper rule of intellectual procedure should be always to begin by assuming that we are in a both-and situation until we are driven by the failure of a prolonged course of intellectual experiment to the conclusion that we are, in fact, in one of those either-or situations in which we have to state and hold our position without compromise. Either-or situations are more commonly met with in the realms of ethical action and decision than in that of pure, truth-seeking thought.

It is with this rule of procedure in mind that I want to turn once more to the contrast between intellectual inference and expectation on the one hand and the facts or events which verify such inferences and fulfil such expectations on the other. We have already glimpsed the possibility that the relationship between revelation and natural theology may be a relationship of this kind. If this is so, the two cannot be validly or fruitfully opposed to each other, because in fact they need each other. Just as inference cannot verify itself or fulfil its own expectations, so revelation cannot be fully understood or appropriated by man unless he is in a position to note which of his inferences it verifies and which of them it disproves; which of his expectations it fulfils and which of them it shows to be groundless. After all, the revelation of God does not come to us in a mental and spiritual vacuum. It is given to living, thinking men, and it has a dynamic relationship to their life and thought alike.

I shall speak of inference and the verification of inference in general terms, but the reader must have in mind that I do so because I regard these general considerations as vitally relevant to our present discussion. I believe that much of the controversy about the relationship of, and supposed antagonism between, reason and revelation can be resolved, and even seen not to arise, in terms of a better understanding of the relationship between inference and verification.

Experience may be said to have a revelatory character, because experience has a way of either verifying or failing to verify inference. Hence it partakes of the nature of revelation. I am using the word revelation broadly, meaning not religious revelation only, because we are surrounded by revelation at every moment. To meet and gradually come to know another human being is to watch him reveal himself. Similarly, sense experience is a form of revelation. The color of the walls of a room is revealed to us when we first enter and behold it. We know no way of calculating rationally what color the walls must be prior to or without entering the room.

I see no possibility of revelation being given except to rational beings, and I see no possibility of the exercise of reason except within some revelational context. Fundamentally, as I see it, the opposition between reason and revelation is similar to the attempt to oppose the left to the right, or the north to the south, or the east to the west, since the two terms involve each other. Rational thought is always thought about a revealed reality or datum, and a revealed reality or datum can have meaning only to an intellectual creature.

The Transcending of Inference

We should note, however, for it is the really important point, that although revelation—the event, the fact—may and sometimes does confirm inference, it never *merely* confirms inference; it always more than confirms inference. Take an example: the young wife, full of joy and trepidation and hope, goes to see her family doctor. He examines her and says, "My dear, you're going to have a baby." It is conceivable that he is wrong—although probably not if he's an experienced family doctor—but it's just conceivable that she has some kind of growth in the reproductive organs; and of course it's always conceivable that she will have a miscarriage. Still she is probably going to have a baby, and normally the event, the revealing event, will among other things verify the doctor's inference.

In another way, however, it will negate the inference, because she will not have *a* baby, she will have *the* baby, a very different thing! No mother that ever lived has had *a* baby—just a pale, tenuous something which verifies the doctor's inference and no more! The revelation always transcends the inference which points to it. The revelation is never identical with the inference, for the inference is always an idea, and the revelation is always a reality.

It seems to me that it is the failure to observe this that underlies a lot of talk about "the God of Aristotle" or "the

God of the Greeks" not being "the God of the Bible," or something of that kind. I really do not know what this means. There are not two Gods, presumably; and surely we should all agree that the cosmic functions of God in Aristotle, for example (no doubt in a vague, confused way which calls for a great deal of analysis and criticism and correction), are carried out by the God whom we worship as Biblical Christians. The mere fact that in a very different context, from a very different aspect, with a very different degree of intimacy, two people give very different accounts of the same person does not mean that they are really two distinct persons!

Sometimes under favorable circumstances, I draw money from my bank which is just around the corner from my home. Usually, out of habit I suppose, I go to the same teller. I can provide a description of him: he's a young man; with dark hair and a rather dark, swarthy skin; a pleasant manner; usually rather well turned out—nice tie, collar always very clean. He works swiftly but always accurately. He has never made a mistake, but then it would be very difficult to make a mistake as far as I am concerned. I should conclude, therefore, that he is a typical and efficient teller.

But suppose that instead of coming to me, the inquirer went to the young man's wife. I wonder what sort of picture he would get from her. I do not know, of course, but he may (I hope he would) get a picture of a loving husband, a very affectionate and dutiful father—possibly a churchwarden at the local church or a secretary of an amateur dramatic group. There are all sorts of possibilities, and, of course, the

27

more she is willing to reveal her intimate experience of life with him, the more rounded the picture will be of, shall we say, a true-hearted, generous, chivalrous man: good neighbor, good husband, good father, and so on.

Will it be valid, then, for the inquirer to say, "Look, we've got two men here! This affectionate father has nothing to do with the soulless efficiency machine." Will he therefore have two men or will either informant necessarily have lied? I think not. We must say at once that because one picture is so much fuller, warmer, more intimate, more profound, it does not necessarily mean that there is no truth at all in the other picture.

I am using this as an illustration of the relationship between inference and revelation; revelation will do more than verify the inference, even in the most favorable circumstances. It will transcend inference to some extent, and to some extent confound inference. I too may very well be confounded if I talk to the teller's wife. I may admit surprise and ask, "Do you mean to say that this man with his slick counting, this man who, when I see him, seems to live for money and taps out figures on his counting machine with such impersonal efficiency—do you really mean to say that he is a romantic lover who moves you to your very depths?" That quick little fellow, who seems almost like a living mathematical table, must now be imagined in another mood as capable of sweeping the young woman off her feet! I may add, "I'm utterly dumbfounded to hear it! It's completely outside my expectations."

Thus it is that revelation may and does confound as well as verify inference. But the inference is not invalid because it is confounded and transcended; it is indeed, in its own degree, verified. Of course, not all inferences are verified, only some. But it is enough for the natural theologian, looking at the thoughts and the hopes and the fears of a non-Christian world, to find at least some inferences which he can verify, even though he must then proceed to transcend and confound them with the tremendous glory of the whole gospel.

Greek and Hebrew

I have already remarked that the relationship of the gospel to philosophy is in many ways akin or parallel to its relationship to Hebrew prophecy. There also we see events at the same time fulfilling and transcending, transcending to the point of confounding, previous outlooks and expectations. Paul noted this parallelism in the first chapter of his first Epistle to the Corinthians when he remarked that the preaching of the gospel is "to the Jews a stumbling block; to the Greeks foolishness." This passage is sometimes appealed to by those theologians who make a particular point of stressing the Hebraic character of the Christian faith. Such writers often delight in elaborating a view which interprets the Greek outlook as the dialectical antithesis of the Hebrew mentality. They insist that any influence of Greek thought on the development of Christian theology must necessarily have been a corrupting one, estranging it from its own sources.

In fact, however, Paul's words assert both an analogy between the two and their relationship to the Christian gospel. Neither Hebrew religion nor Greek philosophy can receive the gospel as long as either of them regards itself as a closed and wholly satisfactory system. In other words, there were Hebrew as well as Greek reasons for refusing to accept the gospel. We may note in passing that the Christian Church has had to wrestle in its history with Judaizing as well as Hellenizing heresies and distortions of the gospel and that, on the whole, in the New Testament period, as perhaps in the epoch of Protestant religion and theology, the former danger presented the greater menace of the two. It is only if and when Hebrew religion and the kind of philosophy we have inherited from the Greeks are open systems, ready to receive new facts and experiences and ready to criticize their past insights and achievements in the light of them, that either can enter into the context of Christian faith and enrich the life of the Church with the values and spiritual and intellectual skills which each richly possesses. The controversy among modern theologians about the respective values of the Greek and Hebrew contributions to Christian theology is a barren and misleading one. It is only when men differ from each other in the same medium and in relation to the same questions that their differences commit them to lifelong opposition. It is precisely because the differences between the Greek and Hebrew outlooks were so great and fundamental that it was possible for them to ally themselves with each other and complement each other in the life and thought of the early Church, with such astonishing fruitfulness and epoch-making consequences.

Of course, Greek thought and Hebrew religion came into contact with each other and mutually influenced each other to a certain extent before the period of the Christian dispensation began, and to some extent they continued to do so, for example, in Philo and Hellenistic-Judaism and in the Jewish scholasticism of Maimonides a thousand years later, outside the limits of Christianity altogether. But it was in the life and thought of the early Church that there took place the most profound and important confrontation of the Hebrew and the Greek, and it was in that context that there was hammered out the mighty synthesis which it is still possible, indeed I should say necessary, for the Christian to regard and interpret as one of the great providential acts of God in human history.

Two Major Problems

Out of the chief types of natural theology, which I have attempted to describe very briefly, there arise two major problems. Particularly from the first, second, and third of the four forms of natural theology, which I described briefly, there arises the fundamental problem: in what sense, if any, may we validly suppose, believe, and say that some vestige of the image of God in man survives the catastrophe of the Fall? In what sense, also, if any, is some kind of analogy of being (*analogia entis,* as the theologians call it) permissible and possible in the thought of fallen man?

This is a problem indeed, but the other problem is an even greater one. From the third and fourth types of natural theology, in particular, there arises the whole question of the scope of theology as a science: can we rest content with a methodological conception of theology which makes it one specialism among many, a particular form of intellectual application and discipline which studies a certain selection of religious and Christian data connected with the original and basic deposit of faith? Very roughly, we may say that theology as a specialism studies the Bible, the history of the Church, and to a rather smaller extent the classic sub-Biblical documents which have appeared and achieved some kind of importance and vogue in Church history, *e.g.*, liturgies and the writings of such great classical theologians as Augustine, Aquinas, Luther, Calvin, and so on.

Shall we rest content with the methodological concept of theology as a specialism or shall we be driven in our modern world, with the tremendous and thrilling revival of theological studies and theological acumen which the twentieth century has witnessed, to an attempt to restate something like the medieval doctrine of a science which is not just *a* science but in some real sense the queen of the sciences— one in which we find the clue to the meaning and interpretation of all the other sciences.

The first of these two problems is of such immediate relevance at this stage of our discussion that we shall turn to it in the next chapter. The second problem, however, we shall for the moment leave on one side, returning to it at a later stage.

CHAPTER TWO

THE IMAGE OF GOD IN FALLEN MAN

The first of our two major problems (whether vestiges of the image of God have survived in fallen man) perhaps arises from what has been said far more obviously than the second. Many contemporary theologians, particularly in Europe, might well point out (in almost as many ways as there are theologians) that in all that we have said so far about some kind of Godward intellectual process of which the premises are naturalistic, the fact of the Fall and the consequences of the Fall for human knowledge and for what we call man's noetic capacities are overlooked. A great deal of authority can be cited from the central traditions of the Christian Church (not all of it necessarily from the great reformers—some also from the scholastics and from the fathers) for holding that the possibility of an intellectual movement toward God would have existed had man not fallen, but cannot be held to exist now that man has fallen.

Calvin's Epistemological Position

I am not at all sure whether all this authority can be quoted for some of the extreme radical positions which are adopted today. As I understand Calvin, for example, his real point is not so much that natural theology as conceived by some of his predecessors is impossible but rather that, because man is fallen and the human intellect is distorted and has become to a very large extent the instrument of his sin, the consequences of natural theology are idolatrous. It leads him to worship, not the living God of the Biblical revelation, but an intellectualized, private God of his own: his creature rather than his Creator.

I will not attempt to substantiate this interpretation of Calvin here, because the task would take me beyond the limits of this book. But I will ask the reader to accept this view as a *prima facie* possible interpretation of much that Calvin had to say; and I hasten to add that fundamentally I am in agreement with such a thesis, though there are certain qualifications which I propose to make. Somebody remarked that about a hundred years ago a certain American professor of theology is alleged to have said, "Of course, I wouldn't claim that Calvin is infallible; I will merely say that I have never found him to be wrong." With humility, I must admit that I could repeat those words without some exaggeration of my real feelings. Nevertheless, on any showing, and whatever one's situation or standpoint in Christendom, Calvin is one of the great theologians. His work and witness must be taken into account with reverence and consideration.

The Confusion Between Finitude and Sin

In much of the reformed theology since Calvin's day, particularly during the last century and a half (roughly since the publication of the first of Kant's three *Critiques*) there has grown up a position which appears to resemble Calvin's, but actually is not the same thing at all. Again, as I understand it, Calvin's position is that the trouble with human reasoning is that it always functions within a context of sin; whereas a very considerable amount of modern reformed theology, which has taken copious draughts of the critical epistemology of Immanuel Kant and his successors, says in effect that the trouble with human reasoning is not so much that man is a sinner as that man is finite.

Clearly, these are two very different statements. If the trouble with human reasoning is that man is a sinner, then indeed the fundamental maladies of human reasoning are in a real and profound sense accidental to his essential being, and therefore tragic. To say that man is a sinner is to set man in the category of tragedy. But to say that the trouble with human reasoning is that man is man (which is what the critical philosophers really say when they teach that it is the finitude of man's being which restricts his rational powers) is not to put man in the category of the tragic; it is to put man in the category of the unfortunate, a very different category indeed.

The Critical Philosophy

It has become more and more clear that the critical philosophy is widely regarded as the philosophical ally or even philosophical propaedeutic to theology, and that it plays, and has played, for a considerable number of reformed theologians, both of the Lutheran and Calvinist persuasions during the nineteenth and twentieth centuries, a role similar to that which Thomism plays in so much contemporary Roman Catholic theology.

It is an added paradox that the Ritschlians, for example, and whole generations of antimetaphysical German theologians really supposed that they had gotten rid of metaphysics simply because they had swallowed Kant's metaphysics! In other words, I wish to suggest that certain imperfections and prejudices and characteristic blindnesses which we find in a good deal of nineteenth and twentieth century reformation theology are not due to the Reformation but to Immanuel Kant, as well as to the confusion between finitude and sin.

This is not meant as a full-blast attack on that very great man, Immanuel Kant. It might have been more just if I had said the Kantians, or merely the critical philosophers and epistemologists, including, of course, the positivists. The trouble is that the only work so many people know of Immanuel Kant is the first *Critique*, and that turns them into positivists. Then we come to a second group who know both the first and the second *Critiques*, and that turns them into antimetaphysical existentialists. Then, very rarely, there are those who also know the third *Critique*, and I think that makes them wonder very much about some of the things they read in the first and second *Critiques!* But by the Kantians I mean primarily the people who, so to speak, sold their all in order to buy the first *Critique*, under the illusion that this is the pearl of great price; and this in effect means that they are antimetaphysical positivists.

The essential procedure of all antimetaphysical positivists is to show, by an elaborate argument which purports to be an inspection of our rational powers by our rational powers (or, if we prefer it, a self-inspection of our rational powers) that reality is divided into a knowable and an unknowable part, phase, aspect (whatever word we choose will be somewhat confusing and difficult). Thus, the mind of man is forever restricted to a certain area of reality which may be called the world of phenomena, or the public world of natural science, or whatever we choose. The rest of reality is the world of noumena or metaphysics, and this is declared to be unknowable.

For a certain kind of theologian, you can see how this seems to fit beautifully the requirements of a revelational, Biblical theology. It means that the proper work of reason is to be found in the natural sciences, and possibly in literary and historical criticism and activities, but that, so far as ultimate (or what we used to call metaphysical) truths are concerned, we are, and we must remain, verily and indeed babes unborn. Therefore, philosophy has demonstrated the emptiness of a niche which only revelation can fill. (There are many different ways of putting this argument, and for this reason I am schematizing it in a relatively simple form that we can grasp easily and apprehend.)

Can a Man Know Anything Utterly?

First of all I want to argue that we can have no conceivable ground or warrant for supposing the existence of that which is in principle unknowable, as distinct from that which is in fact unknown. By definition we can have no experience which suggests the existence of such a thing; and clearly, by definition, we can have no knowledge of it whatsoever.

Of course, it is true that man can know, or rather seem to himself to know, realities which do not exist, or harbor in his mind incorrect beliefs about realities which do exist. That is, man can be deceived and cherish illusions. Men have believed that the earth is flat, and some children suppose for a time that the moon is made of green cheese and is inhabited by one solitary resident. But the problem of human error cannot be resolved, the fact of human error cannot be interpreted, by the simple expedient of supposing that there is some sphere of thought and research in which error is inevitable and then contrasting it with some other sphere in which error is either impossible or at least avoidable. In whatever sphere men think and do research, error is possible; in no such sphere is it inevitable.

Again, men can imaginatively compose for themselves meaningless or nonsense notions by devising incompatible arrangements of words like "a round square" or "a green conception." It is better to describe such notions as nonsense rather than meaningless, for it is only because we know the meaning of the phrases that we see them to be nonsense. The term meaningless has become a popular one in recent and contemporary philosophy, but its vogue is unfortunate. No matter how we define meaninglessness, it remains true that we can only describe a statement or an idea as meaningless if we are in a position to perceive its meaning.

The disease of language, the propensity of savage or sophisticated man to indulge in mere words that mean and point to nothing beyond themselves, is indeed a reality and a real problem for philosophy, but again we cannot deal with this problem by the over-simple method, characteristic particularly of the logical positivists, of laying it down that in some one sphere of thought and research all statements are necessarily meaningless. After all, no sphere of thought and research is immune from the effects of this particular disease.

Thus, human thought is always and everywhere in danger of falling into nonsense or meaninglessness, subject to fits of mere verbalization. But the positivists are greatly mistaken if they suppose that they can vanquish such dangers merely by placing a veto on all future indulgence in metaphysical speculation or by any arbitrary splitting of reality into knowable and unknowable phases or departments. Such a method will avail neither to banish the nonsense from the human mind nor to lead us to a right interpretation of the intellectual handicap inherent in our finitude.

My main charge against the critical and positivist philosophers is that they rightly perceive the finitude of man but misinterpret it. They say in effect, "The mark of the finitude of man is that there are a lot of things which in principle he cannot know." It seems to me much more profoundly true that the real mark of the finitude of the human intellect is that there is *nothing* which man can *utterly* know. The moment they define an unknowable part of reality, which is useless for us to bother about, there always is the suggestion that there is a knowable part which we can really know through and through.

In my opinion, this second suggestion is as unwarrantable as the first suggestion, and even more dangerous and intellectually misleading. Nearly always, the critical philosophy begins by being very humble about the human intellect and says, "It's no good our thinking about all these metaphysical questions because they exceed our rational powers," but it almost always ends by being unwarrantably dogmatic and complacent about that which it supposes we can know. For sheer contemporary dogmaticism, commend me to the logical positivists! They compensate themselves for the vast intellectual and metaphysical sacrifices they have made, the tremendous deed of abdication which they have signed in the name of humanity, by insisting that the little bit that is left is utterly and completely theirs: "Here, in this sphere, you can still dream your dreams of grandeur and glory and intellectual mastery!" In other words, it is a pseudo-humility when a man irresponsibly resigns a kingdom in order to become the autocrat of a cabbage patch.

On the contrary, what we really do know and what we have some warrant in experience for saying, is that all the realities of which we are aware are realities which we cannot entirely contain within our intellect; that whenever man has to do with reality, he cannot know it exhaustively, not even the simplest reality. Hence, he has to invent the various shortcuts to knowledge: for example, all the forms of scientific knowledge which employ a generalizing, pigeon-hole method. This achieves knowledge by subsuming particulars under generalizations.

Take the phenomena of swans. I do not know how many swans there are in the world or how many swans there have been or how many swans there will be, but I do know that a complete list of all the possible general propositions about swans that it is possible to frame will not tell us all the truth about any one swan, let alone all the other swans. Even the finite thing has an infinity of potentially true propositions which may be made about it. The real mark of the finitude of the human mind is that no matter what reality it grasps and wrestles with, in some way the reality always escapes. This to me is the real significance of what some people call "the infinite regress," what Kant called "the antinomy," and, fundamentally, what Kierkegaard called "the paradox." The infinite regress, to my mind, is the sign that we are in touch with reality.

I first met the infinite regress when I was a very little boy. We used to eat a breakfast cereal, which I still see in the shops, called Post Toasties. In those days the box was most fascinating. It contained the picture of a little girl with long hair kneeling in front of a fire. Beside her was a box of Post Toasties, and on that box was a little girl with long hair, beside a fire, and near her was a box of Post Toasties! The artist had given up the ghost quite early, because that third box of Post Toasties had just a little squiggle on it. I was about four or five years old and pointed out to my father that really this never ended, it went on and on, box of Post Toasties, box of Post Toasties, box of Post Toasties, forever.

41

The artist could stop but the philosopher could not! My father replied, "Yes, my boy, but perhaps one day you will think that everything is like that fundamentally." Always, what we are left with is the knowledge that there is more to know. We push on and push on and push on, and we never get to the bottom of reality. The mind of man can never contain all of any reality, not even a box of Post Toasties.

The Corruption of Man's Situation

It seems to me this is the characteristic mark of the finitude of the human intellect: that *there is nothing which is utterly knowable,* not that there are a lot of things which are in principle unknowable. The doctrine that some things are in principle unknowable (the doctrine, that is, that the human intellect is not made for reality and not oriented toward it) seems to me to be identified with the doctrine of the Fall only by confusion. It is not the finitude of the human intellect which bedevils our thinking; it is the corruption and corruptibility of the human social situation, the psychological context within which that thinking is conducted.

In this way, although we may be forced to differ with a good many contemporary reformation theologians, we are actually getting closer to what *the* great reformation theologian really believed and taught. He did not confuse sin and finitude as certain contemporary theologians are inclined to do. Sometimes, as I read these modern theologians, I do not know whether according to them the trouble is that man is sinner or that man is man; and I do not know whether they confuse man's sin with his humanity, but I do know what they ought to mean. They ought to mean that the trouble is that man is sinner, and not at all that man is man.

In other words, it can be no part of our case or belief or argument that man is cut off by nature from reality. Reality must always exceed and transcend man's powers, but I personally agree with Duns Scotus that the intellect is by nature so flexible, so adaptable, and so resourceful that no reality is in principle outside its apprehension, though, because man's intellect is finite, every real thing is in principle outside the grasp of its comprehension, even our own being.

If this is true, we can retrace our steps once more, because now our problem is not the problem of how man can have a natural theology as a finite being, because a natural theology surely must deal with infinitely high matters beyond the power of the human intellect; now the real problem is: what is the effect of sin upon thought? First, however, 1 ought to summarize my reasons for rejecting any belief about the Fall that regards it as totally destroying both the image of God in man and man's capacity to perceive certain analogies between reality and the divine.

The ANALOGIA ENTIS

Barth rejects what he calls the *analogia entis* (the analogy of being), dismissing it as the characteristically Roman Catholic doctrine. (I am not convinced that this is in fact *the* characteristically Roman Catholic doctrine, but I have no doubt at all that most Roman Catholics believe in it.) Barth substitutes what he calls the *analogia fidei* (the analogy of faith); but I do not think his doctrine really meets, explains, those analogies between reality and the divine which are most familiar to us: the New Testament parables.

For example, a certain woman lost half a dollar, and she sweeps under every bit of furniture until she finds it, despite the fact that there are a dozen dollars in her purse. We do not add to the effect if we say, "A certain *Christian* woman lost half a dollar," and "in faith she sweeps." She does not do it in faith; she does it just because she is human. That is where the analogy is drawn. To say "A certain *believing* father had two sons" does not add anything to the parable; the parable simply gives us a human father, not a father who acts as he does in faith, but a father who acts as he does because he is a father. There is no doubt in my mind, as I look at the parables, that this is what the theologians mean by the *analogia entis.*

Sometimes we have the *analogia entis* in its, so to speak, existential phase, as "A certain man had two sons"; and the analogy is drawn in terms of the relationship of the father to his sons. But sometimes, as for example where the analogy is drawn from certain happenings within the life of nature, it has a cosmic basis. The nature parables are not parables of slow growth, but rather parables of secret growth and of an extremely surprising harvest. They are eschatological parables drawn from the life of nature. Here is this tiny piece of matter called a mustard seed, that a breath can blow away, and yet a huge plant comes out of it. It is a secret and above all an extraordinarily surprising process, so quick, so sudden, so complete a transformation. This is certainly the *analogia entis.* We must remember that the parables are not used first of all in the instruction of what we may call the faithful. They are expounded and interpreted later to the inner group of disciples. They are first used as forms of communication with all and sundry, with such human beings as happen to be present.

The Survival of the IMAGO DEI

Would such an analogical process as we have just looked at be possible in a world in which the *imago* had been entirely destroyed by the Fall, so that the *humanum* (the whole life of humanity) could no longer be said to exhibit any vestiges at all of the image of God? To my mind, it would be difficult to conceive how such a process could possibly take place. The parables imply some kind of vestige of the image, and I take it that by saying, "man is in the image of God," and by using the phrase, *imago Dei*, we mean that the life of man presents us with the possibility of deducing valid theological analogies.

The doctrine that man is made in the image of God is present in the Old Testament, although rarely referred to. We cannot determine the comparative importance of a Biblical notion simply by counting the number of occasions on which Scripture explicitly refers to it; on the contrary, its importance is manifested in the extent to which other passages in Scripture presuppose it without any explicit reference whatever. (This is one of the reasons why a merely verbal and literary exegetical treatment of Scripture is insufficient. The interpretation of the Bible must always be a theological as well as a literary activity.)

In the New Testament it is Jesus Christ, the God-man, rather than merely man, who presents the image of God.

Man has to be remade in the image of God in and by and through the redemptive forces let loose among men by the eternal Image who is also the eternal Word of God. (The most exhaustive list of possible prepositions will not, of course, do justice to the subtle reality and many-sidedness of the spiritual processes of which the New Testament speaks.)

Perhaps there is some danger in the simple, unsophisticated statement that man is made in the image of God. This too easily suggests that everything which enters into the present human reality in some sense reflects the Divine Being, and there can be little doubt that the doctrine of the image often meant for the Hebrew religious consciousness in Old Testament times that God has a body, the outlines of which are mirrored or reflected in the human body. It is better to stress the preposition and say that man is made *in* the image of God, or if we prefer it, to say that man contains the image or presents or reflects certain aspects of the image.

Thus, when I look in a mirror, the mirror reflects my face but not the back of my head; and although a part of my image is reflected in the mirror, it is not true to say that the whole mirror is my image. To me it seems impossible to proclaim either that the whole reality of man is the image of God or that the whole reality of God is reflected in such an image of Him as the human reality presents. I prefer to say that certain peak aspects of the human being—rationality, freedom, capacity for love, personality or uniqueness, spirituality, a need and craving for God, a native orientation of mind in a Godward direction, a sense of humor—do indeed reflect certain aspects of the Divine Being. As a result there remains in human life, even fallen human life, the possibility of detecting and elaborating valid analogies by means of which we can approach and grow in a knowledge and understanding of God. It is this possibility that enabled Christ to utter the New Testament parables, and it is this possibility that enables us to devise for ourselves similar means of religious communication in the contemporary world.

The image is that from which we can draw a valid analogy which will give some sort of clue to, or information about, that which the image reflects. Where there is an image there is the possibility of analogy, though it may often be little more than a possibility, and only very rarely an actuality. In this sense, it seems to me that we must hold to the belief that we may properly speak of the survival of some vestige of the image of God in man despite the catastrophe of the Fall.

Again, I do not think that any of the basic religious values which those who go further and deny the possibility of any such survival at all wish to uphold are necessarily abandoned in what I have said. These basic religious values are man's complete dependence upon the power and mercy of God. Certainly, we all wish to assert these values. Every Christian must agree that man is not only finite and contingent and dependent upon the power of God, but also a sinner dependent utterly upon the mercy and the grace of God. These values must be upheld by any Christian who proposes to preach the gospel; for if they are not true, there is no point in preaching any gospel, because man would not need one. He might need a little bracing and exhortation now and then (a little "uplift" as it is called), but he would not need a gospel. Clearly, any man who proposes to preach a gospel must hold this kind of belief about the human predicament and about man's relation to God.

But it has never seemed to me that in order to maintain this position, we need go to the length of denying any kind of survival whatsoever of the image in fallen man. In other words, to say that all men are sinners and dependent upon God's mercy does not seem to me to imply or require a belief in the total disappearance of the image and of all vestiges of God's original purpose and norms for men as a result of the catastrophe of the Fall.

On the contrary, especially if we are thinking in terms of the major and central Calvinistic belief in the power of God, there is a very real difficulty about conceiving the Fall as total. To say that the Fall has entirely obliterated all vestiges of the image of God in man is surely to attribute an immense potentiality to sin—a potentiality which it is very difficult for us to attribute to any activity of the finite and the human, even if we add the sin of the fallen angels to the sin of man. I remember a profound phrase from, I think, the Authorized Version of the Book of Ecclesiastes (whose subsequent fate in many revisions I have forborne to trace, for I like it so very much as it is): "Whatsoever God doeth, he doeth it for ever."

Surely, we must believe that there is still some sense in which the "divinity shapes our ends, roughhew them how we will," that the stamp of God's work and the reality of God's purpose is still upon us, despite our sin.

The Wounding of Man

Indeed, would the tragedy of man be so tragic if his Fall were total? Surely the tragedy of human existence as we know it lies precisely in the way in which it brings conflict and deformation into the very length and breadth and depth of our human being. A total Fall, a complete corruption, might at least have spared us that, for it is not our experience that the conflict is known only in the mind of the converted man who still belongs to a fallen world, who is still tempted and still sins. We find, on the contrary, crowding in upon us every day, evidence of the immense destructive scale and scope of the conflict in every man, wherever he may be. In other words, a picture of man deeply and gravely wounded by the Fall, desperately ill as a consequence of the Fall, and yet still in some sense man, fits the actual situation of being a fallen human being, and our existential experience of that predicament, very much better than any doctrine of total Fall.

Sometimes I wonder (though I forbear to press this) whether in this doctrine of the titanic character of human sin there is not a kind of strange, inverted humanism. I wonder whether, in renouncing forever the illusions of inherent righteousness—the illusion that man is a being who is in process of evolving through time toward an ultimate perfection—there is not a tendency to say in effect, "Well, no doubt man was a bit of a failure in the part of the saint, but see how he plays the sinner! What an heroic sinner he can be, and how boldly he wrestles against God!" In this tremendous stress upon the way in which the Fall has undone man and, according to some theologians, obliterated every vestige of the image in man and destroyed in him every capacity to trace in himself or in his surroundings any kind of analogy to the being of the Creator, I do sometimes sense and detect this kind of "humanism turned upside down." Here the glory of man turns out to be a bestiality which, at least, is a tribute to the power of his sin to thwart the purpose of his Maker.

A Verification of the Effect of Sin

I have suggested that we are wisest and closest to human experience (including our evangelical experience of the Gospel as we find it in Scripture) if we do not regard the Fall of man as quite total, and if we see in man, as we know him and as we *are* him, some surviving vestiges of the image of God and some clue to the being and character of God. These, we have admitted, are not enough to get man very far if left to himself, because of the distorted character of his sinful thinking.

The stress on the distorting pressure of sin upon reason is the part of the Calvinist tradition with which I want to agree very strongly, without any critical reservations at all. Of course, it is not peculiar to the Calvinist tradition. Thomas Aquinas knew about it, and so, indeed, did Augustine. But, they were perhaps prone at times, a little airily, to assume that complete intellectual integrity (a complete swaying and guiding of the reason of man in and by the light of the reasoning of God) is a more frequent event in human history and a moral quality more easy to come by than it really is.

In the modern world we know a good deal more about the wounding of human intellectual integrity by the sin and selfishness of man, because we have had at least two major scientific theories (one from sociology and one from psychology) which in a way have verified what we may call "the theological hypothesis." These are: first, the theory of the ideology—the theory of the distorting pressure of our group interests upon our thought. Second, the theory of the rationalization—the theory of the way in which our complexes and our suppressed and unconscious wishes (and sometimes our conscious wishes) influence the direction and current of our thought, and often overthrow and confound our intellectual integrity.

The theory of the ideology was first stated by Marx, and the theory of the rationalization by Freud. That does not mean that these theories were perfectly stated by either of these writers. Quite clearly they were not. To both men, however, credit must be given for discovering new ideas of the utmost importance. Both of them, although perhaps unwittingly, are really studying the ways in which the Fall and human sin dominate human thought and confound the reason. We now know that a great deal of what supposes itself to be, and is often supposed to be, genuine ratiocination (true honest thinking) is in fact either ideology or rationalization or some combination of both. In other words, as so often happens, and as we should like to see happening more and more (indeed Christian thinkers must be continually conducting intellectual experiments with the object of adding to the known instances of this important process), the theological dogma is turned into a sociological or psychological hypothesis and verified by subsequent sociological or psychological thought and research.

We ought not to be disturbed by these truths. I can never understand why Christians are sometimes horrified by revelations of this kind. For example, when I meet with Christians who are scandalized by the Freudian uncovering of the seamy side of the unconscious, or perhaps by the rather dubious calculations of Mr. Kinsey, I am inclined to say at once, "But, my dear fellow, why are you surprised? I thought you believed in the Fall. The man who believes in the Fall should at least be unshockable!" It is indeed an odd paradox if a man says he believes in the Fall of man yet is shocked at anything human. Let us leave it to the romantic humanists to be shocked at these revelations. Being shocked at this kind of thing is no part of our game, so to speak.

It is strange that so many people who proclaim that they accept the orthodox belief in original sin are so little aware of the meaning and implications of their own theology that they are continually surprised and scandalized by the spectacle of the visible sins of their neighbors. After all, the visible sins are no more than the outward manifestation of the underlying sinfulness, and the orthodox Christian should not be particularly shocked or surprised by their evidence.

Similarly, as we come to know more about the sins and sinfulness concealed in the lower depths of the human mind, the Christian should accept this new knowledge as a further confirmation of his own theological beliefs, neither surprising nor shocking, but precisely what his theology should lead him to expect. The laconic President Coolidge's Baptist preacher was described as being against sin. But more profoundly understood, however, the essentially Christian attitude is against sinfulness rather than against sin, against the underlying causal malady rather than against the outward consequences and symptoms, and in no circumstances whatsoever against the sinner.

One of the troubles with many of the morally censorious Christians, who know not of what theological spirit they are, is that they are not merely shocked and scandalized by the spectacle of real sins, but they are shocked and scandalized by the spectacle of sins which they have, so to speak, invented for themselves by their own puritanical prohibitions. Some Christians believe it is sinful to dance, drink a glass of wine or beer, attend a theater, or play a game of cards. An earnest evangelical character in a contemporary play remarks, "Coffee is so nice. I can't understand why it isn't a sin." But there are groups of Christians for whom even drinking coffee is a sin. The odd thing is that such Christians are almost always pious evangelical sectarians who delight to proclaim that the Bible and the Bible alone provides them with their sole authority and rule of life.

Where in Holy Scripture, we may ask, can we find the smallest warrant for the puritanical habit of inventing new and more categories of sin? Surely, the Puritan's hatred of joy, his unseemly delight in a disapproval of his neighbors, has nothing whatever to do with Biblical Christianity. The trouble with this puritanical misunderstanding and abuse of Christian doctrine is that it tends to make the Church's theology of original sinfulness and actual sin ridiculous in theory and nauseating in practice. There are quite enough real sins without our inventing new ones. In any case, the visible sins are not the heart of the matter. What God is dealing with in and through the Gospel is primarily the profoundly submerged sinfulness inherent in man's present fallen condition. It is precisely because this is true that a scrupulously observant morality, as the Christian preacher has to proclaim so insistently and so often, is not enough.

No doubt a scrupulously observant morality can deal fairly efficiently with most of the sins most of the time, but it cannot even begin to touch the inward and underlying sinfulness. Perservering morality is not enough; man has to be redeemed and re-created. If this is so, any and every kind of new knowledge that reveals and brings home to us the depth and extent of the malady which besets our being should be warmly welcomed by the Christian mind.

Man, as psychoanalysis reveals him, is certainly not a being whose problem can be solved by rigorous prohibitions. Indeed, despite the philosophical and theological confusions which cloud the counsels of so many psychoanalysts, they have on the whole been right to protest against the folly and futility of attempting to solve deep-seated human problems and tensions by the mere mechanism of repression. They are not merely pragmatically right, but they are also theologically right, more profoundly Christian than the Puritans against whose regime they protested. The God who reveals Himself in Jesus Christ is not a repressor who shuts man up in a moral reformatory, but a Saviour who sets man free.

Ideology as Sin

The aim of this digression has been to show how the theories of the ideology and the rationalization, and the new and deeper dimensions of sinfulness which they have revealed, may be interpreted as a very welcome and very real verification of a profound theological hypothesis about man, and the effect of his sinfulness on the whole course of his life and thought. But, let us notice this with some care: ideology and the rationalization are processes which can distort and poison not only our philosophical and metaphysical thinking, not only our thinking in the sphere of natural theology, but equally, let us admit it, our thinking in any sphere whatsoever, including the sphere of what we may call revelational or Biblical and dogmatic theology.

For example, about two years ago I was at a conference in Switzerland where we met many theologians whose native tongue was German. One of the most distinguished of these (whose name would be recognized at once if I mentioned it: a man who has labored long to eliminate from theological thinking every external social or secular pressure and interest) remarked at the end of the meeting, in his loudest prophetic tones (I say prophetic because he is normally inclined to say *no* to almost everything and everybody):

"The great burning reality about which God cares in this present time is the reunification of Germany."

Let me remind you that if one of us had said, "The great thing in God's eyes at the moment is the Atlantic community" or "the Americo-British alliance" or something of the kind, how he would have pounced on us! With what prophetic fury he would have denounced us and rent us and left us without a rag of self-respect to our names. Yet, the reunification of Germany was for him in quite a different category.

55

Thus, all of us can be caught. All forms of human thinking can be affected by ideological motives. Let me use an illustration from another sphere altogether. We observe the same process in the development of Marxist criticism and self-criticism. Obviously, the first difficulty for the Marxist theory of the ideology is the question: "Is Marxism itself an ideology?" At first sight it may appear that Marxism is merely the ideology of the revolutionary proletariat, but the Marxists can never admit this. For them, Marxism is not ideology. Marxism is a science, and science is never ideological (at least, so they supposed at first). Then the problem arises: how and in what sense is Marxism a science? And, in what way must we re-define the word *science* in order to make it clear that Marxism is science, whereas other and fundamentally kindred political and social doctrines are not science.

This is not easy, but at least it gives us a new dogma —science is non-ideological. Science is the one sphere of thought that is immune from all ideological distortion. But what happens in Marxism in the twentieth century? Here, we find the physical scientists suddenly accused and purged because of bourgeois deviations into a pseudo-scientific idealism. Then, the biologists and the economists are purged for more or less the same reason. Apparently, science can be ideological after all. Thus, the original reason for holding that Marxism itself is not ideology falls to the ground.

There is a witty passage in Arthur Koestler's novel, *The Age of Longing*, which charmingly satirizes the consequences of the Soviet discovery that science, like anything else, is subject to ideological pressures. He writes:

In fact, Lord Edwards in his young days had made an original contribution to Lemaitre's theory of the expanding universe. But shortly afterwards the Central Committee of the Commonwealth decreed that the universe was not expanding, and that the whole theory was a fabrication of bourgeois scientists reflecting the imperialist drive for the conquest of new markets.

The "hyenas of expansionist cosmology" were duly purged and Edwards, though he lived safely in England and had nothing to fear, published a book in which he proved that the universe was in peaceful equilibrium, without ever intending to expand. After the second world war, when the Commonwealth began to incorporate the neighboring republics and to spread its frontiers towards East and West, the Central Committee decided that the universe was expanding after all, and that the theory of a static universe was a fabrication of bourgeois science, reflecting the stagnant decay of capitalist economy. After some twenty million factory workers and collective farmers had sent in resolutions calling for death to the "stagnationist vermin," Edwards published another book proving that the universe was indeed expanding, had always been expanding and would go on expanding *ad infinitum*.[1]

By the Grace of God

There is no form of human thought which is immune from some kind of twisting; therefore it is always fallacious to fix upon some particular form of thought and say, "Ah, that consists purely of ideology and rationalization." Let us be quite frank about it. If it is true that the products of thinking in the realms of natural theology can be and sometimes are idolatrous, the same thing is true in the sphere of revelational theology. That too can culminate in some form of

[1] Arthur Koestler, *The Age of Longing* (New York: Macmillan, 1951), p. 83. Used by permission of the publisher.

idolatry. The living God of the Bible is not necessarily identical with the God excogitated by the Biblical theologian.

We are all subject to this danger. All our thinking is infected by a desire not only to attain the truth, but at the same time to affirm social and personal values which, because we are what we are and where we are, we want to affirm. This process is always fundamentally idolatrous, a way of pretending to ourselves and to others that God wishes what we wish, that He confirms and is the source of our prejudices and preferences. But the burden is not to be borne by natural theology alone, or by metaphysics and philosophy alone. Wherever men are men, and wherever sinful men are thinking and seeking the truth, they have to arm themselves and guard themselves against such temptations as these.

Thus, it is always necessary for us to scrutinize and cross-examine our intellectual consciences in order to detect within ourselves, before it is too late, any tendency to make an ideological use of our religious and theological beliefs. There exists a group of Christians in the United States who are banded together for the propagation of the belief (they even publish a small journal devoted to this theme) that what is called a "free economy" has a special divine sanction that raises it above all other economic systems and that it exists where it does exist, and must be brought into existence where it does not exist, in accordance with the will of God.

I once heard a distinguished professor of economics at Geneva, a member of the Swiss Reformed Church, expound precisely the same view. The capitalist free economy was for him the Christian economy.

Perhaps an even more widespread example of the same kind of error is the prevalent tendency to suppose that there is something especially Christian about the democratic way of organizing our political life. I am not thinking here of the way in which many non-Christian thinkers tend to turn democracy into a kind of religion in its own right, with much talk of democratic values, the democratic way of life, and even the democratic virtues, and so on. What I have in mind is a tendency on the part of many Christians to speak of democracy almost as though it were part of their faith.

Now I have no doubt that in appropriate circumstances both a free market economy and a democratic polity can be excellent things. Even then, however, as we know too well, both are liable to corruption. As with all other economies and polities, neither can function efficiently except in a society where workers and citizens reverence justice and fair dealing and are imbued with an integrity of purpose and motive, worship God, and strive to practice the Christian virtues.

In the last resort, all economies and polities are constructed by fallen men in a fallen world. All of them are precarious and in danger of judgment. A free economy will not flourish long, or secure justice and human happiness, in a merely selfish wealth-worshipping society. No democratic polity can secure its foundations or prolong its life in a world of individualists who seek only their own preferences and pleasures. In other words, both of these things

59

can be excellent and desirable forms in their own way, but neither of them is a part of the divine dispensation, and neither of them is immune from the judgment of God.

There is no way of winning total immunity, save by the grace of God. The thinker, remember, requires the grace of God just as much as anyone else—not that the thinker is a peculiar kind of man, for no man spends the whole of his life thinking, and presumably few men pass through the whole of their lives without ever thinking. But whenever a man is thinking deliberately and systematically and saying, in effect, "Under the providence of God, some work of thought is my vocation," let him remember that, just as much as any other man whose life is dedicated to any other form of activity, he needs the grace of God not only to save and redeem him but also to sanctify him and keep him on the right pathway for his particular vocation. This is important for us all, whether we attempt to adumbrate some kind of natural theology or not.

CHAPTER THREE

THE ACHIEVEMENT OF NATURAL THEOLOGY

In this chapter we shall have to consider how far, taking both the past and the present into account, the kind of thinking which we call natural theology has produced any results of positive and lasting value. We shall have to treat the subject in very broad outline indeed. Nothing like a history of natural theology will be possible within the restricted space at our disposal. Instead, we shall have to summarize what seems to me the essence of various types of natural theology with very little attempt to give them the individual flavor which they naturally possess in the context of the work and thought of any particular writer. Again, we shall be able to consider natural theology only in what seems to me to be its very best forms. Of course, the history of natural theology is littered with bad arguments, just like the history of any kind of theology—or any kind of anti-theology, for that matter. In other words we shall confine ourselves in most cases to broadly summarized, non-individuated types of thought which possess some kind of permanent and abiding validity or interest.

The Cosmological Argument in Philosophical Dress

The argument from the existence of the world to the existence of God—that is, to the existence of some kind of directive agency which transcends and yet is responsible for, and therefore implied by, the existence of the world—can choose either of two distinct points of departure. It can begin simply with the mere fact that there is a world, however much or however little we may know about it, and argue in a purely philosophical way about the implications of finite and contingent existence. An argument of this kind will be possible and perhaps valid even if we know nothing whatever about the world except the fact of its mere existence. Alternatively, the cosmological argument may select for its point of departure some kind of scientific knowledge which we suppose ourselves to possess about the world, in which case, of course, its validity may be undermined by the subsequent course of scientific speculation and research.

In the case of any particular writer it is often difficult to determine whether his point of departure is scientific or philosophical. Thus, Aristotle probably began with his scientific beliefs about the nature of the physical universe and the processes characteristic of it—his *Metaphysics,* as the name implies, is intended to be a kind of sequel to his *Physics*—but in later centuries his arguments had much more influence on philosophers than on physical scientists, and they gradually detached themselves from their original basis in Greek science. Thus, St. Thomas Aquinas, the great

Christian Aristotelian, can point out that it makes no difference to arguments of this kind whether the physical universe had any beginning in time or not. This is St. Thomas's way of detaching the kind of cosmological argument that he inherited from Aristotle from any particular scientific belief about the nature of the physical universe. In his view the mere fact of the existence of the physical universe— a kind of existence, that is, which is finite and contingent and altogether incapable of explaining its own reality— proves the existence of God and will prove the existence of God even if its form and appearance were quite different from that which we know from our experience and our sciences it in fact possesses. This is the purely philosophical version of the argument. Not merely this physical universe but any kind of physical universe whatsoever can prove the existence of God.

This gives us the essence of all forms of the cosmological argument, however clumsy or however profound. Physical existence in its very nature is finite and contingent. It does not have to be as it is, for we can quite easily imagine that it may be otherwise. It does not even have to be at all, for we can quite easily imagine its nonexistence. It simply *happens to be*. It has always an inescapably, accidental character. This is what the philosophers mean when they say that physical existence is contingent. Such an assertion is not a scientific proposition, for it is equally true in any conceivable or imaginable kind of physical universe whatsoever. In other words, the observation that the physical universe, any physical universe, must be contingent is not the kind of proposition which can either be confirmed or refuted by any possible inductive survey or analysis of the facts and processes of which it is made up. Any such reality is a contingent reality which might conceivably, that is without logical self-contradiction, have been otherwise or not have been at all.

All forms of the cosmological argument amount in essence to this: an insistence that contingent being can only exist if there is some necessary being which is responsible for the contingency. Contingent being, being that merely happens to be, can only be explained if we infer from it the existence of necessary being, being that has to be, and being that carries within itself the necessity and ground of its own existence. This is not necessarily an argument for what has been called first cause. Quite conceivably, the physical universe may have existed from all eternity and may have had no beginning in time at all. But even so, it cannot explain its own existence. An eternal physical system will still be a contingent physical system, which might have been otherwise than it is and might even not have been at all.

Another way of expressing substantially the same argument is to dwell on the contrast between actuality and possibility. In this world many more things may possibly happen than those which actually do happen. Because I am here in my study composing these particular sentences, I am not in any one of the many other places in which I might equally well have been. Nobody would have said that the laws of reality had been flouted or outraged if, instead, I had taken the morning off and gone to visit a friend or gone out into the town to do a little personal shopping. Every event seems to select one among many alternatives which would have been equally possible, and in selecting this one possibility to negate all the others. Thus, the passage from mere possibility to concrete actuality seems always to depend upon some kind of selective activity which transcends the event itself. Once we see that the existence of this universe as a whole is similarly a fact which selects one possibility from among innumerable others, it becomes clear that the existence of the universe implies one supreme, transcendent selective activity, apart from which the coming into existence of anything else would have been inconceivable.

Considered simply in itself, then, the sheer givenness, the brute factuality of the universe is not rational. Science as such can take the observed facts of the universe for its point of departure, and defer to the facts with a kind of humble natural piety which, from the Christian point of view, is one of the best, most valid, and ennobling aspects of the scientific attitude. But philosophy cannot take sheer factuality as its point of departure. For philosophy factuality itself lies at the very heart of the mystery. Why any facts? Why these particular facts? The question which philosophy asks cannot be asked in terms of the facts simply because the mystery of the sheer factuality of the facts constitutes the essential question. That is why purely philosophical arguments are quite independent of any particular state of scientific knowledge. They have precisely the same degree of validity in an age of biological evolution and atomic physics as they possessed centuries ago before any of these scientific developments were thought of. The answers to such philosophical questions do not tell us more about the facts, or even help us to relate the facts to one another in a more satisfactory way. They simply help to clear up for us the problem of what is involved in the sheer factuality of the facts, any facts, facts known to us or facts unknown.

The validity of this type of argument is thus quite independent of the existing state of our scientific knowledge. But what measure of validity do arguments of this kind possess? It seems to me obvious that *if* we are justified in trusting our reason to take us this far, to push beyond the stage of scrutinizing and relating facts to one another into the deeper waters in which we seek to ask and answer questions about ultimate being itself, then the argument which concludes "that because contingent being exists necessary being must exist" is one which carries with it, to say the least, a very high degree of probability and conviction.

We must admit, on the other hand, that the particular *if* is a very big *if* indeed. Since the time of Emmanuel Kant a considerable number of philosophers have doubted whether the human reason can be trusted to carry us this far. They have held that the human reason is a finite and pragmatic instrument designed by nature to enable us to cope with the facts of life, but certainly not designed by nature to carry us beyond the facts of life into the sphere of those deeper questions about ultimate reality in the service of which traditional philosophy and natural theology have endeavored to employ it. I have already discussed the kind of critical philosophy which seeks to delimit and restrict the scope of the human reason. I think, myself, that this kind of philosophy is probably mistaken in its aim. I am convinced that to delimit and restrict the scope of human reason by a self-critical rational activity is a mistaken and self-contradictory enterprise. Reason cannot trace its own boundaries without transcending its own boundaries. In other words, the so-called critical philosophy is continually guilty of arguing "in a circle."

Nevertheless, although I *think* that this kind of philosophy is probably mistaken, I am not in a position, nor is anyone else, to say that it is certainly mistaken. For this reason I do not care to claim, with many Roman Catholic philosophers, that the cosmological kind of argument, at its very best, demonstrates the bare existence of God beyond all rational doubt. I prefer to say that it makes the existence of God highly probable, much more probable indeed than any alternative hypothesis.

What this kind of argument really depends upon is a faith in human reason, a belief that sheer reason is capable, when functioning with a maximum degree of analytic power and intellectual integrity—which, of course, in a fallen world it rarely does—of conducting us into the very heart of the profoundest mysteries of ultimate being. The philosophical way of believing in God thus rests upon, and is intimately connected with, a profound faith in the human reason as among the very highest of God's gifts to men. It is perhaps no small thing to have thus perceived and defined the close connection between our faith in God and our faith in reason.

Our faith in God supports our faith in reason because it indicates that reason is no mere animal attribute, which man has slowly evolved and perfected through time as a pragmatic weapon by means of which he may wrestle with and overcome his physical environment. On the contrary, it affirms that reason is one of those characteristic spiritual gifts in virtue of which we are able to say that man is made in the image of God. After all, it would not be sufficient if man were merely a rational being in an irrational universe. That would be as futile a situation as that of a being equipped with the sense of hearing in a universe in which there was nothing to be heard. There is not much point in being rational except in a rational universe. To be equipped by nature always to look out for the rational in a universe in which in fact nothing is rational would be a frustrating and an inefficacious condition. Then, too, we cannot make much sense of what we may call the pragmatic success of reason unless we suppose that there is a reason over against us, a reason eminently in and transcendently behind the things we reason about, as well as a reason within us. But if faith in God, which is, among many other things, a faith in an ultimate and utterly effective reason, thus reinforces and sustains our faith in reason itself, then we shall be more inclined to listen to the kind of reasoning which sustains and gives rational conviction to our faith in God by discovering in Him the clue to the mystery of the existence of everything that is less than God. Faith in God sustains faith in reason, and faith in reason reinforces faith in God. At first sight this looks rather similar to a circular argument, but the "circle" is not in fact an argument at all; it is the circle of completeness, the rounded, satisfying pattern which our arguments assume in relation to one another once we have brought them to something like perfection.

The Cosmological Argument in Scientific Dress

In its purest and probably its best form the cosmological argument, as we have seen, is independent of any particular state of our scientific knowledge, but from time to time attempts have been made to elaborate arguments for the existence of God by showing that He is implied by certain particular scientific theories or basic scientific principles. Such arguments have the disadvantage that they may be rendered out of date by further advances in scientific theory, but so long as the doctrines and principles which they employ remain in vogue they may have a certain limited value and force. Most arguments of this kind are not so much arguments for the existence of God as attempts to show that the world must have had a beginning in time. They are thus arguments for the necessity of believing in a creation. But a creation presumably implies a creator, and such arguments are therefore arguments for the existence of God, at least by implication.

Certainly, if it can be shown that the physical universe had a beginning in time and has only existed for a finite time, such an item of knowledge will go far toward confirming the philosopher's view, if it needs any such confirmation, that the physical universe is contingent. Strictly speaking, it does not require any such confirmation. As we have seen, St. Thomas Aquinas was right to perceive that the existence of the universe would be contingent even if it had no beginning in time. Nevertheless, the fact that the universe had a beginning in time, if it can be scientifically established, will certainly corroborate the belief that its existence is neces-

sarily contingent. If, however, scientific forms of the cosmological argument can do no more than corroborate the philosophical belief in the contingency of the universe, they still
require reinforcement by some form of the philosophical
cosmological argument if they are to push beyond demonstrating that the universe had a beginning in time to the
conclusion that such a beginning in time necessarily points
to the existence of a creator who transcends both time and
the physical universe altogether. In other words, the scientific forms of the cosmological argument do not really replace, or substitute for, the philosophical form; they are
more like attempts to verify in scientific terms the minor
premise of the philosophical argument. The philosophical
argument may be schematised in the traditional syllogistic
form somewhat as follows:

Major premise: contingent being is inexplicable apart from
necessary being.
Minor premise: The physical universe is a contingent being.
Conclusion: The physical universe is inexplicable apart
from necessary being.

This brief summary-formula will indicate at once that scientific forms of the cosmological argument can do no more,
at best, than supply us with additional reasons, and we already have very good reasons, apart from the physical sciences, for believing that the minor premise is true. Thus
arguments of this kind cannot do more than make a very
subordinate contribution to the cosmological argument as
a whole.

No doubt, if we view the question from a purely pragmatic point of view the citation of prevalent scientific theories and evidences in support of Christian beliefs does make for effective apologetics. Most of our contemporaries have an almost superstitious reverence for anything that can plausibly be called scientific, and hence they are apt to be impressed by arguments that employ scientific concepts and that appeal to received scientific theories. But the genuine Christian theologian or philosopher is not in the first place interested in effective apologetics. He is not a sophist or paid advocate, chiefly concerned to persuade other people. He is a man with an intellectual conscience chiefly concerned to satisfy his own reason, just as any other scientist or philosopher who works in any other field of study and reflection. I believe that in the long run the Christian thinker will even be more effective as an apologetic force if he puts his primary stress on the virtue of absolute intellectual honesty. The history of Christian thought is littered with defective arguments for Christianity, which have enjoyed, at first, a certain temporary success, but which ended by embarrassing the whole case for Christianity once their defectiveness was generally realized. Real faith disdains the unreliable assistance of bad arguments.

There can be no doubt that many of the arguments for Christianity drawn from passing phases of the development of scientific thought have been very defective. A particularly unfortunate tendency is the habit, characteristic of many Christians who work in the natural sciences, of calling in the assistance of the concept of God to help them out at the point where their existing scientific theories and concepts are inadequate to explain the phenomena. Newton was one of the most celebrated of those who offended in this particular way. The late R. G. Collingwood has an adverse comment on Newton's alleged scientific argument for the existence of God which puts the matter in a nutshell:

> He argues, that since we cannot, on his own principles, explain why all the planets revolve in the same direction round the sun, or why their orbits are so disposed that they never bump into one another, this "supremely elegant structure of the solar system cannot have arisen except by the device and power of an intelligent being," thus exalting the limitations of his own method into a proof of the existence of God.[1]

We are all familiar, of course, with the final result of Newton's gross philosophical error. Laplace, a hundred years later, so refined and extended the Newtonian account of the physical universe that he explained the phenomena, which had so baffled Newton, within the terms of the Newtonian theory. Hence, when Napoleon asked him why there was nothing about God in his book, he replied with the famous words, "I have no need of that hypothesis"—as indeed he had not.

The truth is that an argument for the existence of God of the Newtonian type is not really an argument based on the existing state of scientific knowledge at all. Instead, it is an argument based on the existing state of scientific ignorance, an argument almost surely destined to have its foundations undermined by further scientific progress. It is this bad habit of devising arguments for religion on the basis of a temporary stage in the development of scientific knowledge

[1] R. S. Collingwood, *The Idea of Nature* (New York: Oxford), p. 108. Used by permission of the publisher.

which has given rise to the impression that scientific progress, step by step, destroys the arguments that support our religious beliefs. In one sense, this prevalent impression is correct. Scientific progress has removed, and does remove, many of the arguments which Christians have employed in support of their beliefs. But the arguments which it removes are the bad ones. Thus, the process is not really a threat to Christianity at all, but rather a merciful purgation of Christian intellectualism.

Rather more respectable than drawing arguments from passing phases of scientific thought, is the attempt to show that certain basic scientific postulates, as distinct from developed scientific theories, do clearly indicate the contingency of the whole world-process. Thus, the late Prof. A. E. Taylor advanced an argument based on the so-called laws of thermodynamics:

> One of the first principles of the science of Thermodynamics is the so-called "principle of Carnot" or "law of the dissipation of energy." In virtue of this principle, heat always tends to pass from a body of higher temperatures to bodies of lower. The hotter body tends to impart heat to colder bodies in its vicinity, so that it becomes cooler and they warmer. It follows that at the end of a period of time which, however long, must be finite the heat of our stellar universe must ultimately be distributed uniformly over its whole extent; change, variety, and life, must thus be lost in one dreary monotony. But if we ask why these dismal consequences have not as yet occurred, we are driven to assume that at a remote, but still finite, distance of past time the distribution of heat through the stellar universe must have been one which, on mathematical principles, is infinitely improbable.[2]

[2] A. E. Taylor, "The Vindication of Religion," *Essays Catholic and Critical* (London: S.P.C.K.), p. 37. Used by permission of the publisher.

The point is that if we take this basic principle seriously, we seem to be compelled to acknowledge that any physical universe in which such a law is operative cannot recede infinitely into past time. In other words, the universe must have had a beginning, must have arisen out of a state of affairs not characterized by this particular principle at all.

More recently not unsimilar arguments have been put forward by people working in the field of atomic physics. Such investigators argue that it is now possible to calculate with some precision how long the processes which in this atomic age we take to be the elemental processes at work in the physical universe have in fact been going on. Thus, we know the rate at which lead is changing into thorium; we also know, with approximate correctness, how much lead and how much thorium there are in the world. Such data enable us to calculate with some precision the period of time that lead has been changing into thorium. If the processes with which atomic physicists are concerned are indeed the processes which constitute the very essence of the life of the physical universe, then indeed, such data would seem to compel us to believe that the physical universe had a definite beginning in time.

The validity of arguments of this kind depends on our attitude toward basic scientific principles, and this is a question concerning which philosophers of science differ very sharply. It is always possible, of course, to receive and contemplate the basic principles and most widely accepted doctrines of the various sciences in what I will call a spirit of naïve realism. Such a spirit regards the basic principles of science as referring to and describing an actually existing state of affairs. This means that we regard the sciences as producers of sheer objective truth, in the simplest and most straightforward sense of the word.

This is precisely how many people, perhaps most people, do in fact regard the sciences. There are, however, grave difficulties about this view. All of the sciences have a history, and in the past many principles and doctrines, now outmoded, have been regarded as objectively true, because they confor ned to all the known facts, were fully supported by all ava lable experimentation, and enabled people to predict future events and exercise some kind of technical control over nature. Thus, the pre-Copernican, Ptolemaic astronomer believed that the earth was in the center of the physical universe and that the sun and the planets moved around it. This, of course, is now an utterly rejected theory, yet the pre-Copernican was able in his own day to predict eclipses of the sun and the moon, to forecast movements of the planets, and to interpret in terms of his theory all the known facts that were felt to be relevant.

More recently, we have had other great changes in our basic scientific attitudes, for example the transition from Newtonian to relativity physics, and doubtless we shall have many more in the future.

These considerations make it difficult for us to receive prevalent scientific doctrines and postulates in anything like a mood of simple faith. Considerations of this kind have led many philosophically inclined scientists and many philosophers interested in the analysis and interpretation of science (these are two distinct groups, although they have much in common) to hold that scientific doctrines and principles are no more than convenient and pragmatic axioms which enable us to handle and control our physical environment in practice. If we hold this view, we must indeed base our practice on the loctrines of science, but we must never assert them or reason from them as though they were absolute or objective truth.

Now is not the place to enter into this question in any detail, nor have I the requisite time and space at my disposal. In its own way the pragmatic view raises as many difficulties as the naïvely realistic one, for, we may well ask, how can scientific doctrines or principles have the immense pragmatic effectiveness of, for example, contemporary atomic physics, if they are entirely unrelated to absolute objective truth? It seems obvious that we are not warranted to suppose that scientific doctrines and basic principles constitute the whole truth about the physical universe. But is it really possible for us to suppose, in total reaction against the realistic view, that they are no more than convenient fictions? The truth must surely lie somewhere between these two extreme interpretations of science. The upshot of this present discussion for us, however, is clear. The type of argument we have been discussing only holds good if we assume the validity of a certain way of interpreting scientific theories. These arguments *appear* to be based on scientific data and conclusions, but in fact they are based on a philosophy of science which today is widely called in question and is, to that extent at least, open to grave doubt.

To many readers this implication that the meaning of science for us depends, not merely upon what the sciences themselves have to tell us, but also upon what particular philosophy of science we adopt, will appear a strange and disconcerting one. Yet, such is in fact the case. Just as in a democracy the legislature frames and passes the laws, and then leaves it to the judges in the courts to decide precisely what they mean, so, in the last resort, the interpretation of the meaning of scientific theories is the function not of the scientists themselves but of the philosophers of science, or of the scientists themselves in so far as they are also philosophers of science.

A distinguished contemporary scholar, who has given special attention to the way in which modern science grew out of the Christian philosophy of the middle ages, Mr. A. C. Crombie, stresses the gulf that divides science from metaphysics:

Scientific theory then, tells us no more than it appears to tell us about the experimental facts, namely that they may be related in a particular manner. It can provide no grounds for the belief that the entities postulated for the purposes of the theory actually exist. So, whether or not science makes metaphysical assumptions, as scientific theory it has no metaphysical implications. It can never be used either to support or contradict interpretations of experience written in another language or in a different mood, and propositions in other languages and moods have nothing to do with science. Dives was separated from Lazarus no farther than science is from theology or ethics or a theory of beauty. To try to pass from one to the other is to land in the chaos between.[3]

Perhaps the closing sentences exaggerate a little. The gulf between science and philosophy can indeed be bridged,

[3] A. C. Crombie, *Grosseteste and Experimental Science* (New York: Oxford), p. 319. Used by permission of the publisher.

and has in fact been bridged, in various ways. But the gulf can only be bridged from the philosophical side, and the supports upon which the bridge rests are of philosophical not scientific manufacture.

Still another kind of argument, which has at least a highly scientific flavor, takes for its point of departure some of the analogies and illustrations frequently employed by scientific thinkers in communicating and imaginatively interpreting the achievements of science to that large public which is enthralled and fascinated by science but is not equipped to understand its language. Thus, for example, there was a lengthy period during which many scientific workers were particularly interested in the construction of working mechanical models of physical processes (as they conceived them).

This was the age of "mechanistic science," an age that delighted to liken reality to a vast machine. Of course, this likening of physical reality to a machine was never really anything more than an illustrative analogy, but there is no doubt that many philosophers and scientists took the analogy very seriously. Analogies of this kind are often very useful, but they should always be employed for illustrative and communicative purposes and never asserted as literal objective truth.

And an analogy does not need to be true. Indeed, in the nature of the case it cannot be true. We rightly require of an analogy no more than that it should be illuminating, and some analogies are indeed much more illuminating than others. It is always dangerous in any sphere of thought to take our analogies too seriously, and it is impossible, in any sphere of thought, to avoid employing some analogy or other.

It has, however, been pointed out by some philosophers, —the late Prof. J. E. Turner, for example—that if we do treat the mechanistic analogy seriously enough, it points in a theistic direction. All the real machines with which we are acquainted have been constructed by intelligent beings to serve their own conscious purposes. If the physical universe really is a machine, then it certainly indicates the existence of a supreme intelligent and purposive being who has devised it to serve his own supremely intelligent ends.

This was, of course, no new idea of Prof. Turner's. In the eighteenth century the deistic philosophers and orthodox Christian apologists (e.g. the once celebrated Archdeacon Paley) were particularly fond of likening the physical universe to some mechanical contrivance, such as a watch, and then arguing that such a universe necessarily implied the existence of God just as the watch implied the existence of the watchmaker. Often this analogical argument was given a deistic twist. God had created the perfect machine which, once created, operated forever without requiring any further attention from the celestial engineer. But the deistic interpretation rather spoiled the analogy. We know of no machines which once created require no further attention. On the contrary, machines as we know them must be continually serviced and fed. We feed coal and water to our steam engines; we lubricate and refuel our automobiles. Our machines require our constant attention, not merely because they are imperfect and often operate badly, but because it is part of their essential nature to require our attention, so that only if they are given special care can they operate in accordance with the intentions of their designers. No, if we are to take the mechanistic analogy seriously it requires, not merely the remote, indifferent God of the deists, who creates but does not provide, but the infinitely concerned, responsibility bearing God of the Bible, to whom must be attributed not only the act of creation but also the infinite activities of providence.

The mechanistic argument is a simple and attractive one, and it has a certain force for men who are in the habit of trying to bring the abstract theories of mathematical science to life by imaginatively likening them to the machines with which we are so familiar in our everyday experience. The defect of the argument is, however, obvious. It takes the analogy far too seriously. As we can all see, the physical universe is not in fact a machine, and does not even resemble one to any significant extent. No doubt it is illuminating in certain contexts and for certain purposes to liken the physical universe to a machine, but that is a very different thing from roundly asserting that it *is* a machine. The mechanistic interpretation of science is neither science nor philosophy. It is poetry, and as in all poetry the images which convey the meaning do not have to be asserted or believed in, in order to be meaningful. To say that the physical universe or some portion of it is really like a vast machine is a statement of the same kind as that which the poet makes when he declares that his "love is like a red, red rose." In both cases we can appreciate the force and meaning of the comparison, and we can be deeply impressed by it, but we are not required to believe it or assert it in any literal sense.

The main conclusion of this section of our discussion is clearly a negative one. The attempt to give the cosmological type of argument for the existence of God a scientific flavor is not particularly successful, and it can yield no result of any special importance. At best, efforts of this kind can do little more than corroborate from another point of view some of the conclusions which many of the classical philosophers had reached independently of any scientific considerations. If the cosmological argument pretends that it is a purely scientific argument, it only succeeds in being pseudo-scientific. Nowadays many people are irrationally impressed by a citation of the authority of science. But no honest natural theology can stoop to exploiting this gullibility. Natural theology is a candid and sincere endeavor to appeal to the rational in man. It is not a formula for impressing the irrational. The popular deference to the authority of a science, whose strength, real achievements, and ultimate limitations alike the populace is quite incapable of understanding, is the supreme superstition of our age.

The Existential Argument: Personal Form

As I remarked in an earlier chapter, the existential approach to the problems of religion and the existence of God is not really as distinct from and independent of the cosmological approach as its supporters often suppose. This type of approach discovers and experiences the contingency of the real in the realm of self-conscious human existence rather than in that of the physical universe, and its argument from contingent to necessary being is often so expressed as to be almost indistinguishable from the claim that self-conscious contingent being, whenever it is aware of itself with sufficient profundity, experiences the reality of the necessary being as something inextricably bound up with its own existence. In other words, this type of approach is apt to claim that the existence of God is experienced rather than merely inferred.

This is an antithesis which must not be pressed too far. There is a sense in which it is true that all conscious experience is a very simple form of inference, and certainly it is often true that we may validly infer anything that we consciously experience. I may say that I do not have to infer the existence of the table in front of me because I experience its existence. Some philosophers will reply, however, that to experience its existence is really to infer its existence from the fragmentary sense data which constitute my primary experience. Even if we do not go as far as this and allow for some real distinction between inference and experience, it can only be on the basis that experience is in some way a more profound and more embracing concept than inference. Inference is part of experience; whatever is validly experienced can also be inferred.

We must not distinguish too much between those who claim to infer the existence of God, as something which they find logically *implied* by finite and contingent existence, and those who claim to experience the existence of God as a reality *implicit* in finite and contingent existence. No doubt there is a distinction. If I say that x implies y, I mean that the reality of x is a kind of signpost which points towards the reality of y, a reality y which is both bound up with and external to its own reality. If I say, however, that the reality of y is implicit in the reality of x, I mean that a profounder consciousness of the reality of x will of itself bring the reality of y within the orbit of my experience. In other words, that I am not fully conscious of the reality of x until I have become co-conscious of the reality of both x and y. In so far, therefore, as I understand the Christian doctrine of the relation between God and His creatures, it affirms both these things: the imminent reality of God is implicit in the reality of His creatures, and at the same time the reality of His creatures implies the transcendent reality of God. Thus, both approaches are valid and important, and the distinction between them must not be overstressed.

When we turn to the leading existentialist philosophers themselves, however, we find them profoundly disagreeing about whether the reality of God is found implicit in human existence, if we explore its meaning in sufficient depth and profundity. They may be roughly divided into the religious existentialists, for whom, in the words of Kierkegaard, "it is the God-relationship that makes a man a man," and the irreligious existentialists who, although vividly aware of the limitations, the finiteness, and contingency of man (for them supremely summed up and experienced in the ultimate fact of his mortality), tend to conceive of man as ultimately alone with his inescapable fate. They may, like Nietzsche, dream of some way in which man may ultimately overcome the limitations inherent in his finitude and become God, or they may alternatively, like John Paul Sartre and some of the contemporary French existentialists, think of man as heroically and stoically enduring his fate, and even defying it with his freedom, until at last and inevitably it comes upon him and strikes him down. About what we have called the contingency of man, however, even though they would probably prefer not to use the word, they are all completely agreed. Human existence, as they know it, does not carry its own ground or necessity within it and is inherently frail, finite, and mortal. It can guarantee neither its own continuance nor its own fulfilment.

What divides these two currents of existentialist opinion is not any disagreement about the facts but a disagreement about their interpretation. For the religious existentialists, human destiny and the latent promise of human nature are in fact fulfilled in man's conscious relationship of faith and trust toward God. For the irreligious existentialists, they are never really fulfilled at all. Some bold and hardy spirits, by a supreme and reckless exertion of their freedom, merely come closer to self-fulfilment than others.

As between these two, I cannot doubt that the religious existentialists achieve a more rational interpretation of human existence than the irreligious existentialists. The preoccupation of existentialist philosophy with self-conscious existence, as the most important and revealing element in our experience, is inexplicable and untenable unless we hold that self-conscious spiritual existence is also and ultimately the most important reality in the whole universe. In other words, if human existence is a mere accident in a universe which is blind and indifferent to it, the existentialist preoccupation with human existence is not rationally tenable. The religious existentialists, with their doctrine of the fulfilment of finite selfhood in an existential, personal relationship to the infinite selfhood of God provides us with a scheme which is, from the philosophical point of view, far more satisfactory and convincing. We may say that whereas human existence, for the irreligious existentialist, is in the last resort an irrational and inexplicable tragedy; for the religious existentialist, however tragic many of its component episodes, it is in the last resort a rational, purposeful, and intelligible comedy.

In tragedy terrible events occur, we know not why, and ultimately in vain. In comedy terrible events may occur also, but the conclusion shows us why and shows us that that they are not in vain. Comedy, properly speaking, must be distinguished from mere farce, as Dante clearly saw when he called his epic description of the whole Christian scheme of destiny *The Divine Comedy*. Tragedy is completely locked up in time and therefore ultimately irrational. Comedy is eschatological and rational, always concerned to show how the end makes sense of all that has come before. We may illustrate by comparing Shakespeare's *Hamlet* with his *A Winter's Tale*. The last act of the written tragedy of *Hamlet* is simply the opening of the unwritten tragedy of young Fortinbras, one finite, temporal episode merely leading to another. *A Winter's Tale* on the other hand concludes with an allegory of resurrection and redemption which makes sense of all that has gone before and shows how all things can be transmuted and made new.

The difficulty with comedy, and this is why so many of the greatest tragedies are often finer as literary compositions or even as spiritual documents than the great comedies, is that comedy is usually compelled to express its eschatology in temporal allegories. Comedy, like tragedy, is compelled to end in time, but, of course, there is no ending in time. Hence, the closing scene of a comedy is always allegorical: "And they lived happily ever after." Comedy, thus, cannot be secularized as successfully as can tragedy. Its essential nature is religious and Biblical, and if it does not conclude with straight, candidly confessed eschatology; its only alternative is to resort to lame and unconvincing allegory. Hence, the irreligious existentialists, who are tragic philosophers, often seem to us more candid and convincing than the religious existentialists, who are essentially comic philosophers. At bottom, however, the comic philosophers are the more rational. They have a sense of intelligible purpose informing all things. They have a sense of ultimate achievement crowning all things. They sense that existence has an objective meaning of its own and is not a meaningless something which can only have meaning roughly thrust upon it by crudely extemporizing as they go along.

There we have it. Either existence has an inherent and objective meaning of its own or it has none. Either existence is rational or it is not. If existence has no meaning of its own, we are powerless to give it any by foisting upon it some kind of subjective interpretation. The religious existentialists misunderstand the essential spirit and character of their thought if they allow themselves to have dealings with any kind of irrationalism. Make no mistake about it, existentialism, whatever the existentialists may say, is a rationalism, and a very profound one. It is an insistence on being ultimately rational about the meaning and purpose of human existence; not merely instrumentally rational about the means which we employ in pursuit of our ends.

At first sight this is a somewhat surprising statement. From Kierkegaard onward most existentialists have believed themselves to be in revolt against the arrogance of rationalism, and most nonexistentialist philosophers would agree in interpreting existentialism as an antirational philosophy, and perhaps dismiss it with contempt on that very account. But the antirational passion and prejudice, which we so often find in the writings of the existentialist philosophers, is not really essential to the true genius of existentialism. The essence of existentialism is to insist that our own intimate experience of existence in the world (our experience of the reality of our freedom and of the way in which life again and again frustrates our freedom, our experience of hope and fear and unquenchable spiritual need, our experience of life and its inescapable fragility and impermanence as it confronts the necessity of death, our experience of love and its disappointment and disillusions) is the most vivid kind of experience of reality which we enjoy and that it constitutes the proper and necessary point of departure in philosophy.

The rationalism against which existentialism properly and necessarily protests is a high and dry rationalism which sins against its own ideal by ignoring and abstracting from our experience of existence. This is the dead rationalism which reasons about everything except the concrete existence which is the most real thing that we know. It is the abstract rationalism which Kierkegaard detected, perhaps not quite accurately, in the great Hegel and denounced, perhaps not quite justly, with such unsparing vehemence. This is also the scientific empiricism which is empirical about everything except about our own existence and which patiently studies and humbly defers to every experience except the most vivid experience of all.

The true existentialist has his own kind of rationalism which sees in the life of reason, motivated and sustained by the rational man's profound existential need for the truth at all costs, and taking the whole range of human experience for its parish, one of the very highest forms of human existence. Let our reasoning but insist upon being a concrete reasoning about the central themes of human existence, rather than an abstract reasoning about isolated problems which a sophisticated reasoning has itself defined and created, and we shall see at once that some kind of existentialist philosophy becomes a rational necessity. John Paul Sartre once wrote a little book dedicated to the proposition that "Existentialism is a humanism." This seems to me a proposition too obviously true to require enforcing. I would only add that, properly understood, existentialism is a rationalism also.

Once again the analogy and parallelism between the cosmological and existential kind of natural theology are clearly brought out. Both of them emphasize the kinship between faith in God and faith in reason. The existentialist preoccupation with existence, as the fundamental and indispensable point of departure in philosophy, is not rational and must in the last resort be abandoned unless we can also hold that existence, the kind of reality with which we are so vividly confronted in the intimacies and depths of our self-knowledge, is objectively speaking the most fundamental and primary form of reality. Self-conscious existence can only be our proper point of departure in philosophy if we can at the same time hold that self-conscious existence is the ultimate and primary form of objective reality itself. Thus again, we are led to the view that there is an essential connection between faith in God and faith in reason.

Faith in reason implies more than that reason is the best instrument we possess for doing what we want to do. Faith in reason means that the universe, and the existence within the universe of such beings as we know and discover ourselves to be, is a rational state of affairs, the meaning and purpose of which can only be disclosed to self-conscious rational beings, and the meaning and purpose of which can only be achieved and exemplified in the existence of self-conscious rational beings. Thus, the existence of self-conscious rational beings is the clue to the meaning of the universe. And this can only be true if self-conscious rational existence is the supreme and absolute fact that underlies and sustains all the existence that there is. Once more, then, faith in God sustains faith in reason. And such a faith in reason as I have endeavored to describe ultimately reinforces faith in God.

The Existential Argument: Social Form

We turn our attention now from the subtle intimacies and privacies of self-conscious personal existence to what we may call the social dimensions of personality. Personal existence is not in fact a solitary thing, however solitary some existentialist philosophers make it appear to be. All personal existence is existence in society. It is not of the essence of personality to be solitary. Where this happens it is a tragic accident. There may indeed be deep levels of personal life which we cannot share with our fellows, not even with our most intimate friends, but these are morbid and unhealthy levels unless we can learn in prayer and worship to share them with God. True personal existence is thus essentially and inescapably bound up with other existing persons. It is existence in inescapable communication with *the other*. Indeed only in society can individuals develop into persons, and only in society can they continue to be persons.

Nevertheless many thinkers have labored to establish a kind of antithesis between society, with its rules, regulations, and insistence that members discipline themselves to meet its basic requirements, and individual personality with its demand for freedom and self-expression. In the world, and in life as we know it, such an antithesis often is plausible enough. There is often a real clash between personality and society, but this is a consequence of the corruption of both personality and society in a fallen world. It is not a conflict demanded and brought about by the essential natures of personality and society. Such a conflict is a consequence, as Christians say, of the Fall.

The Fall has brought about a radically unnatural state of human affairs. It has brought about a state of affairs in which personality cannot do without society but, because society as we know it is corrupt, personality cannot be entirely happy and contented within it. Similarly, it has brought it about that society cannot exist and flourish without personality but, because personality is everywhere corrupt, society is constantly tempted to saddle it with a heavy burden of constraint and excessive authority. Hence it happens that human history is characterized by a pendulum-like swing between a state of affairs in which personality enjoys more liberty than corrupt personality can safely be trusted to use wisely and well, and another equally extreme state of affairs in which society is vested with more authority than corrupt society is able to exercise justly and tolerantly.

Properly understood, however, the social is one necessary dimension of personal existence, and we can no more escape from society than we can evade the responsibilities of personality itself. This is an obvious fact which no sanely balanced, truly empirical existentialism can afford to ignore. Existentialism is not individualism, and it mistakes its own nature if it thinks that it is.

The question now before us is this: Can we discern in social life a basic finitude or contingency, a deep seated need for religion and a religious attitude which will enable us to say that an ultimate religious orientation is indispensable to harmonious and fruitful social existence? This is a question with which several important contemporary writers have profoundly concerned themselves. We may mention in particular the writings of Christopher Dawson and many of the basic teachings contained in Arnold Toynbee's *A Study of History*. The former lays great stress on the universality of religion and of the religious origins of almost all the great forms and vehicles of civilized existence. Toynbee attempts to show that the great crises in and through which a people advance to civilization, and maintain itself there, are in the last analysis crises which have an inescapably religious character and call for description in religious language.

Mr. Dawson's insistence on the universality of religion and the necessary role of religion in the creation and preservation of culture is perhaps most clearly set forth and summarized in his book *Religion and Culture*. Here he stresses the religious origins of the state, the politically organized and unified social order, the concepts of law, science, art, and the idealisms which motivate social criticism and social progress. He maintains this point of view on the basis of a wide range of anthropological and sociological data, and then, in a subsequent volume, *Religion and the Rise of Western Culture*, concentrates on displaying and analyzing the essential relationship between Christianity and our own particular Western form of civilization. Of course the facts which he summarizes have been noted by many other contemporary writers. Thus, Bertand de Jouvenel in his important book *Power* stresses the religious origins of the state, a fact which had also impressed Sir James Fraser earlier in this century. Mr. A. C. Crombie, also, in two important and profoundly learned studies, has illustrated the way in which modern Western natural science arose out of Christian philosophical and theological thought and speculation, fertilized and stimulated by its contacts with Arab philosophy during the Middle Ages.

It would certainly appear that there can be little doubt or argument about the facts themselves. It seems overwhelmingly probable that without religion man would never have attained a civilized existence at all, and that without the Christian religion we should certainly not have attained the particular form of civilization which we now possess. The further contention that without religion civilization cannot continue and, in particular, that without Christianity our civilization cannot continue, is, of course, an inference from these facts of more doubtful character. There is clearly a great difference between observing that without religion a civilization would never have come into existence and arguing that without religion civilization cannot continue in existence. It seems at least possible to hold that, although religion was necessary to the birth and maturing of civilization, it is nevertheless not necessary to its further development, and may even be an obstacle to the attainment of its final perfection. To me, of course, this is very improbable, but it is not an altogether impossible point of view.

Certainly, the way in which periods of religious scepticism and widespread alienation from religious practice coincide with periods of social instability, of a loss of nerve on the part of society as it confronts the intimidating ordeals of history, a decline in its belief in its own civilizing mission and will to survive, does seem to suggest that there is a very close and abiding connection between the maintenance of our religious beliefs and institutions and the preservation and progress of our social order. Nevertheless, it must be admitted that the generalizations which such a writer as Mr. Dawson deduces from his facts have not quite the same authority and certainty as his description of the facts themselves.

There are even profoundly religious reasons for dissatisfaction with a kind of argument which seems to suggest that religion should be accepted and practiced for the sake of social survival. It is not the primary function of religion to preserve civilization. It is possible that a religion, widely and sincerely practiced, may tend toward the preservation of the social order, but such a consequence can only be a kind of by-product. Any living religion has profounder purposes and intentions than that.

On the other hand we should remember the inherent limitations of the kind of argument we are considering. It does not even purport to be an argument for Christianity or any other particular religion. Its aims are more modest. It merely attempts to show that religion of some kind is a natural human necessity, necessary to the well-being of men in society. Clearly the affirmation of belief in any particular religion takes us infinitely further, but that is no reason for despising the value of this kind of argument on its own level and within its own limits.

Far profounder is the analysis of the basic factors operative in the birth and growth of civilization which we find in Arnold Toynbee. The terminology in which he defines these basic factors has a religious character which is not accidental but is necessitated by the essential character of the factors themselves. Thus, according to him, civilizations are born and pass through their initial phases of growth in a crisis of "challenge and response." A people are challenged by a set of intimidating circumstances, and their triumphant response to the challenge lays the foundation of their civilized existence. The language is very similar to that in which a modern Christian theologian would describe the

94

process of Biblical revelation. The revelation itself is hidden in a series of 'crisis-events' to which men respond with prophetic understanding and self-committing faith. Our religion is born in a crisis which elicits the response that lays the foundation of both church and creed, and it prolongs itself and deepens its understanding of the position to which it is committed through a series of similar crises. The parallelism and kinship between the two concepts is very plain. The process out of which civilization is born is at least quasi-religious in character.

Again, Toynbee stresses the role of a creative minority in the growth and extension of a civilization. The lives of the members of this creative minority are characterized by a certain rhythm of "withdrawal and return," of which the clearest examples are to be found in the careers of such great religious leaders as Buddha, St. Paul, and Mahomet. There is an apparent withdrawal from society into closer intercourse with the values and realities which are subsequently taken back into society.

We can observe the same rhythm in the history of modern natural science. The applied science which serves social needs and purpose is subsequent, both in logic and in time, to the pure science into which the great scientific discoverers withdraw, and in so doing withdraw from society. But the process itself is at least quasi-religious in character.

Another of Toynbee's key concepts is what he calls "etherealisation." A society may become so successful in its response to the challenge of intimidating circumstances that the circumstances cease to challenge it sufficiently to stimulate it to further creative efforts. What is demanded in these circumstances is a transposition of the challenge to a more inward and spiritual plane, so that the society which no longer finds itself challenged by its physical situation, or the hostility of other societies, may continue to challenge itself from within. Surely, this challenging of itself from within is very close to the concept of a prophetic religion. The prophets challenge their society from within, denouncing its failures and abuses, not because they are hostile to it, but precisely because they love it. It is their labor and their witness which stimulate it to further creative development.

If, according to Toynbee, the processes in and through which civilizations are born and grow are fundamentally of a religious character, it is equally true that for him the disintegration of a civilization has a profoundly irreligious character. Toynbee describes the disintegration of civilization partly in terms of inertia, of a "resting upon one's oars," a failure on the part of the mature civilization to challenge itself any further from within, and partly in terms of what he calls idolatory—a state of mind in which a society comes to give absolute value to its own being and its own achievements. A disintegrating society is a society that worships itself. The theology of such a worship may be some kind of fanatical nationalism, or a humanism which persuades men to concentrate so entirely upon the values which they know, upon the values which illuminate their own contemporary existence, that they can perceive no other values as transcending them. The values upon which the humanist concentrates may be, and probably are, values indeed, but our values, however valuable, will ruin us if we permit them to blind us to all that lies beyond and above them. Thus, for Toynbee, civilization and its growth is the product of a creative spirituality, whereas its disintegration and decline is the consequence of an exhausted spirituality, in which men make idols of themselves and their own achievements.

We may most helpfully contrast and relate Dawson's and Toynbee's approaches to our problem by saying that whereas Dawson indicates the reality of the connection between religion and civilization by building up a vast store of empirical evidence, Toynbee analyzes and interprets the connection by showing that the processes which create and sustain civilization have an ineradicably religious character. What both of them agree in asserting, to fall back upon language which we have employed throughout this chapter, is the contingency of the secular. The secular, the merely temporal and this-worldly, aspects of civilization do not add up to an independent, self-contained whole. We may agree that civilization sometimes appears to be secular in both its spirit and intention, but this is only because we so often ignore the way in which any civilization is rooted in a view of life and the world which is essentially religious. The "world" in the New Testament sense, the merely secular (which the Bible so often contrasts sharply with the Kingdom of God and the Church), is thus an abstract and unreal thing, a tragic illusion. It is society abstracting itself from the realities upon which it depends. Thus it is reduced to worshipping itself, because it recognizes no reality above itself which can and will judge and redeem it.

Wherever we look—outwardly at the physical universe which provides us with our native environment, around us at the life of the society to which we belong, or within us at the intimacies and depths of our own personal existence —we are impressed by the inescapable fact of contingency. Nowhere do we find completeness; nowhere do we find a kind of being which can conceivably either give birth to itself or sustain itself; nowhere do we find anything which carries within itself the ground and explanation of its own existence. The social form of the existential argument points toward the same conclusion as the other types of natural theology which we have so briefly characterized.

The Final Assessment

This ultimate convergence of view, this almost precise parallelism between the types of argument which we have so rapidly surveyed, is in many respects the most impressive thing about them. Probably no one of the arguments which we have considered will by itself produce any high degree of confidence or conviction, but when we set these several considerations side by side and note the unanimity with which, when we analyze what they say, they agree in proclaiming the same fundamental message, our rational nature can hardly fail to be impressed. After all, it is not as though there were any considerable reason on the other side for not believing in God. A theistic philosophy is not logically self-contradictory, nor in any other way repugnant to our reason.

I do not believe that any philosopher can possibly hold that it is impossible for the theistic account of life and the universe to be true. There are, in fact, almost no arguments against the existence of God. There are certainly many difficulties, for example the so-called problem of evil, but then there will certainly be some difficulties in our ultimate philosophy whatever it may be.

In the nature of the case, a philosophical view can do no more than barely outline the form of reality in which it believes. In the realm of philosophy, as we have already seen, we are compelled by the nature of philosophy to infer the reality which our philosophy asserts and to turn the reality into a concept, whereas the reality, whatever else it may be, is certainly not a concept. In the realm of philosophy we are never confronted with that which our philosophy asserts in all its concrete reality. That is why no philosophy, however profoundly and confidently theistic, can ever be a substitute for religion, or of itself prompt and sustain a religion. Of course, the philosophizing of religious men will be religiously motivated, but the religiously minded philosopher, most of all, will always be conscious of the fundamental distinction between religion and philosophy.

To return to the main point, it is certainly not a logical impossibility that the theistic philosophy should be the true one, and it is significant that there are no worthwhile arguments against the existence of God. Atheistic propaganda usually confines itself to criticizing arguments which have been put forward for the existence of God, and it must be admitted that some of these criticisms are often just, because many of the arguments which purport to prove the existence of God have been exceedingly bad ones. Nevertheless, they are not all bad, and I believe we are justified in claiming that taken together they indicate that it is extremely probable that the theistic philosophy is the one which is, at least, most significantly gravitating in the direction of the truth.

I do not think we can hold that theistic philosophy demonstrates the existence of God beyond all possibility of rational doubt (for reasons which I have already indicated), but I think it no exaggeration to suggest that the convergent arguments for theism, and what we may call in the widest sense a religious attitude toward life, are so strong and establish so high a degree of probability that we may assume their substantial truth.

Of course, this is not enough for the Christian. He will say that he has other, more profound and more empirical ways of confirming the truth of the theistic hypothesis. For him, God has not merely been validly inferred by philosophers, but God has actually spoken to men and revealed himself both in Jesus Christ and in the life and experience of the Church. To live and think and worship and pray within the context of the Christian revelation and the Christian Church is to discover that within oneself there is a sharpening of the cool philosophical assessment of probabilities into the basic, rocklike convictions upon which one's whole existence is founded.

Of course, the Christian is fully justified in reporting this experience, and in regarding it as supremely significant. But this experience gives the Christian no ground for depreciating the testimony of philosophy, nor does his personal witness to what God has done for him in Jesus Christ in any way replace or supplant the testimony of philosophy. The philosophical testimony remains valid and illuminating within its own limits.

We must always remember that no philosophical argument for a theistic and religious view of life in the world is an argument for becoming a Christian. The arguments for becoming a Christian do not arise in our minds until we begin to make an honest survey of what we may call the Christian facts. By the Christian facts I refer to such things as the acts of God in Jesus Christ and our experience (intellectual, moral, spiritual, social) of life in the Church. It is the analysis and interpretation of these facts which provide us with our reasons for becoming and remaining Christians.

These reasons are good ones. There is nothing irrational about becoming and remaining a Christian. I am convinced that the man who talks loosely and vaguely about "relying on faith rather than on reason" does not know what the words faith and reason really mean. Surely, it is clear that there can not conceivably be any reason for becoming a Christian prior to some kind of analysis and interpretation of the Christian facts. But in this life, the most normal role of reason is to analyze and interpret the facts with which we find ourselves confronted and to suggest appropriate action in regard to them. But although our reasons for becoming and remaining Christians are based on an examination and interpretation of the unique Christian facts, we may nevertheless welcome arguments which seem to suggest, if they are valid and always provided that we are rationally convinced of their validity, that even a chain of reasoning which takes as its point of departure all the facts known to us *except* the Christian facts tells as far as it goes in the same direction.

The kind of philosophizing which we call natural theology can thus contribute no more to Christian theology than a certain limited amount of corroboratory detail, "a touch of verisimilitude to what is in itself a by no means bald and unconvincing narrative" (to borrow, with appreciation, the phraseology of W. S. Gilbert). But even this is no small thing. Natural theology proclaims that because the world, even this fallen world, is God's world, the experience of life within it points mutely and short-sightedly toward the reality which the gospel reveals. If the God who reveals himself to us in the gospels is indeed the creator of the world, this is perhaps no more than we should have expected.

CHAPTER FOUR

NATURAL THEOLOGY IN A NEGATIVE MOOD

So much then for what we may fairly call the positive achievement of natural theology. A rational analysis and interpretation of the facts which confront us in our experience of life and the world, even if we ignore for the moment the specifically Christian and religious types of fact, does seem to point in the theistic direction. At all events we are warranted in saying that if reason is to be trusted at all in such matters the theistic hypothesis is at least a very likely one. The question before us in the present chapter is this: Can natural theology continue the argument a little further and plausibly attempt to show that all known alternative hypotheses are by comparison improbable or even impossible?

If such a negative argument can be made out and sustained it would clearly and enormously strengthen the many stranded positive arguments which we endeavored to summarize in the last chapter. Personally, I think that such an argument can be elaborated in a rationally effective manner.

Not only is theism rationally speaking a probable hypothesis, but the various alternatives which have from time to time occurred to the human mind are, and can be shown to be, by comparison, very improbable indeed. We will now consider briefly what the best known and most important of these alternatives are. Some of them we have discussed already; others have not as yet engaged our attention.

Scepticism, Agnosticism, and Positivism

Very few philosophers indeed have endeavored to maintain a total and dogmatic scepticism about everything. Clearly, a comprehensive scepticism of this kind would necessitate being sceptical even about scepticism, and thus finally indicate the possibility of a way out of scepticism altogether. One is reminded of the advice of the sceptical father to his son. "My boy, always be doubtful about everything. Only a fool is ever certain of anything." "Are you quite sure that's true, father?" replies the son. "Yes, my boy, I'm absolutely certain of it."

The prevalent impression that the natural mood of philosophy is a sceptical one is perhaps due to a misinterpretation of the method of systematic doubt employed by many philosophers in the course of their philosophical arguments. The method of systematic doubt is in fact a dialectical device employed in order to discover what there is in our experience, if there is anything, which cannot possibly be doubted or, alternatively, to diagnose and define the doubts which reason must seek to banish from our minds before we are justified in feeling certain, or relatively certain, about anything. Thus the great French philosopher, Descartes, attempted to doubt everything, but finally came to the conclusion that there are three things which cannot in fact be doubted: the personal existence of the man who is doing the doubting, the lucid truths of pure mathematics, and the existence of God. Similarly, Socrates, as he is presented in the dialogues of Plato, normally proceeds by the method of questioning everything in which people believe in order to arrive at more adequate and certain definitions of what they believe in. Yet it would be a great mistake to say that either Descartes, Socrates, or Plato were sceptical philosophers. They were in fact anything but philosophical sceptics. We must carefully distinguish the methodological doubt of the great philosophers, which is no more than a very useful dialectical device, from the real doubts of the sceptical philosopher. The former employed the method of doubt during the course of their arguments for the sake of arriving at more certain conclusions. The latter may not do very much doubting in the actual course of his argument. His doubt is in his conclusions, and that is what makes him a sceptic in the proper sense of the word.

The more common and intelligent form of scepticism is the kind of critical philosophy which we have already discussed. It attempts, as we have seen, to distinguish between a sphere of discovery and enquiry in which knowledge is possible and another sphere of discourse and enquiry in which it is held to be unattainable.

This kind of philosopher is usually described as a positivist when we think of him in relation to the kind of knowledge which he regards as attainable by man, and as an agnostic when we think of him in relation to his declaration that other kinds of knowledge are unattainable. Thus, most sceptics are positivists and agnostics at the same time. Indeed, positivism and agnosticism are usually two differents aspects of the same philosophy.

Our criticism of this kind of philosophy has already been made clear. It misunderstands and misinterprets the consequences of the finitude of the human mind. Our conclusion was, when we discussed this question in the second chapter, that although we are incapable of knowing everything about anything because our minds are finite, yet we have no warrant whatever for believing that there is any reality which is entirely and in principle unknowable. In other words the positivist agnostic is much too positivist about that which he thinks that he can and does know, and much too agnostic about everything else. Reason will support neither the extreme optimism of his positivist mood nor the unqualified pessimism of the agnostic phase of his thought.

No doubt there have been some agnostics who cannot properly be called positivists. Such people will argue that the case for and against a metaphysical hypothesis like the existence of God is about evenly balanced, and that we have therefore no alternative but to suspend our judgment. This does not seem to me to be true. There are no positive arguments for atheism, corresponding to the positive arguments for theism. Indeed, it is difficult to see how there could be. A positive argument for a negative conclusion is in the very nature of the case a very rare thing. One is reminded of the story of the hedgehog who was discovered by a jack rabbit feverishly endeavoring to bury himself in the middle of the summer. "Whatever are you doing?" asked the jack rabbit,

"Haven't you heard," replied the hedgehog, "Congress has decided to investigate all the porcupines." "But you are not a porcupine," the jack rabbit assured him. "I know, but could I ever prove it?" moaned the hedgehog in despair. The moral of this story is perhaps political rather than metaphysical, but it does indicate the dialectical difficulty in which we find ourselves involved whenever we try to devise positive arguments for a purely negative conclusion.

But even if for the moment we accept the possibility that the arguments for theism and for atheism might conceivably be evenly balanced, is it really possible for us to suspend our judgment about a matter of this kind? The answer to this question must clearly be in the negative. It is never possible to suspend judgment about any question which involves action. To suspend judgment about a question which involves action is really to vacilate in indecision. Vacillation and indecision are quite different from a rational suspending of judgment. The question "Shall I believe in God or not?" is not really the purely theoretical question which it appears to be. "Shall I believe in God or not?" can and should be restated in another form. It really means "Shall I worship God or not?" For to believe in God without worshiping Him is not really to believe in *God* at all. Now clearly it is not possible to suspend judgment about a practical question like, "Shall I worship God?" The agnostic who sincerely supposes that he is suspending judgment on this matter is in fact, and perhaps without really wanting to, all the time coming down on the negative side. No doubt there are some purely theoretical questions about which we can and should suspend judgment, at all events for the moment. (For example, the question whether or not the planet Mars is inhabited.) But the question, "Shall I worship God or not?" is not a question of this kind. Here no true suspending of judgment is possible. How fortunate it is that the arguments for and against the existence of God are not really so evenly balanced as the agnostic supposes.

Atheism

Very few great philosophers have been dogmatic atheists, although a small minority have taught that God, or the gods, if He exists or they exist, is or are not concerned about us and that in consequence we need not in practice concern ourselves with Him or them. Normally, atheism takes the form of a criticism of such conceptions of God as are fashionable at any particular stage in the development of culture, and of such arguments as are put forward in an endeavor to prove the existence of God. As I have already suggested, such criticism may be of positive value. It is often the theists who provoke men to atheism by the unworthiness of their conceptions of God, and by the feebleness of the arguments with which they endeavor to support them. It would be very unwise for the religious man to dismiss all atheism as a negligible and irrelevant blasphemy. On the contrary, the best kind of atheism can teach us many salutary lessons. It warns us against forms of belief in God which are unworthy and sometimes more truly blasphemous than any kind of atheism can ever be. In a sense genuine atheism is a highly spiritual state of mind. The best kind of atheist is revolted and frustrated by ways of declaring the truth about God which quite plainly fail to meet the spiritual and intellectual needs of a spiritually and intellectually awakened man. In a way, indeed, the theist and the best kind of atheist are not so sharply opposed to each other as they seem. What the theist really asserts is not the total adequacy of any particular idea of God, not even his own idea, but the reality of God. What the atheist denies is not the reality of God—that, alas, is too far from his conscious experience for him even to deny it—but the adequacy of the ideas of God that are put before his mind by the believers. On the whole, indeed, atheism seems to me in every way the best alternative to theism. It is perhaps a pity that genuine atheism of the best kind is so very rare, for it has much to teach us of positive value.

Perhaps the most familiar form of atheism in the contemporary world is the Marxist variety. This can hardly be counted among the higher and more spiritual forms of atheism to which I have alluded, but it has two interesting characteristics which make it worth mentioning. It rejects theism not so much because it holds that the arguments for theism are defective or invalid—although, of course, it does do this—but because it regards belief in God and an ultimate destiny for man which "doth not yet appear" as an unhealthy belief which robs this present life of any consequence and value.

No doubt it is true that there have been some pervertedly pious people who have been led to the conclusion that the reality of God and the whole spiritual dimension of our experience make everything else comparatively unimportant. This is not, however, the outlook of the Bible or of historic Christianity as a whole. The belief that God made the world and that human life has an ultimate destiny and significance makes everything that happens here and now of supreme importance. It is, on the contrary, the belief that human existence is so to speak going nowhere, is a mere transitory phase in the evolution of the cosmos, which implies that life is objectively speaking, unimportant. If we are in fact going nowhere it cannot matter so very much precisely how we go. It is only if our journey has a specific destination that it becomes important to choose the right road and keep it in good repair. The idea that we shall be wiser and more resolute in dealing with the problems of this present life if we ignore its context and ultimate meaning is a quite incredible and totally invalid paradox. The true implication of the Christian gospel and the Christian interpretation of human existence is that the world really matters because it is God's world, that people really matter because they are God's children, and that the way they live their common life together in society and human history really matters because it is in society and human history that we must prepare ourselves for life in God's kingdom.

An even more notable feature of the specifically Marxist atheism—although one which it shares with several other kinds of atheism—is its way of introducing God, so to speak, under another name. In Marxism there is indeed some recognition of a force other than man and stronger than man which takes charge of human history and controls human destiny. This is what the Marxists call "the dialectic of history," a historical force or law of history operating within human history which ultimately determines the course of events. Often among communists we find something very like a kind of piety, which treats this dialectic of history as an almost personal force which is slowly but surely working its purpose out and which must be served by men with sincere devotion and self-sacrifice. It is this which gives to communist enthusiasm an almost religious or mystical quality, and it is on account of this reverent and obedient attitude toward the forces controlling history that some observers have been led to describe communism (rightly, in my view) as a kind of religion.

It is certainly true that we often find something very like a recognition of God among those who reject the name of God. Thus, among some purely naturalistic thinkers, nature and natural processes are taken to be the ultimately decisive force in life and are treated with the kind of reverence with which religious people approach God. The divine name is rejected but there is still some recognition of an objective controlling factor in human affairs which demands to be reverenced and obeyed. Of course, such conceptions of God are necessarily defective and idolatrous from the Christian point of view, but from the point of view of natural theology they are not without significance. They indicate that even some of the atheists feel compelled to recognize, although of course they would not admit it, the kind of intellectual need for an ultimate principle of reality and truth which leads those who are not prejudiced against the use of the word to declare the necessary existence of God.

Dualism

Some religious teachers, and perhaps a few philosophers, have been so profoundly impressed and influenced by the reality of evil that they have concluded that there exists not one God upon whom everything else that is not God depends, but two opposed ultimate principles, a principle of ultimate evil and a principle of ultimate good. The creation as we know it is a vast area of conflict between these two ultimate principles. This belief has taken many different forms, but by far its most common form throughout the Christian era has been a belief that it is the principle of ultimate evil who created the material universe, and that the God whom Christian men worship is the creator of spiritual reality alone. This easily leads to the conclusion that material and bodily existence is inherently evil and the source of all evil. The moral conflict is thus essentially a conflict within man between his spirituality and the demands and cravings of his fleshly nature.

In Christian history this kind of belief is usually called the Manichean heresy after Manichaeus, an ancient Persian teacher who was reared in the teaching of the Zoroastrian religion. For the first fifteen centuries or so of the Church's history heresies of this kind turned up again and again in many different places, and to some extent infiltrated the Church itself and influenced the thought and teaching of even rigidly orthodox defenders of the faith. During the last five hundred years, it appears to have died down, but in fact this kind of heretical teaching has manifested itself in a new form in the puritanism which has disfigured the life of so many Christian churches and sects since the Reformation. Puritanism is not, of course, explicitly Manichean in its teachings, but its general attitude toward life and its particular horror of the kinds of sin which are most obviously "the sins of the flesh" show that it has a profound affinity with the old Manichean heresy.

We may trace in this kind of thinking two basic errors, one theological, one philosophical. The theological mistake is that of supposing that the root of our sin is our physical or fleshly nature. This is a grave error. All sin is by nature not a physical but a spiritual process. Or, in other words, only spiritual beings are capable of sin. Even the sins which look like "sins of the flesh" are in fact sins in which a spiritual being abuses the physical nature and potentialities entrusted to his spiritual care. Thus, for example, there is no "drink evil." A physical thing like a drink cannot conceivably be evil. The crux of the evil of drunkenness is the abuse of drink, the greedy and intemperate use of something which is in itself neither good nor evil. Similarly if a wife murders her husband by poisoning him with arsenic, we should not dream of calling this the "arsenic evil." It is the spiritual woman, not the arsenic, who is guilty, and she has misused arsenic in order to inherit her husband's fortune, or for the sake of marrying some other man.

If, however, we take a New Testament point of view of the basic moral issues of human existence, we shall see that the so-called sins of the flesh are not even the worst sins. In the New Testament it is pride and lack of love rather than over-indulgence and sensuality which utterly destroy and pervert human souls, and so it is that even the publicans and the harlots go into the Kingdom of Heaven before the highly respectable Pharisees.

The Old Testament tells the same story. Thus in the great

113

myth of the Fall of Man which we find in the second and third chapters of Genesis, the serpent does not lure Eve to destruction by tempting her sensuality, by telling her that the forbidden fruit has an exquisite taste of which she must not allow herself to be cheated by the Divine prohibition. On the contrary, he tempts her spirituality. "If you show yourself strong enough to disobey God," he tells her in effect, "you will become like God, sharing his knowledge of good and evil and transcending the contrast between the two." This perverted desire of the spiritual creature to place himself on equality with God is indeed the sin of sins, and the heart and root of all sin. Yet it has nothing to do with the fact that we possess a physical nature, for it is only possible in a spiritual being. We do not sin with the lowest part of ourselves, but with the highest part of ourselves. Indeed, so far as we know, we are the only beings whom God has placed in this world who are even capable of sinning, and it is because we are capable of sin that we are fit for salvation. Manicheanism and puritanism—of course they differ in many ways, but fundamentally, I believe, they are agreed—are thus completely mistaken about the nature and cause of evil, and this mistake lies at the root of all their other errors.

The philosophical error is perhaps the more obvious. If God is indeed that primordial being upon whom everything that is not God depends for its existence, then there cannot be two gods. If there are two gods or two ultimate principles of being, then in fact neither of them is God, for the existence of each of them is limited by the parallel existence of the other. To acknowledge more than one God is in fact, as the early Christians saw so clearly, to be an atheist. Once we properly understand what the word God really means it becomes obvious to us that there can only be one God, only one ultimate creative principle upon whom everything else depends for its existence. Even more obvious is the difficulty of seeing how, if there are two creators who do not collaborate together in harmony but are eternally hostile to each other, their respective creations can fuse together in what at all events appears to be one world or one universe. After all on very strict Manichean principles each individual human being, a union of body and spirit, is partly the creature of the principle of evil and partly the creature of the principle of good. If we interpret him in this way how can man conceivably be one creature? It is true that fallen man is aware of conflict within himself; but if the dualistic philosophy is true, this conflict is an ultimately irreconcilable one, not one from which he could hope to be redeemed by any conceivable redemptive act of God.

Evil is certainly a problem, but it cannot conceivably be interpreted and understood in such terms as these. Christian theism sees the mystery of evil as essentially the mystery of its presence in a world created by the just and loving and utterly righteous God. No doubt the mystery must always remain. The problem is not the problem of understanding the mystery, but the problem of learning how to live with evil creatively, so that faith shall not be confounded, hope dissipated and charity turned into bitterness and hate by the evil which enters into our experience. This is the problem which we see so triumphantly solved by Jesus Christ in His incarnate life, and in particular at the moment of its great climax upon the Cross. The only way in which we can begin to enter into the heart of the mystery with some kind of understanding is to see the possibility of evil as somehow inherent within the possibility of good. We have already remarked that it is only because man is capable of sin that he is fit for salvation. Inherent in the very nature of finite spiritual being, in its splendid dignity and tremendous potentialities, is the possibility of its self-perversion. Sin and evil are, so to speak, by-products of finite spiritual existence. Not to create beings capable of sin would be not to create beings fit for salvation. In the divine mind, clearly, the risk was worth running and the price worth paying. Once we have learned to interpret evil in this way, we have no alternative but to acquiesce in the divine verdict.

Pluralism

Pluralism is the belief that the universe is composed of many realities, all of them equally ultimate and equally real. Ancient pagan polytheism, the belief in the existence of many different gods and goddesses, is one form of pluralism, but there are many modern forms of it which recognize, logically enough, no divinities at all. Thus, there is a personal or spiritual pluralism which believes that the ultimate reality is simply a plurality of personal existences. There is also a scientific, possibly materialistic, pluralism, which believes that the ultimate realities are the units of matter or force, whatever they may be called, in terms of which physical science interprets all physical phenomena. But although pluralism may exist in many different forms, the basic philosophical difficulty remains always the same. In effect pluralism means that there are many distinct realities existing side by side with one another and in some sort of relationship with one another, but the relationship of different things to one another is not something external or added on to their own individual nature. The different things of which the world is composed need one another and depend upon one another, and the existence of one is unintelligible apart from the existence of others. Thus a cow is distinct from the air that she breathes, the cud that she chews, the water that she drinks, and the parents who brought her into the world. Yet apart from the air, the cud, the water, and the parent bull and the parent cow, she could not exist or even have come into existence. In other words all the distinct entities of which our world is composed are what we have called contingent realities. They do not explain their own existence; they cannot account for their own existence; and therefore their reality cannot be the ultimate reality of which we need ask no further questions. They are real but not ultimately real, and the mere affirmation of their reality cannot possibly constitute a satisfactory account of their reality. If they were all of them ultimately real, that is ultimately independent of one another, we could never account for the plain fact of their immediate dependence on one another, nor for the fact that they live a common life in one universe. Philosophically speaking, pluralism is perhaps the least satisfactory of all the known alternatives to theism.

Pantheism

At the opposite end of the scale from pluralism is monism, a philosophy which usually implies, or is at least closely connected with, pantheism in religion. According to this philosophy the universe, far from being composed of a vast collection of separate entities, is in fact a single spiritual being, and what appear to be separate beings and things are in fact no more than different phases or aspects of this one being's activity and self-manifestation. Just as for pluralism the reality is the many, so that in consequence pluralism cannot explain the unity of the many, so for monism and pantheism the reality is the one, so that these doctrines cannot explain the diversity and plurality which meets us on the level of immediate experience. (Theism, of course, explains this problem of the one and the many by saying that both are real in their own form and degree: the necessary being or ultimate creative principle is one, and the contingent beings or created and dependent, finite realities are many. In these terms we can indeed make sense of the ultimate unity of the many, and the diversity of reality at the level of our own experience.)

Pantheism identifies God with everything that exists, interpreted as constituting one single composite or collective being. Thus, God is another name for everything. There are two difficulties about this view, one ethical, the other logical or metaphysical. If God is simply the totality of all being considered as a unity, if He is in everything and everything is in Him, then none of the distinctions we make between different things and forms of experience can have any ultimate meaning. All is God, and all things are lost and confounded together in the dark night of the divine being. So far as many of the distinctions with which we are familiar are concerned, this would no doubt not matter very much, but there are some distinctions which we cannot make intelligently or intelligibly unless we suppose that they have ultimate meaning and validity. Consider, for example, our ethical distinctions between good and evil (*e.g.* between justice and injustice) and the philosophical distinctions apart from which many of the highest forms of ethical experience would be impossible (*e.g.* the distinction between different persons which is necessary if the great values which we find in personal experience, faithfulness, trust, love, and so on, are to have any ultimate meaning or worth). If God is indeed identical with everything, then injustice is as divine as justice, and the distinction between persons who trust, love, and sacrifice themselves for one another is an ultimate illusion. Some pantheists and monists talk glibly about a god who is *beyond* good and evil, but, in fact, if the words good and evil have any real meaning it is impossible to be *beyond* good and evil.

There are three possibilities in relation to the distinction between ultimate good and ultimate evil. Either we hold fast to the good and abjure the evil, or we surrender to evil and isolate ourselves from the good, or we merely ignore the whole distinction as unimportant and irrelevant. Of these three possibilities the last is in fact the most evil of all. It is not possible to be *beyond* good and evil but it is, alas, possible to sink so low as to be *beneath* good and evil, and this is the worst and most depraved form of spiritual existence. The god of pantheism is in fact beneath good and evil in this sense, lower and more depraved even than the traditional idea of Satan, neither embodying the good and existing as the fount of all goodness, nor recognizing the good sufficiently to war against it, but existing from all eternity in sheer indifference to or total ignorance of the basic conception which establishes the possibility of the higher forms of spiritual experience. The god of pantheism is in fact not really god at all, but simply a kind of personification of everything in general.

Pantheism in practice sometimes seems a warm and attractive thing because it is akin to the spirit of some of the highest and noblest types of poetry, for example, much of the best poetry of William Wordsworth. This is the kind of poetry in which men interpret their aesthetic enjoyment of the spectacle of nature and their feeling of our kinship as fellow creatures with the natural order in a religious way. It is certainly true that for many men the enjoyment of the spectacle of the beauty of nature is an occasion of genuine religious experience. "The heavens declare the glory of God; and the firmament showeth His handiwork." This kind of poetry can be found even in the Bible itself. But it is a manifest intellectual confusion if we suppose that because the spectacle of the beauty of nature often moves the human spirit to adoration and worship, that it is therefore the beauty of nature itself which is adored and worshiped. If we intensely enjoy the music of Beethoven, it is Beethoven himself rather than the music whom we admire and praise. The apparent pantheism of so many of the greatest nature poets is due to an intellectual error of this kind. Our own detection of the error should not, of course, prevent us from enjoying and being spiritually edified by the poetry. Pantheism as a philosophy and religious doctrine is not any less preposterous because a great deal of pantheistic sounding poetry is noble and inspiring. The great poet justifies his existence by the beauty of his poetry. We ought not to require of him that he should necessarily be at the same time a great philosopher and a reliable theological guide.

Deism

This alternative to theism is now almost, perhaps quite, abandoned and forgotten, but we may mention it here for the sake of completeness. According to deism, God created the world but, having created it, He interests Himself no further in the course of its existence. We have already remarked that this theory was very largely sustained by a belief that the universe is a perfect machine. The celestial mechanic started it going, but it is so perfectly designed and manufactured that it requires no subsequent intervention on the part of its designer and creator. The difficulty about this analogy, as we have seen, is that this is not in fact the way in which any of the machines with which we are acquainted behave. A greater difficulty is that this theory requires us to believe in a totally completed creation. It reflects and depends upon a scientific picture and interpretation of the universe which was only possible in pre-Darwinian times. That is one reason why deism nowadays makes no appeal to any kind of philosopher at all. Religiously speaking the idea of a god who cared enough about the world to bring it into existence, but not sufficiently to concern himself with it any further is quite incredible, and it would require more simple faith than most of us have at our disposal even to imagine what it would be like to profess so ridiculous a creed.

We have attempted no more in this chapter than a very brief and summary discussion indeed, but we have at least been able to indicate that the achievements of natural theology in what I have called its negative mood are by no means unimportant. When we look at the possible alternatives to theism—which are also and equally, of course, alternatives to one another—they do not appear to be a particularly impressive collection. I have ventured on the perhaps somewhat questionable opinion that atheism is the best and most respectable of them, if only because it takes the question of the existence of God with radical seriousness. Nevertheless, atheism cannot stand by itself. It amounts, after all, to no more than a declaration that theism is not true. It requires to be supplemented, therefore, by some alternative account of the universe. This can hardly take the form of either dualism, pantheism or deism. In fact, therefore, atheism is almost certainly driven to some form of pluralism, so that in most cases the objections to pluralism are also additional objections to atheism, and the objections to pluralism seem to me quite decisive and insuperable.

It is possible for a philosopher to hold that the arguments in favor of a theistic philosophy are not absolutely convincing beyond all possibility of rational doubt, but I think that he may well be constrained to admit that at least the case for philosophical theism is immeasurably stronger than the case which can be made out for any alternative to theism. If we can indeed say that either A or B or C or D must be true; that A is probably, although perhaps not quite certainly, true;

that B, C, and D are either very improbable or altogether out
of the question; then surely we are justified in concluding
that for all practical purposes we may assume that A is so
very probably true that its high degree of probability is in
effect almost indistinguishable from sheer certainty?

CHAPTER FIVE

A THEOLOGY OF NATURE?

We remarked at the end of our first chapter that the very conception of a theology of nature raises the whole question of the scope and logical structure of theology itself. It is not the purpose of this chapter to supply a theology of nature in even the barest outline. I regard the idea of a theology of nature as no more than a project. It cannot be claimed that Christian thought has ever produced a developed theology of nature in the past, nor that it is actively engaged in producing such a theology now. We have to ask ourselves whether a theology of nature is a feasible theological project? What kind of speculative doctrine a theology of nature, if we had one, would be? And what would be the value of a theology of nature, if we had one, in relation to current controversies and perplexities?

Two Kinds of Theological Thinking

The historian of Christian theology may usefully distinguish between two distinct types of theological thought (research and speculation) that easily harden into two different kinds of theology. One kind of theology confines itself to the specialized study and interpretation of what we may call specifically theological data, theological things and experiences in the narrower sense of the word. This kind of theology tends to be existentialist and redemptionist in its tone. Its first emphasis is upon man's experience of being a sinner, of the inescapable consequences of sin, and of man's powerlessness to help or save himself or to surmount the crisis of his own existence. Its second emphasis is on the way in which God in and through Jesus Christ has come to man's rescue and done that for him which he cannot do for himself.

In this kind of theology the doctrine of atonement, redemption, or salvation (all these classical theological terms are concerned with the same empirical reality) is the primary theme of the Christian gospel, and the basic or architectonic idea of Christian theology. It is the architectonic idea because this particular type of theological thought tends to answer all other theological problems in terms of the doctrine of redemption. Thus, in classical theology, all enquiries which seek to answer such questions as who or what was Jesus Christ, and what do we mean when we claim that He is God-made-man are called Christological enquiries. They seek to determine the *logos* or rationale of the Christ, to make sense of the Church's experience of and attitude toward its Lord. Now the kind of theology which we are trying to describe has its own characteristic way of handling this question. It seeks to understand the mystery of the person of Jesus Christ through the study of what we know of the work of Christ. Christ, as men know him in the Church, is the Saviour and redeemer of sinners. We may therefore ask ourselves what kind of being must a historical figure possess if He is to be the Saviour of sinners?

In order to answer this question, we have to consider the nature of sin and the needs of sinners, and thus arrive at a kind of mental picture of the kind of saviour that sinners require. In this way we arrive at our understanding of the incarnation. The incarnation is the coming into the world of the kind of being who would be able to save us from our sins.

There is nothing peculiarly evangelical or post-reformation about this kind of theology. On the contrary, we discover similar processes of reasoning even in the early classical period of the growth of Christian theology which we call patristic. Thus, the fourth century heretic Apolinarius taught that Christ did not assume a complete human nature, but only a partial, outward-seeming human nature. The orthodox objected that if this were so, He could not be the Saviour of the whole of our human nature, because what He did not assume He could not save. In order, in other words, to save human nature, the Christ must unite the whole human nature to God. The point of this objection was that those who made it assumed that whatever else we know or do not know about the Christ we are at least certain that He is the Saviour of the whole human nature.

This kind of theology has many advantages to recommend it. It has the virtue of keeping very close to the basic Christian religious experience and to the actual way in which the Church preaches and must preach the gospel. It reduces to the barest minimum the difference of atmosphere between what the Church says when it proclaims the gospel and what it says in its more intellectual setting forth of its theology. Many theologians, particularly those who like to call themselves evangelical, desire their theology to sound as much like their preaching as possible. This is understandable, because nowadays most theologians are clergymen (it may be questioned whether this is not really a misfortune for the Church) and most clergymen are expected to be preachers, or at least to preach very frequently (which is perhaps not quite the same thing). This kind of theology has also a further advantage. Since the whole of its thinking is based upon a single point of departure from within the Christian experience, and one particular doctrine or doctrinal theme provides it with a single architectonic idea, it can easily be expressed in a highly systematic, streamlined way.

Nevertheless, it has certain disadvantages. There is much in God's creation, and in human life and experience, with which this kind of theology does not seem to be concerned. It succeeds in making theology appear systematic, rounded, and complete only at the cost of drastically narrowing its scope. Nor is it quite clear that its point of departure is in fact a possible or proper point of departure at all. It begins with man's existential experience and his certainty that he is a sinner. But can man really explain what he means when he declares himself to be a sinner without some reference to a doctrine of creation and the purpose of God in creating man, in the light of which he is able to perceive that he is in fact a sinner? Sin is presumably a failure on the part of man to be what he is meant to be and to become what he is meant to become, a tragic falling short of his own proper stature. Sin is the failure of the whole human race to occupy its own proper level and fulfil its own proper function in the created order. But how can we say this unless we have some idea of what it is that we are falling short of, what it is that we are failing to become? In other words, our experience of sin and our doctrinal declaration that we are all sinners presupposes what is from the logical point of view a more fundamental doctrine. It presupposes the doctrine of the creation of the world by God as the instrument of His loving purpose, a purpose fulfilled in the perfect humanity of Christ by the power of God, and therefore in principle a purpose which may be fulfilled in us despite our sins in so far as our humanity is joined to and becomes one with Christ's humanity in the life of the Church.

In saying this we have pointed the way toward a rather different kind of theology. From this new point of view it will appear that the doctrine of creation is logically more fundamental than the doctrine of redemption, and that the problem of the Incarnation—the question who or what was Jesus Christ—must be answered in terms of the doctrine of the creation as well as in terms of the doctrine of redemption. We now see that the perfect humanity of Christ is the living embodiment in human history of the purpose of God in creating human nature and human history. The Christ reveals to us not only the fact of human redemption but the purpose of the creation. From this point of view we see that the Christ is a cosmic figure, the very crown and summit of the creation, the logos or principle of creation which was in the beginning, the "last thing" or principle of judgment which shall triumph at the consummation of all things. He is for us the first and the last, and in Him all things consist.

This leads us to a kind of theology for which the basic, architectonic, theological ideas are those of creation and incarnation. This is often called incarnational theology, and it is one which from Hooker onward has been the peculiar possession and characteristic of the theological thought and speculation of the Anglican communion, distinguishing Anglical theology rather sharply from that traditional in the Lutheran and Reformed churches.

In pre-reformation theology we find, side by side with each other, tendencies in both the redemptionist and incarnationalist directions, but no very clear decision between the two. In the middle ages the whole question was raised in a very simple but striking way: Would Christ have been born among men if men had not sinned? After a very balanced discussion of the whole issue, St. Thomas Aquinas came down rather tentatively on the negative, redemptionist side, although it is true to say that on the whole the theology of Aquinas tends to be incarnationalist. In this context, he argues that all that we certainly know is that men have sinned and that Christ has become incarnate, and to suppose that there may have been an incarnation without any sin is to venture into realms of unprofitable speculation.

Duns Scotus, however, took the other side. He held that the purpose of God in creating the world and mankind was one which from the beginning envisaged the incarnation. The purpose of God in creating the world and mankind is not one which is fulfilled in the mere act of creation, but rather one which will be fulfilled at the consummation of all things. The Incarnation is thus, for him, necessary to the fulfilment of the whole plan of creation because the purpose of God in the creation is not fulfilled in the world and in the drama of human existence as we know it, but rather in the Kingdom of God which will issue out of it.

The position maintained by Duns Scotus has for us two very important advantages, of the second of which Duns Scotus, himself, was quite unaware. In the first place, it is closer to the New Testament. The New Testament does indeed speak again and again of Christ as the Saviour and redeemer of sinners, but elsewhere, particularly in the fourth gospel and in the Epistles to the Colossians and the Ephesians, it presents Him as the cosmic Christ, the crown and fulfilment of the whole creation and the clue to the meaning of the creation. More than that, Duns Scotus's view is in harmony with the eschatological emphasis which we find running right through the New Testament. In these eschatological passages Christ is repeatedly presented, not merely as the redeemer of sinners here and now, but as the last thing, as the final principle of judgment and victory in and through whom the whole purpose of the creation will be accomplished and the whole meaning of it laid bare.

But if this incarnationalist kind of theology has the advantage of being so much closer to Holy Scripture as a whole (the redemptionist kind of theology, at least since Luther, has always tended to lay special emphasis on certain favorite New Testament passages, chiefly Pauline, and to allow the rest of the New Testament to fall into comparative obscurity) it has also the secondary advantage of fitting in, very illuminatingly, with much that we now know about the processes which characterize the life of the universe.

The New Testament and the kind of incarnationalist theology which we find in Scotus knew nothing about the concept of evolution, and yet they are both evolutionist in their outlook. Evolution suggests that the real meaning of a process is not to be found in the way in which it begins but in the way in which it consummates itself. The eschatological passages in the New Testament suggest precisely the same doctrine. The concept of evolution suggests that in a very real sense the creation of the world is not yet finished; the process of creation is still going on. The kind of incarnationalist theology which we find in Duns Scotus suggests very much the same thing. For him, as we have seen, the incarnation is not only necessary to the process of redeeming man but it is also necessary to the process of creating man, a process which will only be consummated in the Kingdom of God.

Until very recently, almost all theologians were agreed (and almost all non-theologians also) that the creation of the world had been completed. The Christian theologian tended also to believe that the human part of the creation at least had been spoiled by sin, and the purpose of the creation to that extent obstructed or even nullified, so that man stood in need of a redemption which would restore to the creation its original integrity and visible conformity to the divine purpose. This kind of attitude, as we have noticed, was out of harmony with the eschatological outlook which we find everywhere in the New Testament. But on the whole it is true, and not too harsh to say, that for many hundreds of years Christian theologians of all schools of thought have contrived to ignore, or at least push very much into the background, that eschatological outlook which is so very much in the foreground of the New Testament itself.

We must, however, not be too hard on the theologians. They tended to assume that the creation was finished very largely because most of the best science of their own day assumed the same thing. Darwin, in other words, has rendered a great service to theological thinking, and made it possible for us to apprehend shades of meaning in the New Testament which generations of our predecessors scarcely noticed.

Our realization of the importance of this conception of an unfinished creation is clearly expressed in a letter written by the late Archbishop Temple shortly before his death:

What we must completely get away from is the notion that the world as it now exists is a rational whole; we must think of its unity not by the analogy of a picture, of which all the parts exist at once, but by the analogy of a drama where, if it is good enough, the full meaning of the first scene only becomes apparent in the final curtain; and we are in the middle of this. Consequently the world as we see it is strictly unintelligible. We can only have faith that it will become intelligible when the Divine purpose, which is the explanation of it, is accomplished. Theologically, this is a greater emphasis on eschatology.[1]

[1] F. A. Iremonger, *William Temple* (New York: Oxford), pp. 537-8. Quoted by Dorothy Emmett in the chapter which she contributed to this volume. Used by permission of the publisher.

From the point of view of such an approach to theology as this, it will easily be seen that Christ is interpreted as much more than the Saviour of sinners. He is indeed the Saviour of sinners, but He is also the clue to the meaning and purpose of the whole universe. Hence, for this incarnationalist theology the scope of theology, its proper sphere of interest, comprehends the entire creation. This observation gives us a catholic theology, in a slightly new sense of the word catholic.

This catholic theology is very far from being the theology of all catholic theologians, although it is probably true that almost all catholic theologians, as distinct from evangelical theologians, tend in this direction. This kind of theology is catholic in the sense we use when we say that a man's literary or artistic tastes are catholic, meaning that his mind is unrestricted by prejudice, unmarred by blind spots, and wide open to every variety of literary or artistic experience and value. This theology is catholic because it is, in principle, an attempt to give a theological account and interpretation of everything that is or will be. It is only from the point of view of such a theology as this that a specific theology of nature is a feasible project.

Perhaps one word of warning may be timely and proper before we conclude this particular part of our discussion. We have been talking about the distinction between two different kinds of theology. Controversies that stem from these can be very profound and far reaching, and they may sharply divide us from one another on the intellectual level. But let us notice that these are not really controversies about religion at all; they are controversies about theology and theological procedure. We can differ about such questions on the intellectual level and yet remain at one with one another on that profounder level where we confess our faith and worship our God.

Theological differences need not, indeed should not, involve religious differences or ecclesiastical divisions. The redemptionist type of theologian believes in the incarnation; the incarnationalist dare never forget that he is himself a redeemed sinner. The controversies between us are concerned with the manner and scope of theological thinking. They are not controversies about the substance of the Gospel itself. There we can agree in a common act of faith.

Nevertheless, these theological issues, although certainly not the profoundest issues, are grave and important. Our theologizing will do much to determine the way in which we present and communicate the Christian gospel to the world and the way in which Christian thought will relate itself to the thinking and the doubting and the self-questioning of men in the world. In a world in which there are many intellectuals to be saved, and in which the intellectuals fashion climates of opinion by which even the minds of non-intellectuals are often decisively influenced, the precise form which the Christian intellectualism (another name for the Church's theology) assumes and the terms in which it asserts itself are matters of crucial importance. They are closely related to the success or failure which attend the Church's efforts to fulfil its evangelistic functions and to discharge its evangelical responsibilities.

Theology and Science

Theology has usually been related to science in the setting of the rather hackneyed and dreary "science *vs.* religion" controversy. The main aim of the Christian apologist, when thinking and speaking in this context, is to show that the kind of truth which we find in Christianity is not really incompatible with the kind of truth which science supplies. He may try to do this, for example, by arguing that the evolutionary account of the growth of the universe and the emergence of man are quite in harmony with the essential point and teaching of the colorful poetic myth with which the Book of Genesis opens. Alternatively, he may try to show that theology and religion answer questions different from those which science answers and that they are concerned with phases or aspects of reality or experience different from those with which the scientist is concerned.

There is indeed much of value that can be said along these lines, but it is doubtful if we can ever get to the very heart of the matter in this way. The trouble is not so much that some of the things which the natural scientist sees and teaches may at first sight appear to contradict or to be out of harmony with essential religious and theological teachings. These are but minor frictions, which will almost certainly be lessened and thus ultimately disappear in the course of time, as our knowledge increases and our analysis becomes more profound. The real tension between science and religion, and this particularly from the point of view of those working or interested in science, is the difference between the logical categories and methods employed in these two different fields. The scientist is apt to feel, as he peruses and considers some work of philosophical or theological thought, that its standards of rational judgment and its methods of seeking truth, even perhaps its criterion of truth itself, are very different from those with which he is familiar in his own sphere of research. If there is any truth in religion in general, or in Christianity in particular, it seems to him to be a kind of truth which he can never reach by employing the methods he employs in the sciences. He is apt to demand that it be possible for him to make sense of Christianity in the same kind of way that he is accustomed to make sense of the data of his own science. Thus, he complains when he finds that this cannot be done and feels that there is apparently no making any sense of Christianity at all.

This raises the question of the relation of the human mind to the logical categories and methods which it employs on different occasions, and in relation to different types of problems. There are two possible approaches to this issue, one holding in effect that the human mind is and ought to be enslaved by its categories and methods, the other holding that the human mind is free in relation to them.

The first approach we may call the dogmatic one. According to this view there are certain categories and methods which constitute the very essence of reason itself. The only valid kind of thinking is the kind of thinking which employs these categories; all other modes of thought are invalid and ultimately meaningless. This approach lays down precisely what these categories and methods are, and gives us what purports to be a universal definition of the very nature of science (*i.e.* that science is a mental discipline which thinks in terms of *x*-categories and employs *y*-methods to the total exclusion of all others). In other words science is known and recognized neither by the purposes which it serves, nor by the motives which inspire it, nor by the kind of result that it achieves, but by the logic and rules of procedure to which it conforms.

The worst consequence of this view is that it fails to do justice to the differences among the many distinct sciences, differences which are dictated by the great variety of the subject matter of the sciences concerned. This habit of dogmatizing about the categories leads to a demand that all the sciences should ideally look alike, that is, that they should all possess the same logical shape. Because of the tremendous success and prestige of the physical sciences in the modern world, this usually takes the form of a demand that all sciences, if they are to be acknowledged as sciences, should resemble the physical sciences in their logical structure. This cramping dogma has often made things difficult in the biological sciences which, in the view of many workers in this field, require categories, for example the category of purpose, with which the physical sciences can dispense. In what are called the social sciences, the necessity of making all "scientific" enquiries look as much like physics as possible has lead to distortion, and often ridiculous results. Those, like the so-called logical positivists, who are most ruthless in asserting this dogmatic view of the scientific categories, and who insist on working them out to their last logical consequences, usually hold that speculative disciplines like philosophy and theology can have no meaning at all.

There is a very obvious, although in some ways rather subtle, initial objection to any view of this kind. The belief that only the categories and methods employed in the physical sciences have rational validity cannot itself be discovered by employing the methods of physics and it cannot be asserted within the terms of its categories. There is no scientific way of demonstrating the truth of the proposition, or of verifying the hypothesis, that the scientific categories and methods of the physical sciences are the only rational ones. The assertion is thus a dogmatic presupposition, presumably presupposed and asserted under the influence of some kind of belief that without such a presupposition faith in the validity of science is impossible.

Our second possible interpretation of man's relation to his categories calls such a belief into question. From this point of view, the hallmark of truly scientific procedure is the devising of logical categories and methods appropriate to the subject matter being studied. Its emphasis is upon the resilience and flexibility of the reason, its mastery of its categories, its freedom to employ one set of categories in one sphere of discourse and quite a different set in another.

We catch perhaps the first glimpse of the possibility of man's freedom in relation to his categories in the third of Kant's three great *Critiques*. In his first *Critique*, Kant had seemed to assume that the categories of pure reason are the basic, elemental categories of the human mind, the same wherever men are men, so that the categories we use in one sphere of discourse are necessarily the categories which we must use in any other. In his third *Critique*, however, Kant faces fairly and squarely the possibility that in the biological sciences the very nature of the subject matter may demand the employment of categories other than those which are required by the subject matter of mathematical physics. At this point, he speculates rather tentatively that man may after all have a certain freedom in relation to his categories, that there may be several sets of categories among which we may validly choose in accordance with their appropriateness to the particular kind of intellectual problem with which we are wrestling.

Since Kant's time the probability that this may indeed be so has been heavily reinforced by the discovery that even in the realm of mathematics important alternatives exist and real choices may and must be made. Thus, from Euclid to the second half of the nineteenth century men knew and employed only one geometry. This geometry assumed that space had the character of a large, three dimensional box. Today, we know that many alternative geometries are possible, and one of them, not very happily entitled the geometry of curved space, has assumed great scientific importance because of its employment in relativity physics.

This use of the so-called geometry of curved space in contemporary physics must not be misunderstood. The point is not that we used to believe that space is boxy but that modern science has now discovered that space is really curved. I remember a woman once saying to me, "What's all this nonsense about space being curved? Look at it; you can see for yourself that it's nothing of the kind." This is to mis-understand the nature and function of a geometry, which does not reproduce facts but interprets relations.

Space is neither curved nor boxy, but spacial relations can be validly interpreted and described in terms of several distinct geometries. Which geometry we in fact choose to employ will depend upon the precise purposes which we have in mind. Thus, for example, even in this age of relativity-physics, the land surveyor still employs a three dimensional geometry because this is the kind of geometry which suits his purposes. Historically speaking, in fact, three dimensional geometry was essentially a geometry for land survey-ing. It was the experience of the Egyptians in building the pyramids that lay behind the Euclidian geometry. It was only when the physicists stopped being universe surveyors *à la* Newton and became interpreters of physical events *à la* Einstein that the classical geometry proved inadequate and had to be replaced by another. But we must always bear in mind that *neither* geometry is *true*. A geometry is no more than a set of categories, a tool of analysis, useful in one context and less useful, perhaps even useless, in another.

Thus, even a study of trends of development in the physical sciences during the last half century supports a belief in man's rational freedom in relation to his categories. Once such a point of view is established, we shall cease to require or expect that the kind of truth given to us in Christianity and Christian theology must, if rational men are to accept it, necessarily be a kind of truth which can be discovered by the methods which the sciences employ or must be expressed in terms of the categories to which a scientific training accustoms the scientific mind. We shall not expect or demand either that science shall be able to make sense of Christianity or that it must express Christianity's meaning within the limits of its own highly specialized terminology.

There is, however, a valid demand which may be made from the other side of the fence. It ought to be possible for Christian theology, using its own categories and methods, to interpret and make sense of the fruitfulness and success of the scientific method, when employed in the service of its own proper purposes and in relation to its own highly speccialized subject matter. This is the problem to which what I have called a theology of nature must address itself. It must answer two very fundamental questions: How is it that created reality is, among many other things, a possible and proper subject for successful scientific scrutiny and analysis? It must also answer an additional, although closely related question: How is it that man is the kind of being who, among many other things, is capable of analyzing, and to some extent knowing, created reality by the employment of a scientific method which he has himself devised? Such problems must be solved by theology in terms of its own doctrine of creation and its own doctrine of man.

I believe that the clue to the solution of these problems is to be found in the Biblical assertion that man is made in the express image of the God who has created everything that is not God. The possibility and success of science points, more clearly than anything else within the limits of our natural experience, to the fundamental kinship between the Creator who called the facts of our experience into being and the creatures who, alone among all the creatures, possess this awe-inspiring capacity to probe and understand them.

The fact that man is capable of achieving a scientific knowledge and understanding of the world in which he finds himself is, after all, something of a problem. So far as we know no other creature of the world is capable of attaining scientific knowledge or anything remotely resembling it. In a very real sense scientific man in knowing and interpreting the world in his own scientific way stands over against the world, distinguishes himself from the world, we might almost say transcends the world. Again, in seeking for and to some extent discovering a sheer objective truth about the world in the course of his scientific researches, when we see them conducted with the highest degree of intellectual integrity, man as scientist transcends both the peculiarities of his own private psychology and the interests of the social group to which he belongs; that is, he pushes beyond the possibility of mere rationalization or ideology. In a very real sense man as scientist transcends even himself. Such a transcendence of one's environment and one's selfhood is only a possibility for what theology calls a spiritual being. The very fact of scientific achievement is one which calls for a theological account and interpretation of man. Science is in fact an inherently spiritual activity; it is itself a form, and a very high form, of spirituality.

Indeed, one of the intellectual developments which most of all menaces science and scientific activity from within contemporary thought is the widespread tendency among those thinkers who are particularly impressed with the importance of science and its successes to conceive of what they call a purely scientific account of man himself, which may easily and paradoxically suggest that man is not in fact the kind of being who is capable of becoming a scientist. According to many writers, a really scientific view of man must interpret him as being utterly conditioned and determined by the world in which he lives and by the unalterable peculiarities of his own private psychology. Such a being would not be capable of the objectivity, the intellectual integrity and the transcendence of his world and his condition which the scientific ideal demands of its devotees and practitioners. What science really requires and implies is not the kind of picture of man that is given in what is sometimes called the Scientific World View, but the theological picture of man as the child of God whose mind is adequate to the task of knowing and interpreting the world because he is made in the image of the Creator of the world.

Again, the success of science is really a verification of its conviction that this world is the kind of world which can only be known by empirical means. We cannot know or interpret the world by any kind of pure, deductive, rational analysis which attempts to decide what the world in the nature of the case must be like. In the long run we can only find out what things are like by observing them carefully and experimenting with them resourcefully. But what kind of world is it which can only be known scientifically by using the empirical method? The answer seems pretty clear: The world which can only be known by the empirical method is the world as it is conceived and defined in the terms of the Christian theology, the created, contingent world which does not have to be but merely happens to be, which might conceivably have been otherwise than it is, which might quite conceivably not have been at all. The success of the scientific method thus contributes in a most striking way to the verification of the metaphysical account of the world which we find in classical Christian theology. Indeed, it is perhaps no accident that the scientific method as we now know it was first invented and devised in a mental climate which was dominated by classical Christian theology. The philosophical justification of the attitude toward the world adopted by the first pioneers of modern science, and the methods which they devised in order to seek the truth about it, was the account of the world given by the theologians. The pioneers of modern science thus correctly diagnosed the logical and methodological consequences of the Christian doctrine of creation.

The proper way of relating theology to scientific thought, then, is not to attempt to show, desperately (and ultimately in vain) that Christianity is, after all, something to which the scientific mind can do justice in its own terms, but rather that the scientist himself and the phenomenal success of his science is something to which the theologian can and must do justice in his own proper terms. The honest scientist is mistaken if he supposes that he cannot with intellectual integrity accept Christianity unless he can somehow force its truth into the mold of his own scientific categories. What his intellectual honesty really requires, and must demand, is not that his science should be capable of interpreting and apprehending his Christianity but that his Christianity should be able to make sense of his science. Thus, the proper context in which to relate theology to modern sci-

ence is not that of the stale "science *vs.* religion" controversy, but that of the theology of nature, which we can now
see to be indispensable, not only for apologetic purposes, but
also for the intellectual completeness of our theology itself.

The Analogy Between Theology and Science

We have alluded to the obvious difference between theology and the natural sciences. Nevertheless, they are in
certain respects analogous and akin to each other, and we
ought not to close this discussion without laying some emphasis upon this kinship. Great as the differences are, theology has in fact much in common with the spirit of the
natural sciences. Indeed, I would venture to say that theology is closer to science than to what is sometimes called
the philosophy of religion. The so-called philosophy of religion is simply a collective name for the various kinds of
philosophy whose conclusions tend in a religious direction.
At its best, it is another, and less specific name, for the kind
of natural theology whose achievements we briefly assessed
in the last chapter. But Christian theology is not itself a
part of the philosophy of religion; it is a rational assessment
and interpretation (with many prophetic, that is pragmatic, applications to the problems of human existence in
the world) of those specifically Christian facts which constitute the special subject matter of theology. It is the possession of a special subject matter, a particular set of facts
and experiences to the elucidation of which it devotes its
energies, that distinguishes theology from philosophy of
religion and that approximates it to the sciences. Theology,
like the sciences, is grounded upon fact and experience,

145

and, like the sciences, it must in the long run defer to them.

The underlying kinship between philosophy and the sciences is the true theme of Bishop Butler's great work *The Analogy of Religion*. This is a difficult book for the modern reader because it addresses itself to a particular eighteenth century controversy, that between what used to be called natural religion and revealed religion, a controversy which has long ceased to have any vitality or meaning. The eighteenth century is over, and its particular intellectual difficulties and scruples no longer trouble the conscience or the reason of contemporary man, whether Christian or not. The result is that Butler's book reads like a brilliant contribution to a dead controversy, meaningful no doubt in its own time but no longer meaningful to us or relevant to our needs and interests.

The book only comes alive if the reader translates it, so to speak, as he goes along, constantly asking himself what Butler would have said if he had written from the same point of view in our own time. His main point is that both science and theology are confronted at bottom with the same problems and the same difficulties, the problems with which the human mind is inevitably confronted when it ceases merely to elaborate its own ideas or to deduce the logical consequences of its own presuppositions, and instead disciplines itself to the scrutiny and interpretation of sheer fact. The difficulties, he tells us, which confront us when we seek to make sense of the data of revealed religion are fundamentally identical with the difficulties which confront us when we seek to think in naturalistic terms. There is an inevitable tension between reason and fact, whether the facts which concern us are the natural facts with which the scientist deals, or the unique facts located in past time which are the subject matter of the historian, or the very special class of facts in and through which God has revealed himself to men (which are the special and proper objects of theological scrutiny). Reason, no doubt, would in one sense be happier if it were not compelled to saddle itself with the heavy discipline of deferring to the facts, if it felt itself free, as some philosophers have, to wander without constraint wherever the flow of ideas seemed to take it. On the other hand, reason inevitably craves a worthwhile subject matter, and such an absence of discipline as it sometimes seems to demand does in the end prove self-frustrating. It is by displaying its power to endure this endless tension between reason and fact that the human mind manifests its vitality and endurance. The recognition of the reality of this close parallel between the mood and method of theology and the mood and method of natural science should do much to help theologians and scientists understand and appreciate one another more adequately than they have tended to do in the recent past.

The Role of Theology in the History of Science

Another factor which may tell in the same reconciling direction is our new appreciation of the important place of theology in the story of the development of modern science as we now know it, particularly in its very early stages. Until recently, this particular aspect of the history of science was almost completely ignored, but contemporary research is making us more aware of it.

Most of the giants and heroes who dominate the story of the earlier phases of modern science were what we may call amateur theologians—Galileo and Boyle, for example, rather good ones, and Newton a very bad one. This suggests that in their minds there was no clear-cut break or cleavage between theological thinking and scientific thinking.

If we direct our search to an earlier period, to the later middle ages, we shall find people who concerned themselves sometimes with what would be called theological thinking and sometimes with what we should now call scientific themes. These did so without recognizing any fundamental difference between them at all. Thus, Robert Grosseteste, who taught at Oxford and subsequently became Bishop of Lincoln in the thirteenth century, is an important, without being a particularly great, figure in the story of the development of medieval theology and Christian philosophy. In the story of the early development of modern science, he is a supremely significant figure, in some ways more outstanding than the better-known Roger Bacon. His great achievement was the hammering out of a synthesis between the methods of pure rational analysis employed by the scholastic philosophers and the empirical trial and error methods employed by medieval inventors and technicians. (The rapid advance of technical development during the later middle ages is something which has also been overlooked in the more conventional history books.) This fusion of empirical and technical methods with techniques of pure rational analysis was perhaps the achievement which made the development of modern science, as we know it, possible; yet Grosseteste, himself, was apparently unaware of the way in which he was continually stepping out of the realm of what we should now call theology into the realm of what we should now call science. For him, these two worlds were one world, and their problems and perplexities all of one piece.

In the last resort, we may still hold that Grosseteste was right. There is in fact only one world, and theology and science are both concerned with the same world from different points of view. The distinction between them is obvious and important but not fundamental. It is certainly not a distinction which, once we understand it properly, need divide the theologian from the scientist either in sympathy or in spirit, nor should we permit it to blind us to their common history, their common roots in Christian civilization —characteristically and uniquely a spiritual civilization which treats the material, visible world with seriousness and reverence.

CHAPTER SIX

THE USEFULNESS AND GRANDEUR OF NATURAL THEOLOGY

There can be no fruitful communication between the Church and the world unless there is some coincidence of the range of interests of men in the Church with the range of interests of men in the world. Men can talk with one another only in a language which they all understand, and about things in which they share some common motivating interest.

I can think of no danger in the contemporary intellectual situation more alarming than the perceptible tendency of a certain kind of Christian intellectualism to become so inbred and introverted that it has nothing to say to the world about anything in which the world is interested, and no interest of its own that anybody outside Christianity can conceivably share. Here is a real danger that may turn Christian theology into no more than an interpretation of the private religious experience of the Christian man. Of course, different Christians will interpret the term, "private religious experience," in different ways. It may be interpreted from the evangelical point of view, existentially, as the experience of conversion and Christian existence in the sight of God; or it may be interpreted by the catholic primarily in terms of liturgical life and our participation in the corporate life of the Body of Christ; or, again, it may be interpreted primarily in terms of mysticism, as by the religious individualist. But however we interpret the meaning of the phrase, it is possible to concentrate upon it in so narrow and introverted a fashion as to make it appear irrelevant to the experience and range of interests of any man who is not a Christian.

A mere interpretation, however intelligent and profound, of experiences which we have and which the vast majority of other people do not have (so far as their conscious minds tell them) will not establish a platform for communication. The necessity of a common platform, of a Christian sharing in the interests of non-Christian men in the world, emphasizes the importance of natural theology. In order to communicate with the world, it is necessary to have something to communicate which can be understood in terms of the world's experience and intelligibly propounded in the world's language, and which is concerned with something about which those with whom we wish to communicate desire to hear.

That is why I cannot but feel that Dr. Paul Tillich's fondness for defining theology in terms of what he calls "ultimate concern" is a rather unhappy and unfortunate one. My quarrel is with the phrase itself rather than with what

Dr. Tillich appears to mean by it when he expounds his conception in detail. No doubt all men are ultimately concerned about something or other, and no doubt also the theologian is ultimately concerned about all that concerns him, which is, in a sense, everything. But as things are, we must admit that the question of ultimate concern is one which divides men and makes their ultimate concerns appear irrelevant to one another. What unites men and constitutes a sphere of discourse in which they can meet and communicate is what we may call the area of "proximate concern," the immediate problems which arise for all of us out of the common human condition in which we find ourselves. It is only by showing that Christianity and Christian theology are as much at home in the sphere of proximate concern as in the sphere of ultimate concern, have as much to say about the immediate problems of the human condition as about the ultimate reality of God and the ultimate destiny of man, that we can establish a point of communication with man as such.

Christian Intellectualism

Many well-meaning critics of Christian intellectualism are apt to charge the Christian theologians and intellectuals with using words which are too long and employing conceptions which are too subtle for the common man to understand. But that is not the real problem. Such a criticism is not really a criticism at all, for it says no more in effect than that Christian intellectuals are real intellectuals, which is just what they are meant to be and must be if they are to do their own special work in the Church effectively. It would be a lamentable thing, indeed, if the Christian intellectuals were no more than pseudo-intellectuals, concealing a fundamental intellectual naïveté beneath a thick covering of sophisticated language.

It is not, in the last analysis, long words and subtle conceptions which prevent communication between the mind of the Church and the mind of the world. Indeed, the use of everyday and imprecise language, and the employment of only a simple conceptual apparatus may well lead to a complete breakdown of communication in a world in which all the problems are exceedingly complicated. I remember a friend of mine telling me that he was once invited to preach in a London church whose congregation consisted very largely of members of Parliament, industrialists, bankers and people whose vocation in life compelled them to spend the week wrestling with vast, well-nigh unfathomable problems.

After the service a banker churchwarden remarked to my friend, in a mildly critical way, "You know, in some way I prefer a rather simple sermon about the simple Gospel."

My friend replied "What on earth would be the use of a simple gospel to a man like you?"

The churchwarden sighed and said rather wistfully, "I should find it very restful."

Of course, we can sympathize with the churchwarden, but the Christian Church cannot conceivably resign itself to proclaiming a restful gospel!

The real obstacle to communication is not long words or subtle conceptions. The problem lies elsewhere. What do we desire to communicate? Where do our interests converge and overlap with those of the people to whom we wish to speak? What have we got to say to men in the world about the things in which they are already interested? The real problem may be described as that of making a valid and fruitful transition from a merely devotional, Biblical, and churchly theology, which confines itself to working out and defining the basic theological concepts and categories, to a prophetic theology which openly employs them in the interpretation of the problems of human existence.

I do not wish to be misunderstood. Obviously, the task of discerning and defining the basic Biblical and theological concepts and categories is a very important theological discipline, indeed it is the primary function of the theologian. It is, in the last resort, his dedication to such an activity which constitutes him a theologian. But the basic theological concepts and categories are more than self-sufficient ideas which ask only to be exhibited in their purity and clarity before the respectful eyes of an admiring church. They are also hypotheses which require to be verified in terms of the experience of men in the world. Merely to discern and define the basic and primary Christian ideas and say in effect to the world, "Here they are, do not do anything with them—they may not be tough enough to bear the strain—confine yourself to inspecting them with a reverent gaze and from a decent distance," is hardly science, even in the rather special sense of the word in which theology may reasonably claim to be a science.

A real science fulfils itself and expresses its genius in the activity by means of which it verifies its hypotheses, its basic concepts, in terms of experience and experiment. The same is true in theology. The verification of the validity of theological conceptions is to be found in a prophetic activity which manifests the power of theology to interpret and handle the world's problems, to unravel its perplexities and shed precious shafts of light on its dark places. Theology verifies itself in prophecy. This means that the theologian must be a man obsessed by an insatiable curiosity which prompts him to search into the nature of all that conditions human existence, to interest himself in everything in which he finds other men interested. Wherever and whenever the theologian addresses himself to his task in such a frame of mind, some kind of natural theology, some kind of theological concern for the natural, will inevitably manifest itself in his Christian thinking.

The Alternatives

What are the alternatives to this theological and prophetic approach to the problem of communication? As we look round on the very varied evangelistic activities which are being carried on in different parts of contemporary Christendom, we can indeed perceive several alternatives, most of them rather unpleasant and of doubtful validity.

There are, for example, the rather crude techniques—although here and there we find more sophisticated and refined versions of the same kind of thing—of those who are called revivalists. Their method is to hammer at people with a constantly reiterated, highly emotional presentation of the Gospel until the latter are battered into a kind of intellectual insensibility. Not unsimilar, are the activities of those, operating on more exalted social levels, who gather together their spiritual clientele at luxurious weekend house parties and morally challenge and gregariously herd them into a kind of self-conscious salvation.

The fundamental error of those who resort to methods of this kind is that they fail to display any proper reverence for intellectual integrity. They are disobedient to the Pauline injunction to think upon (that is, reverence) the things which are just, pure, true, lovely, and of good report. Intellectual integrity is not, of course, the only virtue, but it is undeniably a very noble one, and one which the modern world, at its best, has learned to respect very highly.

We must show ourselves capable of respecting, not only intellectual integrity wherever we find it, but also the modern world's respect for intellectual integrity. I believe it to be true that we can only speak profitably to men about their many sins if we show ourselves capable of appreciating their few virtues. We do not have to proclaim the Gospel in a world which is entirely black, devoid of one single redeeming feature. No doubt it would in some ways be easier to proclaim the Gospel if that were indeed the case, and we may wish, in a certain mood, that it were so. However, we must be realistic; it is not the case. A reverence for the very real virtue of intellectual integrity is one of the best characteristics of the contemporary mind. It is vitally important that we should share that reverence in our private minds and also make it outwardly visible that we do so. We do not desire that men should become Christian against their reasons, on the strength of an excess of religious emotion or by an arbitrary act of will. On the contrary, we desire that men should come to Christ with the whole of their being, and that means, among other things, with the free consent of their reason.

Again, there is a certain way of theologizing and proclaiming the Gospel which rather resembles the way in which a harping wife afflicts and sometimes dominates her husband. The preachers may appear to nag at the world, quarrelling with it as a matter of course, almost on principle, about whatever it does and whatever it is suffering. Some unwise parents treat their children in the same way. To the children themselves, it seems that they are the targets of an endless stream of criticism which falls upon them with equal weight whatever they do. The result is that real and important criticisms fail to make their point, because the children feel that their parents are against them anyway. There are some kinds of preaching and some kinds of theology which seem motivated by a kind of anger against the world. The theologian, especially, dare never forget that the wrath of the theologian is a very different thing from the wrath of God, and almost invariably unspiritual in its motivation.

We may recollect how the prophet Jonah was unwilling to go to Nineveh to preach the word of God there until he was told what his message was to be when he arrived: "Yet forty days and Nineveh shall be destroyed." This encouraging news overcame all his reluctance, because that was precisely the kind of thing he enjoyed saying in places like Nineveh. The mantle of Jonah seems to have fallen upon not a few contemporary theologians, but the prophet who prophesies in the spirit of Christ dare never pronounce a message of doom unless the pronunciation of it breaks his own heart. He dare never declare the judgment of the Lord upon mankind unless the judgment falls first and most heavily upon himself. The doom of the world is also the doom of the Church and the doom of the prophet. In any case, men do not and will not come to Christ merely in order to escape their doom. They come to Christ, if they come at all, in order to find and know the God made manifest in Christ. There is no other reason for becoming or being a Christian.

The Way of Natural Theology

Intellectual difficulties which prevent people from making the act of faith, in so far as they are honest and sincere, demand our sympathy and respect. The suggestion that men should be urged to overcome them by suppressing them, though it may seem to bear fruit in a surprisingly large number of cases, is always unwise, even in some ways immoral, and it is often self-frustrating in its ultimate consequences. An act of faith which is only made possible by the suppression of honest intellectual scruples results in a subsequent life of faith which will continually be weakened from within by the lurking presence of the suppressed intellectual doubts. Intellectual doubt cannot be suppressed; it can only be dissipated by careful intellectual analysis. In a way, natural theology may be likened to psychoanalysis. It seeks to disperse, by a process of patient and dispassionate analysis, the roots of doubt and those half-concealed, sometimes altogether unconscious, intellectual difficulties which prevent a man from coming to God, and offering himself to God, with a faith which comprehends his entire being.

Of course, an intellectual process of this kind will not of itself suffice to bring a man to God. It has frequently been noted that no man was ever argued into becoming a converted, committed Christian. That is true. It is equally true, however, that no honest man who has gone through a period of intellectual doubt—and few mentally alive people can grow up in our world without ever experiencing its sting—can become a Christian without any argument at all, although the argument may, in some cases, be a purely internal argument which takes place in his own mind.

Even though the argument which natural theology conducts never suffices by itself to turn men into convinced, converted Christians, it may nevertheless be necessary, in order to remove many of the impediments which must be removed before honest men feel able to become Christian with integrity. From this point of view, the argument of natural theology may be recognized as a process of great importance and significance. And to conduct that argument in the name of the Father and of the Son and of the Holy Ghost is indeed a very high office and vocation which no man should despise.

Natural Theology, an Unfinished Mission

If, then, it is essential to the nature of natural theology that it seizes with joy and avidity upon points of convergence, points at which for the moment it can feel itself at one with some current tendency, it follows that natural theology cannot be a fixed doctrine, written down once for all in a book in which it can be read and learned. What do people mean when they say, as some theologians do, "I do not believe in natural theology"? Does such a man mean, "I do not believe that it is natural to be theological, or I do not believe in being theological about nature"? He may of course mean these, but I think that he usually means, "I have seen certain propositions written in a book, purporting to be propositions in natural theology, with which I do not agree." So, of course, have we all. But, for that matter, we have all read in books propositions purporting to be propositions in revealed and Biblical theology with which we equally disagree.

Natural theology is not, and cannot be, a completed doctrine, something written down once and for all by a Thomas Aquinas or a Bishop Butler or some other distinguished worthy of the past. Natural theology, indeed, is a project rather than a doctrine, a process which in the nature of the case cannot be completed as long as time, and the debates of time, and our novelty-laden human experience shall continue. Natural theology is an essay in the art of communication, something which has to be renewed and rethought in every age, in the light of what the existing points of convergence happen to be at the time, and they certainly differ very greatly at different periods in the development of thought and civilization. Natural theology is always and necessarily contemporary theology. The different manifestations of its spirit hold for an age rather than for all time, though some of its greatest achievements may survive and bear restatement in new language again and again.

The natural theologian is a kind of missionary, and to become a natural theologian involves a kind of *kenosis*, the sort of self-emptying which we recognize supremely in the

Incarnation. ("Who being in the form of God emptied Himself.") The natural theologian, having at his disposal the whole treasury of revelation and theology and the Gospel, nevertheless seeks to empty his mind and stand for a time where other men stand, hoping to find his way back to his true home from where they are, and to bring some of them at least with him. This is no small operation of the spirit, and it finds its sanction in the very heart of the Gospel itself.

Thus some kind of natural theology, some kind of spiritual and intellectual mood and phase of the Church's life in which the Christian theologian empties himself, in order to discover his intellectual kinship with those who dwell outside the Christian community, is a necessary moment in the life and thought of the Church. So long as we find ourselves in a world which is always in theory, and sometimes in practice, intellectually honest, the Christian Church will never be able to dispense with its natural theology and its natural theologians. In any case, as I have also argued, no system of theology can ever be complete without its chapter entitled Natural Theology, for the God who stands self-revealed in the Gospel is the Creator of the world, and only when interpreted in the light of His loving purpose does the world and the life men live in the world disclose its real meaning and its eternal worth.

Graceful Reason

The word "graceful," understood in its true sense, means more than elegant and beautifully proportioned motion. To speak of graceful reason is not to ask the question whether reason is capable of a precision and economy of effort which makes the study of its operations an aesthetic delight. Incontestably it can, and I have often felt that to trace the masterly mental processes of a supreme artist in the use of reason, like Bishop Berkeley or St. Thomas Aquinas or Plato, is rather like listening to a great violinist performing almost magical wonders on his fiddle. But the title of this book speaks of "graceful reason" in a more profound and a more literal sense. Can reason indeed be filled with grace? Is it something in man which God can and does use? Is it in its own essential nature, and can it become in the living human use of it, an organ of spiritual experience, a means of sounding the depths of our intercourse with God, and then of deepening them still further?

When we understand what the New Testament means by grace, we see at once that, although all human things are made for grace, no human thing can attain grace in its own right. The grace of God is something which has continually to be poured by God into the human vessel, something which men can only possess if God gives it to them. We can only be graceful if we are filled with grace. Is reason just such a receptacle?

This book is nothing if it is not an attempt to show that we may give an affirmative answer to precisely this question. Reason is more, and not less, rational when it takes for its proper theme the truth of God, when it seeks to unite the truth which we find in the gospel in one synthesis with the many truths with which life in the world is continually confronting us. There is no truth but truth, and the many truths will not finally coalesce into one truth until the last day, until that consummation in which the meaning of everything will be laid bare. Meanwhile, loyalty to the truth displays itself in the searching rather than in the finding, and the life of reason is one in which we observe with joy and admiration the truths we know coalescing into unities before our very eyes. And such provisional unities as we do observe point always toward that ultimate unity which is presented to us in the Christian revelation and which, in satisfying the entire being of the Christian man, satisfies his reason also.

Well may we cry, as we contemplate the insight and fruitfulness of even inadequate and sin-stained reason in a fallen world, and particularly where we see it rising to its height in consecrated service to the truth of God:

Hail Reason, Full of Grace!